T0372512

Brands on a Mission

Brands on a Mission explores the importance of creating a performance culture that is built on driving impact through purpose, and the type of talent required to drive these transformational changes within companies – from CEO to brand developers.

Using evidence from interviews and stories from over 100 CEOs, thought leaders and brand managers, the book presents an emergent model that organisations can follow to build purpose into their growth strategy – and shows how to bridge the gap between Brand Say and Brand Do. Readers will learn from the real experts in the field: how Paul Polman, former CEO of Unilever, built purpose into the DNA of his company; what keeps Alan Jope (new CEO, Unilever) and Enmmanuel Faber (CEO, Danone) awake at night; and how brand developers from Durex, Dove, Discovery and LIXIL have made choices and the reasons behind them. In this book you will learn how a soap brand Lifebuoy taught one billion people about hygiene, how a beer is tackling gender-based violence, and how a toothpaste is tackling school absenteeism amongst many others. Renowned experts like Peter Piot (Director, London School of Health and Tropical Medicine), Michael Porter (Professor, Harvard School of Business), Jane Nelson (Director, Corporate Responsibility Initiative, Harvard Kennedy School) and Susie Orbach (leading feminist and formerly professor, London School of Economics) also share examples, data and their everyday experiences of helping corporates create a culture of purpose. And leading NGOs and UN experts like Lawrence Haddad (Executive Director, GAIN) and Natalia Kanem (Executive Director of UNFPA) will recount how the public and private sector have worked together to create an accelerated path to reaching the Sustainable Development Goals by 2030.

The book provides a clear pathway of how to take brands through the journey of developing impactful social missions and driving business growth, and is an essential guide for both managers and students alike.

Myriam Sidibe is one of the world's leading voices on brands that improve public health. From within Unilever, she created a movement to change the handwashing behaviours of one billion people, the single biggest hygiene programme in the world. She is a senior fellow at Harvard Kennedy School and Board Member of Wateraid UK and Kilimanjaro Blind Trust.

"Purpose-driven marketing, when done right, can create social impact that can improve millions of lives while simultaneously improving company competitiveness. Too many companies, however, pursue hype that delivers no real results. Myriam Sidibe draws on her 15 years at the intersection of branding and public health to describe how to do it right. This book is a valuable starting point for any marketeer with a brand on a mission."

Michael E. Porter, Bishop William Lawrence University Professor,
Harvard Business School

"The days of getting big and rich then giving back as a means to repair the damage are over. There will be neither talent nor time for this model. Brands will only succeed if they are on a mission that serves the people's power. Myriam's book explores why and how brands can achieve this, and invites everyone to join. What is at stake in this book is no less than reinventing the role of the market economy for social justice."

Emmanuel Faber, CEO Danone

"This sprightly volume introduces Mother Teresa to Mad Men. It shows how product branding, so often maligned, can bring substantial social value."

Professor Richard Zeckhauser, Frank P. Ramsey Professor of Political Economy,
Kennedy School of Government, Harvard University

"In this fast-paced book, Dr Myriam Sidibe conveys the 'how' of successful branding through purpose. This notion is generating intense interest, especially among young people of the 'Sustainable Development Generation' the world over, who identify with the principle of taking action towards the social good. The real-life examples are practical, useful and inspiring."

Dr Natalia Kanem, Executive Director of the United Nations Population Fund

"Dr Sidibe's work provides an extremely valuable contribution to public health, and the role all parts of society need to play – from governments, to local communities, to NGOs, to business and academia."

Professor Peter Piot, Director and Handa Professor of Global Health, London School
of Hygiene and Tropical Medicine

"Brands on a Mission is essential reading for anyone who wants to drive positive change through their brand, not just talk about it. For anyone who believes that brand 'purpose' means something more than a warm and fuzzy ad. And for anyone who wants to understand how to align multiple organisations and interests behind a common goal. Myriam's story is unique, but its lessons are universal."

Andy Last, CEO MullenLowe Salt

"An inspiring new perspective on rethinking the role of businesses in public health."

Camilla Cavendish, author of Extra Time: 10 lessons for an ageing population

"Partnering with both the brand Lifebuoy and the company Unilever was a tremendous boost to our fight against trachoma. This book is an admirable guide to how to create such partnerships effectively in pursuit of the Global Goals."

Caroline Harper, CEO Sightsavers

"The best marketing goes way beyond promoting a company's commercial goals; it connects brands to deeper consumer needs and public good. Myriam Sidibe inspires marketing and business leaders to find that sweet spot between their corporate interests and their purpose. She shows how marketing spending can change the world for the better."

Deb Gordon, author of The Health Care Consumer's Manifesto *and former Chief Marketing Officer, Network Health*

"We need more voices from Africa and even more African women leaders that challenge the status quo and contribute to the economic development of the continent. Dr Sidibe's work is inspiring and gives hope for business models that keep the well-being of our mothers and children at the heart of the debate."

Landry Signe, author of Unlocking Africa's Business Potential, *Brookings fellow*

"A must read for any leader who wants to ensure that their business model stays relevant for the turbulent decades to come. Practical examples on how to position your brands to be a force for good and keep relevance."

Paul Polman, Co-Founder and Chair of IMAGINE, and Co-founder of the Business and Sustainable Development Commission, Former CEO of Unilever

Brands on a Mission

How to Achieve Social Impact and
Business Growth Through Purpose

Myriam Sidibe

Routledge
Taylor & Francis Group

LONDON AND NEW YORK

First published 2020
by Routledge
2 Park Square, Milton Park, Abingdon, Oxon OX14 4RN

and by Routledge
52 Vanderbilt Avenue, New York, NY 10017

Routledge is an imprint of the Taylor & Francis Group, an informa business

© 2020 Myriam Sidibe

British Library Cataloguing-in-Publication Data
A catalogue record for this book is available from the British Library

Library of Congress Cataloging-in-Publication Data
Names: Sidibe, Myriam, 1976- author.
Title: Brands on a mission : how to achieve social impact and business growth through purpose / Myriam Sidibe.
Description: Abingdon, Oxon ; New York, NY : Routledge, 2020.
| Includes bibliographical references and index. | Identifiers: LCCN 2020002104 (print) | LCCN 2020002105 (ebook) | ISBN 9780367428334 (hbk) | ISBN 9780367855437 (ebk)
Subjects: LCSH: Brand name products–Social aspects. | Branding (Marketing) | Consumer satisfaction. | Success in business. | Advertising–Brand name products.
Classification: LCC HD69.B7 S53 2020 (print) | LCC HD69.B7 (ebook) | DDC 658.8/27–dc23
LC record available at https://lccn.loc.gov/2020002104
LC ebook record available at https://lccn.loc.gov/2020002105

ISBN: 978-0-367-42833-4 (hbk)
ISBN: 978-0-367-85543-7 (ebk)

Typeset in Bembo
by Wearset Ltd, Boldon, Tyne and Wear

To my parents, Michel and Christine Sidibe, for the purpose genes, and for keeping the purpose journey real and authentic.

And to my life partner, Yan Welffens, for his patience and belief in me.

Contents

Foreword

Addendum - March 2020
The coronavirus crisis has brought to light the fragility of our economic system but also presents an enormous opportunity to show the power of stakeholder capitalism and cooperative leaderships. Companies that understand that lesson from the crisis will do well moving forward.

January 2020

To paraphrase Charles Dickens, it's the best of times and the worst of times. The world has made enormous progress in the past 50 years, with innovations across many sectors lifting billions of people out of poverty and improving their welfare accordingly. More people have access to clean drinking water and sanitation than ever before. As a result, deaths from diseases caused by drinking unclean water and poor sanitation have declined rapidly. People live longer, healthier lives and have access to economic opportunities to improve their lot more than at any point in history.

This growth in economic opportunity has been accompanied by a greater respect among businesses for human rights, too. More responsible, respectful corporations are sharing the benefits of progress more equitably than in earlier boom periods when growth often came with far greater human costs.

But for all there is to celebrate, we must not become complacent. Returning to Dickens, it's the worst of times because, despite major advances, progress towards addressing the challenges that remain is now slowing down. We cannot help but notice that with this growth has come widening wealth inequality. Coupled with social and political grievances, inequality is driving political instability in many countries, weakening our governments' and other institutions' ability to address the greatest global challenges.

Lifting the remaining people out of poverty and improving their welfare will require innovative approaches and testing new ideas. The world is wising up to this. For all the advances that have been made, we can no longer write cheques to charities and NGOs and hope they can fix these problems. Continuing with the status quo will not enable us to achieve the ambitious targets – the Sustainable Development Goals (SDGs) – the nations of the world unanimously agreed to at the UN General Assembly in 2015.

The funding gap is one part of the problem: the UN estimates that it will cost US$2.5–3 trillion to meet these targets but total overseas development aid spending in 2018 was just US$153 billion. New sources of financing are being developed and growing rapidly, but even optimistic analysis of current trends suggests that a funding shortfall will be a key barrier to the world reaching the SDGs by the 2030 deadline.

A more inclusive approach to growth and development will be an essential facet of ensuring everyone has access to greater well-being and opportunity. The Business and Sustainable Development Commission, set up by Paul to initiate awareness of the goals amongst the private sector, estimates that pursuing sustainable and inclusive business models could unlock economic opportunities worth at least US$12 trillion a year by 2030 and generate up to 380 million jobs, mostly in developing countries. This is not just a critical move for the billions of people around the world still living in poverty and suffering from preventable debilitating and deadly diseases. It provides growth opportunities for businesses large and small that are seeking new routes to sustainable expansion in an increasingly volatile and uncertain world.

But what does inclusive growth mean in practice, and how can companies realign themselves to create it? Inclusive growth means going beyond corporate social responsibility (CSR) at times towards embedding a movement of responsible social corporations, leveraging their resources and expertise to address critical global challenges in a commercially sustainable manner. In appreciating the need to make near-term social investments, businesses can realise long term commercial rewards. A responsible social corporate (RSC) goes beyond philanthropy, corporate social responsibility and impact investing. None will create the transformation the world needs, and businesses pursuing them will not realise the full benefits to their own operations and bottom line.

Companies looking for inspiration would do well by looking to Unilever's Sustainable Living Plan. This aims to expand the size of the business while making a meaningful contribution to the health, well-being and livelihoods of those left behind by growth, while avoiding negative effects on the environment. Many of the goals are driven by the brands directly in their business models, whilst initiatives like Unilever Zero waste factories, green energy, sustainable sourcing, fair wages are all wider corporate strategies.

In launching the plan, Unilever sought novel thinking and partners from across the development landscape, admitting that it did not have all the answers, but that it was committed to collaborating to find them. To date, Unilever has made great progress across its targets, improving the lives of millions of people, and experienced outsize growth, especially among brands with a social purpose at their heart.

Many businesses around the world are realising the opportunities for growth and impact that can be unlocked by pursuing a strategic approach to inclusive growth. Many more need to embrace this evolving social contract where basic human rights are not only respected but become the basis of business' relationship with stakeholders. We regularly speak to business leaders looking for ideas and resources for how they can embed this new way of doing business into their own work. As a guide for aspiring intrapreneurs, *Brands on a Mission* is a fine contribution to this library. Myriam Sidibe is a pioneer in identifying the issues that companies can address through their core business operations and building a practical approach to creating positive change alongside commercial growth. *Brands on a Mission* focuses on what consumer brands can do to improve the world, especially on health and well-being issues, which alone have the potential to unlock a US$1.8 trillion economic opportunity.

Embedding social purpose in business is not always easy, but it is worthwhile – the examples in the pages that follow are testament to that. A thoughtful reading of this book will help anyone working on the hard issues that come up when companies embrace a social purpose, with advice and stories related to each step in a widely applicable model.

All that's left to say is "good luck" and to stick at it. Creating innovative ways to bring growth and social progress into lock-step have been some of the most thrilling and rewarding experiences in our own careers. We believe that if you try to do the same, you will be thankful. And so will the people your work helps. It's only through thinking like this that we will create a better world where everyone can be happy, healthy and have opportunities to create better lives for themselves and their families.

Paul Polman, Co-Founder and Chair of IMAGINE, and Co-founder of the Business and Sustainable Development Commission, Former CEO of Unilever.

Professor John Ruggie, Berthold Beitz Professor in Human Rights and International Affairs at Harvard Kennedy School.

Acknowledgements

If you want to go fast, you go alone. If you want to go far, go together.

(African proverb)

Looking back across my career so far, I've had the good fortune to work in many different worlds. I cut my teeth in public health, before moving to the corporate sector to put my research into practice. For now, I'm back in academia, but this time on the teaching and writing side, focusing on what business can do to make the world a better place. For what the next chapter holds, I am not yet sure, I'm excited to see where I go from here.

As my career has evolved, I have had the opportunity to work with some truly gifted people, and am grateful to many fellow colleagues and mentors who have opened my eyes to the potential for developing new models for public health impact, and those who have supported me along the way.

For my academic world, I am talking most recently about my time at the Mossavar Rahmani Center for Business and Government at the Harvard Kennedy School. The last two years have been fantastic, you welcomed me at a time of transition in my career when I needed to reflect and get more confidence in what I believed intuitively I knew already. You gave me a great academic home, financial and intellectual support, and a belief that I could get this done. My senior fellow colleagues provided amazing support. I especially thank Richard Zeckhauser, John Haigh, Scott Leland, Susan Gill, Jane Nelson and my faculty sponsor Leemore Dafny. This Center is a gem, providing businesses with what they need to embrace a better understanding of public policy. I have made some great friends and a special shout out to Deb Gordon and her family. My other important academic home is the London School of Hygiene and Tropical Medicine. To Val Curtis and Robert Aunger in particular, who have read my work, critiqued it and constructively challenged me all along. I know that this volume is not to their standards of perfection yet, but you will have to wait for the next book for that.

To my research team over the past 18 months, headed by Ben Tidwell, Post Doc Fellow, and the amazing research assistants that helped develop the case studies in this book: Gunjan Veda, who almost went on to write an entire book on Dove and self-esteem; Rafael Beleboni, on the Lifebuoy case study, bringing his diplomat eyes to the UN conversations; Hoang Bui, for #NoExcuse Gender-based violence and Durex global condoms; Marc Anani Isaac, for the Discovery case study and general amazing responsiveness; to Celine Mazars on gender-based violence insights from South Africa; and to Ashiana Jivraj on the oral health insights. I can't wait to see you all at the book launch party.

And to my very small core production team: John Landry, the absolute best editor, who managed to put himself in my skin and my sometimes messy words; Andy McConnell, for pushing me on adding practical exercises, and Harriet Woollard, the ultimate task finisher, who played an especially important role in getting the content of the book ready for production.

To my agency family, MullenLowe salt, a huge thank you for all your support for many years.

To the companies and brands that have generously open their doors to me to share their insights on their social purpose journey, I hope you will like what you see. A big thank you to these brand teams in particular: Durex from RB, Discovery (Vitality), Carling Black Label from AB InBev, Blue Band from Upfield, Danone, LIXIL. And to the 100 people I have interviewed from various companies I thank you for your time and inspiration.

Many more colleagues have inspired, challenged and supported my work on brands and health, some by reading and critiquing selected chapters, others as sources and sounding boards. For this I single out particularly for thanks Steve Miles, Avinish Jain, Richard Wright, Rene Lion, Esha Sheth, Anila Gopal, Stacie June, Eric Ostern, Marianne Blamire and Andy Last. Special thank you to Helen Trevaskis for the book cover – this book without you in it would not have been complete. Thank you also to my great coach, Liam Black for pushing me to just keep going, when the road ahead wasn't clear at all.

To my UN and NGO family, a special mention to Sid Chatterjee, Ruben Vellenga, Desta Lakew and Ann Thomas, who not only read with interest the insider perspective of the private sector but also gave me a more nuanced perspective. You have all my respect.

And keeping the best for (almost) last, to my Unilever family. I have spent 15 years in this amazing company, and I have made friends and colleagues that genuinely feel like family, as close as blood. The ethics of this company is what allowed me to do things that no company has ever done before, all the way to writing this book. I can't list the names of all of you, but you know who you are. I have learned everything I know from you. To HR: I know I am the worst nightmare for anybody in HR, constantly challenging and pushing your limits, but thank you for putting up with me. To my intrapreneurs inside Unilever, this is our story. I take inspiration every day from your drive to make a difference.

None of these individuals, nor any institution with which I am affiliated, bears responsibility for the opinions expressed in the book or for any errors in fact or judgement – those are mine alone.

Of course it would have been impossible to do this without my family and friends supporting a dream that they perhaps don't quite understand. And to my children Yaackim, Soraya, Yerim and Yeelen (the Y children) for their patience with me during this project. A special mention to Soraya who moved to Boston with me, to live that Harvard-mummy-daughter year and regularly checked on the progress of my chapters. To all my children for keeping me grounded to what is expected of a mum.

For me, writing this book has first and foremost been a learning journey. And it is work in progress, bound to evolve in time as we all do. After all, we are all *Brands on a Mission*.

Introduction

An intrapreneur[1] born for social purpose

I always knew I wanted to work with the most vulnerable people. I was born in 1976, the daughter of parents from Mali a former French colony in Africa; I grew up there until I was 12 years old, and Bambara, the local dialect, was my first language. My parents made a living helping people escape from disease and poverty, and our dinner-table conversations for as long as I can remember were about social justice.

The hard part was figuring out where I could contribute to social justice most effectively. I explored joining an NGO, the UN, the World Bank and Academia. It never occurred to me to work in a for-profit corporation. But eventually I found that industry was the right place for my talents, and turning industry towards social justice is what the world needs now.

Looking back now, I can see how my family background set me on this journey. My father, Michel Sidibe, is a French-trained economist who rose through the United Nations organisation and served for ten years as Under-Secretary-General and Executive Director of UNAIDS. From him, I learned resilience and commitment to the cause, from fighting against homophobic laws, to making lifesaving drugs (such as ART) accessible to millions around the world. He remains my public health hero, and he is now the health minister of Mali. My mother, Christine Sidibe, named me after Miriam Makeba, "Mama Africa", a South African who fought against apartheid and was exiled to French Guinea, where my mother was growing up at the time.

In 1991 my father was promoted to be UNICEF's programme manager for all of Francophone Africa. We moved to New York City, and I joined the United Nations international school and learned to speak English. I even gave a speech to the UN General Assembly on women's rights and equality, at the age of 14. Moving to New York City liberated me and even in my broken English I could share with my fellow students my anger about the way many women are treated and the obvious lack of equal opportunities, even more apparent in Africa where I had just emigrated from. I personally never lacked amazing strong women as role models and was taught early on to speak out.

My father's mother helped raise me as my parents were very young when they had me, both in their first year at university. My grandmother was a

French woman who ran away from her family when she fell in love with a Malian soldier posted in her village in Poitou-Charentes during the Second World War. She settled in Mali with her husband and they shared 50 years of devotion. Many of my personal convictions come from her, especially her deep courage and her non-attachment to material things. My grandfather, her husband, was also a man of deep principles.

They needed all of that to manage early on. Theirs was one of the first biracial marriages in Mali. The French colonial administrators were uncomfortable with a white woman living in "African quarters". Neither of the families approved of the match. When their first two children died of illness in infancy, gossips started on how even God was against this union. But my grandmother kept going and had three children who survived, including my father. She embraced Mali while keeping her French values, especially in food where she developed some delightful "fusion" dishes. Neighbours enjoyed her guava marmalade, and ginger juice with a twist of vanilla.

Figure I.1 Grandparents, Jeanne Poitevin and Fode Sidibe, France 1944.

My father was committed to Mali too. He and my mother went to university in France, but they returned after graduation and settled us into Malian life. My three siblings and I attended rural schools with few resources. I have vivid memories of carrying my stool to school on my head. We had to carry our own water too, and we took turns cleaning the school toilets.

What's so wrong with helping people?

When I finished high school in New York, my parents insisted that I first get a practical degree so I could always get a job; after that I could do whatever I wanted. I chose McGill University in Canada and studied engineering, focusing on agricultural engineering and biosystems, the most socially

Figure I.2 Parents, Michel and Christine Sidibe, on their wedding day, France 1975.

Figure I.3 With my younger siblings, Yacine and Anissa, Mali 1984.

Figure I.4 With my grandmother, Mali 1991.

important topic I could find. It wasn't easy to learn about soil chemistry and plant DNA, when my English was still halting, but I graduated.

Graduation ceremonies for Canadian engineers include a ritual: each graduate receives a ring made from metal retrieved from a bridge that collapsed. The ritual reminds engineers that they work for people and that people's lives depend on their best work. That became a motto for my professional life.

Finally, at the age of 24, I completed a master's degree in water and waste engineering at Loughborough University in the UK. Eager to apply all this knowledge to social justice and public health, I joined the International Rescue Committee, an American non-governmental organisation specialising in emergency contexts. They shipped me to rural Burundi, a small country in central Africa ravaged by ethnic conflict. I went to Bubanza, a rebel zone, to build water systems and toilets in internally displaced camps.

My two years there gave me direct contact with people in need. Though it was rewarding, something felt not quite right. We kept talking about the "beneficiaries", a terminology that bothered me deeply, as did the constant focus on the donors who paid for everything. Our success depended on writing grant applications for funding, and those grants measured success by how many toilets we built. But I kept seeing a lot of empty toilets, as the "beneficiaries" weren't using them.

I wondered, was my career going to be constantly chasing donor money to build unused toilets? Was I going to make decisions for powerless people? As a young African woman, I wanted to be part of the development of my continent. But my work felt undignified for the beneficiaries and unsatisfying for me. So, if the humanitarian route wasn't for me, what else was there?

That something else soon appeared. In 2001 I was invited to a conference in nearby Rwanda, where I described the concept of mobile sanitation that I had just developed for refugees. There I met Val Curtis, then a lecturer at the London School of Hygiene and Tropical Medicine. She was on the lookout for young talent who could be trained at Europe's premier school of public health. She was focused on promoting hygiene, and she said: "We could do with someone like you in our group".

It was a dream opportunity at what I saw as the mecca of public health. Sandy Cairncross, the guru of water and sanitation, was also there. I followed up and applied for a new programme at the school, the Doctorate in Public Health, which they were designing for future leaders. It included courses at the London School of Economics on policy and management and required only three-quarters of the research of a PhD. I was accepted, but without a stipend to support myself.

At the same time, UNICEF offered me a job as a sanitation officer in Rwanda. It was a level-three professional position, and I was only 26. My dad saw this as the break of a lifetime. It meant entering the UN system and switching to sustainable aid work, not emergency response. It also had great potential for career growth. UNICEF would see me as a young, highly trained African woman, a resource to nurture and develop. It could be a great career move. Coming from Mali, this meant everything.

Nevertheless, I went for the public health doctorate. My longing for academic learning was just too strong, and perhaps I also needed to chart a different path from my father. I took my savings from my work in Burundi and moved to London.

The doctorate degree included a year of courses jointly in health policy and epidemiology between the London School of Economics and London School of Hygiene and Tropical Medicine. I spent a year in East Timor as part of my degree, seconded to the Ministry of Health in the newest county in the world, writing their environmental policy and learning Tetum. Meanwhile, I was pregnant. I delivered our baby Soraya, but my husband and I divorced soon after that. I stuck to my plan and just hoped to find money along the way. My opportunity came a year into the programme, when Val told me about the Hygiene Centre she had set up with donations from Unilever, the multinational soap company. She had the funds to support research into children's motivation to handwash with soap.

It was something I was interested in, and it would help me finish my degree, so I moved to Senegal with my baby daughter for two years to carry out this research. Those were fantastic years, setting up a research team, and working with the national Senegalese office for hygiene. I conducted "structured observations" of thousands of children coming out of toilets, data for what became my thesis on getting schoolchildren to use their school toilets and to wash their hands with soap. The Lancet had just published a review on how handwashing with soap could save lives significantly, and my research was to be an important contribution to this knowledge gap.[2]

I returned to London to write my thesis, with almost all my savings exhausted, but somehow I finished my degree.

Joining a corporation

It was during this rebellious time that I discovered Unilever, or rather we discovered each other. It wasn't in my plans; nothing in my upbringing, values or academic journey had prepared me to join a corporation. But in 2005 the managers of one of Unilever's soap brands, Lifebuoy, recruited me. Another graduate student at the school had done an internship for Lifebuoy for a year, and they wanted to hire her to manage partnerships with public health organisations. She declined in order to concentrate on finishing her doctorate but put in a word for me.

I remember going for my first meeting in London. I was still a few months from finishing my degree, a single mum, and I needed the money. I liked the heritage of Lifebuoy soap, which was created in 1894 to combat cholera in Liverpool, UK. But I wasn't sure about managing partnerships, especially with the UN, notorious for being difficult. So, I demanded that the job description include a broader goal of developing a programme to change behaviour around handwashing, a chance to apply my research findings.

I decided to give Unilever a try, especially as they agreed to give me time to finish my degree. After a few months there, I fell in love, not with a fancy marketer but with a word. Crazy as this sounds the word was "consumer". I realised that Unilever didn't treat its audiences as beneficiaries, but as consumers. Instead of offering hand-me-downs and pity, Unilever treated consumers, however vulnerable they might be, with respect and dignity. That's because consumers have a choice: they choose with their wallet what to do with their money.

It was an exciting moment. This changed everything for me. I had found the polar opposite of what made me feel so uneasy in Burundi: from giving resources to beneficiaries who had no choice, to making solutions attractive to consumers who did have a choice, however humble their circumstances.

I wasn't interested in joining the corporate structure or helping with corporate social responsibility projects that recreated the same donor-project mentality that pervades the aid world. Instead I wanted to sit with what I considered the most powerful function in the world, Marketing. Fifteen years later, I'm still there.

For me, the little girl taught to fight for social justice, the daughter inspired to make a difference, the student trained in public health, this felt like the perfect home. Marketers had a lot at their disposal, the greatest platform for impact, because they were experts in changing behaviours. I was hungry for that knowledge, and I enrolled in marketing courses with eager 24-year-olds to understand the 4-Ps (product, price, promotion and place) and other basics. I spent the next ten years with Lifebuoy's marketing team, attending daily meetings on everything from packaging to fragrances, from product designs to ad copy, and even pricing and profit margins. It was all about developing the world's most far-reaching antibacterial soap. I wanted to bring handwashing to the maximum number of people where it mattered most, in the areas of highest mortality and morbidity.

Surprising as it may seem, I've never felt that I've compromised on my public health values while at Unilever. Instead I've been in a position to make a big difference. We co-founded Global Handwashing Day in 2008, an advocacy day now recognised by the UN and celebrated every 15th of October by 500 million people in 100 countries. I used my doctoral research findings to help develop the "School of Five", a handwash programme for schools that has been translated into 19 languages to reach 450 million children in 35 countries. Lifebuoy's behaviour change programmes have reached one billion people over the past ten years.

To get there, we needed partnerships, but with a new approach. We were negotiating a programme on handwashing in India. At the time, Lifebuoy was the largest selling soap in India. It was present in 87 per cent of households, and more people knew the Lifebuoy advertising jingle than the Indian national anthem. UNICEF at the time was a major promoter of hygiene and

Figure I.5 Global Handwashing Day, Kenya 2019.

sanitation, and had amazing experience in rural programmes and a strong relationship with the government. However, they lacked the marketing power and tools of the private sector. With a common aim, it seemed a natural fit for a partnership. If UNICEF wanted to promote handwashing with soap in India it would be difficult, if not impossible, to do it without Lifebuoy. Their reaction to our proposal at that time perhaps gives the clearest indication how much has changed in the last 13 years. Not only did the UNICEF team want no mention of the brand, or association in any shape or form, but I was told that they were ashamed to be in the same room as me because they thought I had "sold out" to industry.

It is important to realise that we were dealing with respected colleagues who had spent their professional lives in difficult areas fighting for protecting the most vulnerable children. Yet here I was pushing for a transparent relationship and somehow equating in the same sentence profit and lives needed to be saved. This was the prevailing mentality at the time, that any association with business was to be, at the very best, through a cheque. This probably goes down as the most difficult moment in my life, that feeling of being rejected by the people I considered my own.

It is in that moment that I understood that I had moved to a different side, the side of the private sector where I would always be looked at with scepticism and doubt, because of this other motive of profit. Finally I said, "You must be running out of lives to save if we can't get the biggest soap in India to be part of the programme." They told me I was disrespectful. A term that I would hear often in the early days, alongside the term "difficult". I could see that this was rooted in a deep misunderstanding of each other, so I decided ironically to become the voice of the brand managers working so hard to develop this soap brand for the same population we were all trying to reach. I became determined to make my stint in the private sector count.

Unilever became a force for good not by the old CSR approach of writing cheques to NGOs, but through the power of its entrepreneurial, creative spirit, the scale of its businesses and most importantly that it viewed the poor people of India as consumers, not beneficiaries. Instead of shielding Unilever as it entered the world of public health, I became a sword fighter. We made the point of never giving only cash to our partners – a stand that amounted to a rebellion inside Unilever against the prevailing CSR mindset.

Instead we developed a new blended financing model (see Chapter 6). We forged ahead with iconic partnerships, from Sightsavers to the UK's Department for International Development. Most important, we created a framework for brands with a social mission, one that other Unilever brands have since followed. That framework, developed further in my year sabbatical at Harvard University, is the core of this book.

A few people at Unilever were crucial in guiding me along. Steve Miles, my first boss at Lifebuoy, exposed me to the brilliance of the marketing mind and showed me how marketers rule the world. We came up with ten principles for Lifebuoy partnerships, including the one about not giving money to partners. You have to remember, Lifebuoy at that time was a regional brand with €280 million in revenue and giving money away to partners had no role in a growth strategy. As we worked on embedding behaviour change programmes into our marketing, he gave me a new title, Manager of Social Mission. I loved the mystery of that title. Since no one knew what it meant, I was free to do what I needed to do to become the best public health marketer.

As I explain in Chapter 2, Paul Polman's arrival as CEO in 2009 made a huge difference to our internal standing. His Unilever Sustainable Living Plan pushed everyone to pay attention to the brands' social purposes. He also brought an openness to the external world that turned our business models of embedding purpose in the brands into a whole new way to pre-empt competition.

Samir Singh, who succeeded Steve Miles at Lifebuoy, was another great boss. His ambitions for Lifebuoy's growth were as big as mine for handwashing with soap, and his leadership was phenomenal. We were the perfect match in many respects. He understood what it took to succeed as an African in a global corporation, as he himself came from India. It's about going beyond the token voice at the table and getting the equal respect that says, "I will give you seniority and resources, and you will give me everything you've got to deliver our vision." Lack of diversity and therefore the lack of role models is very hard at any time, let alone when you are trailblazing. I spent four years in Mumbai at Hindustan Unilever Limited, the Indian arm of Unilever and Lifebuoy's strongest market. These were the best years of my professional life, where purpose was palpable, from the thriving talent around me, to a blooming business where I could make a difference immediately.

Fifteen years later, with maturity and first-hand experience, I do not romanticise capitalism as much, and I have a better appreciation of multi-sector collaboration. I understand the concerns with the word "consumer" and its limitations for reaching the world's poorest people. However, I also know how to tie clear incentives to social good, and I continue to believe that we can reconcile consumerism with social purpose. The years at Lifebuoy gave me a competency that I've applied to other Unilever brands tied to public health, especially Pepsodent toothpaste for oral health, Domestos toilet cleaner for sanitation, and Knorr bouillon cubes for nutrition.

In all of this work, I focused on Africa, Asia and Latin America, emerging nations where business has the greatest opportunity to improve the health of mothers and children, the foundation of social justice. I joined Unilever's Africa leadership team, which meant that I could not only develop the brand models but also lobby for their integration into the country plans. I realised it wasn't enough for brands to have a tangible, authentic mission. They also need five things to sustain efforts in the long run (*the Purpose Tree*): deep-rooted focus on behaviour change, truly engaged partnerships, broad social advocacy, the measurement of results and support within the corporation as a whole. This will yield business, social and environmental impact. These five "roots" form the structure of this book.

What is this book?

This book is not a celebration of Unilever's brands, or any brands on a mission. It presents what I hope is a realistic account of how brands promote public health issues in relation to consumerism. I've framed it as a how-to guide, to help readers either start the journey or boost their effects on the ground. It can help brand managers and marketers find affordable interventions to meet their profitability goals while still making a difference for people. It offers chapters on each of the five pillars, preceded by a general chapter to explain why brands benefit from embracing an explicit social purpose. Each of these chapters offers hand-holding exercises to help brand managers navigate through the journey of embedding a social purpose. And because each public health challenge, and each brand, is a little different, the book also presents six illustrative case studies of brands on a mission.

The book runs counter to the popular perception that business leaders are unaware and incapable of dealing with major social challenges. But it does advise brand leaders on navigating the organisational structures and corporate politics that can impede the delivery of real solutions. I have fought many battles in my 15 years in Unilever. I've learned many tricks for steering through systems and getting things done in large corporations that intrapreneurs should find useful.

Likewise, the book urges the public sector to get off their "moral high horse" and seek real partnerships with companies, partnerships that draw on the best of both sectors. After all, even the strongest public sector in the world will never get more people to wash hands than the world's largest soap company.

Notes

1 League of Intrapreneurs. *Transforming business from within.* www.leagueofintrapreneurs.com/ (Accessed: 18 December 2019).
2 Curtis, V. and Cairncross, S. (2003). "Effect of washing hands with soap on diarrhoea risk in the community: a systematic review", *The Lancet Infectious Diseases*, 3(5), pp. 275–281. doi: 10.1016/S1473-3099(03)00606-6.

1 Why brands need a social mission

In the past decades, it's become clear that corporations are the great source of both wealth and inequality.[1] With corporations becoming almost as large as nation states, we need a new model of enlightened capitalism. How do we link real business models with alleviating real suffering. And what can brands and marketing, the heart and fuel of many of these corporations, do to help? Profits, while essential over time, are not people's main motivators.

That model becomes easier to develop in the current competitive environment. Most consumer brands, at least in the West, are being challenged. In the past they could charge a high price because their products had higher quality or were more convenient for buyers. But good-quality store brands and other generic rivals have now proliferated. Consumers now see little difference and are buying the cheaper version, forcing the conventional brands to lower their prices. It's a downward spiral, because that disappearing price premium paid for the innovation to better serve consumers' needs and wants.

An even bigger problem may lie in talent. Premium brands depend on having smart, engaged people looking ahead and solving problems for consumers. But talented people have many career options nowadays, and they're more likely to work for a technology or financial firm, or a start-up with plausible ambitions to change the world. Why spend your career developing incremental improvements to largely similar versions of the same product for people who have plenty of stuff already?

Fortunately this problem comes with its own solution. Affluent societies have become so efficient and disciplined that consumers no longer need to buy a premium brand to ensure basic quality and availability. These consumers, and by extension employees, now have the luxury to worry about people other than themselves. They're looking to help those who are less fortunate, if not directly, at least with their wallets. And that's where conventional brands can regain their differentiation.

To set themselves apart in the marketplace and sustain their profitability, brands can embrace a social purpose. Besides helping to improve the world, the mission brings long-term commercial benefits to the brand and to their corporations as a whole. Pursuing sustainable and inclusive business models could unlock economic opportunities worth at least US$12 trillion a year by 2030 and generate up to 380 million jobs, mostly in developing countries. In health and well-being alone it is an opportunity worth US$1.8 trillion.[2]

Take Unilever's overall purpose, which is "to make sustainable living commonplace". The company believes it has the opportunity and the responsibility to be a force for good in the world, and its brands are the main vehicles for making that happen. By helping to solve social problems, the company may well create larger future markets for the brands and retain consumers that are looking for authentic brands that make a difference in the world.

This book focuses on the challenges of public health, because that is my background, and that's the discipline in marketing that I'm trying to foster. But any of the UN's 17 Sustainable Development Goals (SDGs) could provide a fine social purpose for a brand. I do draw the line at industries such as tobacco, sugary soft drinks and guns. I am talking about products that either can have a good impact directly, or can be consumed in moderation without causing harm.

The opportunity for brands

Before we jump into describing how brands can regain their differentiation, it's important to explain, why brands? After all, we have governments and charities to address social problems. Shouldn't brands just do what they do well, serve individual consumers, and leave those bigger structural challenges to the public and non-profit sectors? After all, brands helped to elevate the standards of living of millions of people in the twentieth century, and mostly without explicitly trying to solve social problems. Why change now?

For all the progress we've made, there are still hundreds of millions of people struggling with the basics of life. The United Nations has set 17 Sustainable Development Goals[3] on a range of social and environmental problems, from hunger to climate change, and most people aren't satisfied with the improvements of recent decades. We need to step up the pace.

Take the problem of poor sanitation mentioned in the previous chapter. If we could solve sanitation problems by simply giving everyone access to a proper toilet, then the governments and non-governmental organisations (NGOs) could take care of it. But, as I learned in Burundi, the basic hardware isn't enough. You need to get people to take care of the toilets, because dirty, smelly facilities will push people away (see Chapter 11). And you need to invest in infrastructure, which means cleaning out the tanks periodically, setting up septic systems or (ideally) building a full-fledged sewer system. Without those additions, people eventually abandon the toilets and go back to their old unhealthy ways, or catch diseases in the place that is supposed to protect them.

The scale of the challenge is huge. Over two billion people lack access to a safe toilet. A quarter of all people in the world are at risk of diseases spread by poor sanitation. Here's where a Unilever brand, Domestos, comes in. Domestos is a premium brand of bathroom cleaning products primarily for affluent consumers. But its leaders, along with the leaders of Unilever, weren't content to just keep selling to those customers. They were in the sanitation business, and they wanted to improve sanitation for everyone, not just people with a lot of disposable income.

Domestos is a business, not a charity, so they didn't want to just donate products and send employees to remote villages. Nor did they want to simply write a cheque – that's the tired path of corporate social responsibility, which consumers see right through and no longer provides differentiation, if indeed it ever did.

Whatever Domestos did to improve sanitation, it had to fit in its business model. It didn't have to fit perfectly – in that case, it had to do more than the usual economic returns. They had to find the middle ground between philanthropy and business as usual.

They treated this problem like any other marketing challenge. They researched the target consumers and learned about their environment, motivations and habits. They left the sanitation infrastructure to governments and NGOs – this wasn't their expertise – and focused on behaviours. Then they drove through two big initiatives.

First, they developed a new toilet cleaning powder, which came in small single-use packets costing only two US cents (US$0.02). Each packet had enough cleaning power to thoroughly clean out a toilet. With clarity on the price, the team designed a product to tackle the cleaning and hygiene needs for a squat toilet – separate from plumbing or sewer infrastructure – whilst generating an acceptable margin. They started with India. They marketed this product in the same way as any other Domestos item, often creatively because most of the target market lived in remote villages without the usual media channels. They wanted to make going to the toilet a dignified, rather than degrading, experience.

Second, Domestos launched a programme to train school janitors in how to clean toilets, starting with South Africa. Access to decent school toilets is a major problem. Besides spreading disease, poor sanitation discourages teenage girls from attending school because they have no place to change their sanitary pads. When I did research for my dissertation in Senegal, schools had an average of one toilet cubicle for 800 students, similar to Domestos' targets. Now janitors in South Africa were learning the proper, efficient cleaning procedures, equipped by Domestos and supported partly by the school.

These two programmes show the mission in action. The social purpose was an important driver for Domestos to come up with those individual-use packets. They might have spent their R&D funds instead on new features for existing products, maybe new scents or a proliferation of bottle sizes and delivery mechanisms for every conceivable situation. Those ideas had a better chance of meeting Domestos' margin requirements, at least in the short run. If you do not care about social purpose, then you're likely to play it safe and focus on your existing, affluent markets. But the social purpose helped Domestos to think about future growth in sanitation, which would surely be in South Asia and Africa. By entering those future markets now, Domestos positioned itself for future sales.

If a brand does not embrace a social purpose, then it definitely does not provide free training for janitors and teach children about toilet use habits. The return on that investment almost certainly will not meet Domestos' requirements in the short term. The programmes make sense only if you factor in the mission. But it's a social mission within the business, not a charity, because it creates value for everyone. Domestos covers its costs and gets a likely return on its work, in the form of future brand growth, while school children get better sanitation.

This mission-oriented work therefore benefits Domestos in ways that probably do not show up in its business model, unless that model is projected to the long term. It stakes a position in a future market. It differentiates the brand with affluent consumers. It makes Domestos' employees feel better about working there. And perhaps in some larger political sense, Domestos and Unilever are helping to justify society granting them a licence to operate.

Still, why couldn't the government or NGOs do exactly what Domestos is doing? For two reasons. One is a simple question of resources. Domestos has a substantial global marketing capability, as well as the budgetary resources to sustain certain programmes over time. This recurrent investment frees non-profits and governments to focus on infrastructure or other pressing public health issues. Even if the socially-driven programmes account for only, say, 10 per cent of total marketing spending, that's still a substantial amount from a global brand such as Domestos.

The other has to do with expertise. When the AIDS epidemic got everyone's attention, governments and NGOs provided many free condoms. Health clinics got baskets of condoms and pushed them onto everyone who visited. This made a huge difference in halting the epidemic, but now the rates of infections are stuck and condom acceptance is a big problem. The quality of some of these free condoms is doubtful, and people clearly prefer premium branded condoms.[4]

A different kind of problem emerged when, for malaria advice, governments spent donor money to buy bed nets, distributing them to people for free. They thereby undermined the private sector provision of bed nets, making people dependent on handouts. And it was claimed many of those free bed nets were used for purposes other than disease protection.[5, 6]

It's become a maxim in public health: you cannot just give people a free product and assume they'll use it, even if the product is in their rational best interest. You have to present it in a way that's desirable to them, and spend some resources on promoting and teaching its use.

Marketers know all about this desirability challenge – it's the core of their job, and they're pretty good at it. Not always in socially desirable ways. In 2006 alone, the six largest global alcohol producers spent more than US$2 billion on advertising, and exposure to alcohol advertising has been shown to contribute to excessive drinking.[7] The billions of marketing dollars from food companies have contributed to rising obesity and heart diseases. Today, corporations are arguably responsible for the most serious emerging health problems that people face, and they alone have the global power, reach and authority to change the fundamental causes of these conditions. If we could show an alternative in which doing good is still profitable, we could change that dynamic. Committed marketers can use their skills to make a difference where governments and NGOs fall short. Public health professionals are indeed getting better at persuasion, but they still lag in giving consumers the rewards (functional and emotional) that come with using branded products.

In any case, it's not a competition. Sanitation is such a large, multi-faceted challenge that we need everyone to tackle the problem, private and public sectors, ideally with some sort of coordination if not close partnership. While focused on toilet cleaning, Domestos has also helped to promote sanitation infrastructure. It's not in their realm of expertise, but they've helped others working on the problem. The brand has partnered with UNICEF to fund their sanitation programmes, bringing infrastructure to over ten million people. Now here is a good way to spend cash – improving the enabling environment where your purpose-driven brands operate.

Domestos has also brought to affluent markets a chance to get involved in these programmes through cause-related marketing campaigns. To further support improved sanitation, the brand co-founded the Toilet Board Coalition. Charlie Beevor, who heads Domestos, chaired the Coalition as of 2019, and he points out:

> We've been incubating start-ups through the coalition, mentoring sanitation entrepreneurs in sub-Saharan Africa, in South Asia and Southeast Asia. We are looking to build the evidence base for models in urban, peri-urban, and rural situations, because obviously there isn't a one size fits all. That's very much a longer term play.[8]

While embracing the mission, Domestos understands the benefits in terms of differentiation with its main offerings. Beevor adds that:

> A toilet cleaning brand is typically not a brand that people choose to engage with. But when you raise the awareness of the sanitation crisis to hundreds of millions of privileged people who never think about access to sanitation, they say that's unacceptable. And very often they prefer and reward brands that are seen to be investing part of their profits, and also their resources, in being part of the solution along with other brands and NGOs and government bodies.[9]

It all comes together. Brands need a new avenue for differentiation, because their traditional appeal is no longer compelling in itself. The world needs brands to apply their marketing expertise and resources to help with major social challenges. And by resources, I mean much more than a portion of their marketing budget – their talent as well, especially around inducing people to change their behaviour.

Globally, health and well-being are better than ever, but a large number of people still suffer from preventable diseases. Every year, millions of children under five still die of diarrhoea and pneumonia.[10] Besides the sanitation related woes, malnutrition – including obesity as well as undernourishment – affects one in three people.[11] Oral diseases, such as cavities, are the biggest cause of school absenteeism and low work productivity.[12] Thirty-seven million people are still living with HIV-AIDS.[13] Mental health is increasingly under the spotlight: 80 per cent of girls express body dissatisfaction, which often leads to low self-esteem, depression, substance abuse.[14, 15] Toxic masculinity and unhealthy stereotypes are fuelling a rise in depression among young men, along with domestic violence.[16]

Many of these issues can be addressed by changing habits and attitudes. An estimated two-thirds of healthcare costs are driven by lifestyle choices.[17] We know that people at risk of HIV infections should use condoms; that we all should wash our hands with soap and brush our teeth before going to sleep; and that we should exercise more and eat a better diet. Yet we often do not behave in our best interests. We know what's good for us, but often act otherwise.

This disconnect between desirable, health-promoting behaviours and our actual day-to-day habits is the source of many of the world's pressing public health challenges. This is a great opportunity for brands to embrace a social purpose. Marketing as a discipline can make consumption conscientious and improve both society as a whole and their individual customers.

Marketers may worry that a social purpose will turn off consumers, or at least divert resources that could have been used to win over buyers directly. But brands on a mission are usually rewarded, not penalised, by their customers. Research on the world's 50 fastest growing brands, from 2001 to 2011, found a causal relationship between a brand's orientation to a higher purpose and its financial performance. Brand consultants Millward Brown and former Procter & Gamble marketing officer Jim Stengel developed this list, and they argued that a higher purpose helps brands build deeper ties with customers. They also found that investment in these idealistic companies – the Stengel 50 – over the 2000s would have generated 400 per cent higher returns over the S&P 500.[18]

At Unilever, where I have spent much of my career, the most sustainable brands (brands that endorsed a social mission at their core) grew 46 per cent faster than the rest of the business and delivered 70 per cent of its revenue from 2017 to 2018.[19] Most of this growth happened in emerging nations where achieving the SDGs is crucial. CEO Alan Jope argues that:

> We are on the front edge of a new model of business where authentic purposefulness leads to better financial outcomes, better profits. Actually

there's no trade off. In fact, the more you do on purpose, the better your business performance will be.[20]

Brands on a mission are a subset of the larger movement towards "shared value" – where companies create measurable business value by identifying and addressing social problems that intersect with their business. First introduced by Michael Porter and Mark Kramer in 2011,[21] it has helped to unleash business to address fundamental global challenges. The idea is to do more than simple philanthropy. Rather than write a cheque (though writing a cheque has its value at times), companies can tackle challenges that benefit society and their businesses. A high-tech company, for example, helps provide high school instruction in computer coding, mostly by donating equipment and by encouraging employees to volunteer. Kids in the community benefit from an improved education in twenty-first century skills, while the company is boosting the supply of skilled workers for all companies (including their competitors). They share the value that they (often jointly) create.

The concept of shared value focuses on the products and services that companies offer. With *Brands on a Mission*, I'm extending this approach to the special dynamics of brands. Products and services are important, but in so many cases they aren't enough – we need marketing expertise and resources too. And not just to design better products, but to use advertising and promotions to encourage new habits. Marketers are also good at creating educational programmes to drive the messages deeper, in a more concrete, hands-on way than is possible with advertising.

Marketers have a special challenge with shared value. Realising the benefits of differentiation, some brands broadcast their social purpose before they do much actual good. Their marketers are using social purpose to boost the brand's reputation, rather than embracing the purpose itself. Making a real difference with social problems is hard enough; to succeed, it has to follow from an authentic, company-wide commitment to the purpose. Otherwise the mission is just window-dressing, or what we call "purpose-washing" – similar to green-washing, where purpose-driven activities serve mainly for publicity purposes. We end up with what Anand Giridhardas describes in *Winners Take All*: "social purpose that just furthers the charade of elites disrupting the old order without giving much back".[22]

Purpose-washing brands gain one of the benefits of social purpose, differentiation, but only for a short while. They lose out on positioning for future markets, and they might even make employees feel worse about working for them. And they'll lose the trust of consumers who find out.

Michael Porter points out that:

A lot of consumer goods have ranked low on purpose and social impact. But this is changing with innovative products emerging that take on major societal challenges, such as micro-nutrient fortified foods that improve health outcomes. It is essential that purpose-based positioning and marketing deliver real social benefit. Today's consumers are looking for true social impact, not mere hype and window dressing.[23]

For a social purpose to be real, brands shouldn't try to imitate charities. Marketers have to be transparent about their business model, how it both generates profits and addresses a social problem. It's fine for them to occupy a moral high ground, but they can only sustain it by developing a successful business.

At the same time, marketers need to respect what governments and NGOs have already accomplished in the social sector – and acknowledge all sides of the story of reducing poverty, disease or other social ills. If marketers are going to pioneer new ways of addressing social justice, they do not need to start from scratch.

For me, driving a social mission has been about making a difference in society through a brand aligned to the needs and aspirations of society. The core challenge is to bring the two together: a profit-oriented brand, and real suffering in the world. How do we translate our ideals into a sustainable part of our business? How do we develop business models that drive real social impact? Purpose-driven marketing is the art and science of infusing values in promoting a product to address a major social challenge – while still engaging with consumers and staying relevant to the core promise of the brand.

Fortunately, many NGOs and government officials are now coming around to the power of brands. Rather than pushing companies to be conventionally philanthropic, they are realising that a profit motive can add scale and momentum to their own efforts. And a profit motive keeps companies and brands in check. Tying financial incentives to social good is linked to the performance culture of companies and brands. Innovative partnerships between public and private sector can bring sustained funding and superior approaches to behaviour change. How to make better use of the "muscles of businesses" is key, and it starts with understanding the ecosystem of a social problem and seeing how a business model can help.

Marketing is about creating brands and the benefits that come from them, both products and communication, that mobilise people to do things differently. "It is a great time to be a marketer on a mission because both the public and private sectors are interested in finding a way to work together" adds Steve Miles, my ex-boss and former leader of the Dove brand at Unilever. And many marketers are eager to embrace a social purpose. I've spent my professional and personal life working and interacting with a range of people on social challenges, and actually some of the most principled people I've known were in the private sector. I've met many brand managers and brand directors who were concerned with making a difference and pioneering ways to do that in their day jobs.

When people think of marketing, they tend to dwell on the negative elements of "manipulating" consumers to buy what they do not need. As described in books such as *Salt, Sugar and Fat*, cunning marketers have led people into obesity, diabetes and poverty by tricking them with useless prod-ucts.[24] *Lethal but Legal*[25] explains how decisions made by six industries (food, tobacco, alcohol, pharmaceutical, gun and auto) have had a greater impact on health than those made by scientists and policymakers. Yet as Oxfam argues, those of us who buy, cook and eat the food are more powerful than we might think, influencing corporations to adapt to meet our demands. We can work with brands on a mission to respond to our needs.

Instead of getting consumers to buy what they do not need, marketers can encourage them to be engaged in social issues. And in doing so, people get engaged with the brand too. After all, most businesses are moving away from Milton Friedman's principle that companies should work solely on maximis-ing shareholders' wealth. The Business Roundtable recently issued a "State-ment on the Purpose of a Corporation", signed by the CEOs of 181 of the largest US corporations, representing 30 per cent of total market capitalisa-tion. The one-page declaration concluded that: "Each of our stakeholders is essential. We commit to deliver value to all of them, for the future success of our companies, our communities and our country."[26] This represents a clear move from shareholders to stakeholders. Likewise the Chairman of Black-Rock, Larry Fink, the giant global investment manager, in his 2019 letter to CEOs told the companies in which it invests that "profits are in no way inconsistent with purpose – in fact, profits and purpose are inextricably linked".[27]

Making it happen

I've seen brands take on a social purpose in two ways. One is to go back to the founding of the brand and understand its reason for existing. Brands often forget their original purpose in the chase for growth. Marketers focus on functionality and new features. But that does not mean the original purpose is irrelevant.

Lifebuoy antibacterial soap began as a soap specially formulated to fight cholera in nineteenth-century Britain. It was therefore an easy extension to embrace a twenty-first-century mission of fighting disease in developing countries through better handwashing.

The same principle applies well beyond obvious products for public health – including makeup. Ukonwa Ojo, former Chief Marketing Officer for Coty, recommends "going to the archives of the brand. Most of the time you will find a compelling reason why the founders did what they did, and even though years have gone by, that reason is still powerful."[28] CoverGirl, one of Coty's main brands, was launched in 1961 to make the cosmetics used in fashion magazines available to ordinary women and girls, so they didn't feel marginalised. CoverGirl still has the same mission, just defined in different ways. It was the first line of cosmetics to have a brand ambassador with a hijab, so girls with this covering do not feel alienated from the beauty conversation.

Some brands have pursued a social mission for decades, without talking explicitly about purpose and before the term became fashionable. Unilever's Indian subsidiary is perhaps an extreme case, and one focused on the corporate rather than a product brand, but it's still illustrative. Nitin Paranjpe, now Unilever's Chief Operating Officer, has spent most of his 31-year career at Hindustan Unilever Limited. In the 1990s, he says, no one spoke of brands with purpose:

> The leaders of the company used to say, "If it is right for India, it will be right for us." Because we saw ourselves as being in that country for a hundred years, and the only way you will succeed is by integrating yourself with the needs of the society. My proudest example of purpose was the Shakti programme to build a distribution network into remote villages. The idea was simple, how can you develop people's skills while expanding our reach? We taught women how to sell products and to do so in small places where conventional distribution was too costly. We were working at the intersection of what is good for business and what is good for society.[29]

The other approach is to discover a major social problem related to the product, regardless of why the brand started in the first place. That connection is essential – a mission disconnected from the product will not work, because it will not be authentic, and because it will not support the brand's business model.

Unilever's Dove brand (Chapter 2) began in 1957 as a soap to combat dry skin with special moisturising agents. When moisturising became a commonplace offering, Dove's marketers looked around for a new problem to address. Starting around 2000, they embraced the mission of overcoming notions of perfect beauty that caused women to think less of their own bodies. A poor body image can drive a range of social problems, from low productivity and stunted careers to depression and suicide. Dove developed a series of provocative advertisements, some critical of its own industry, while becoming the largest provider of self-esteem education to girls around the world.

Taking on a social purpose can be invigorating, but marketers have to be careful not to jump onto an issue, exploit it for brand benefit, and move on to the next opportunity, especially when the public sector criticises their efforts. To be credible and authentic, they must first invest some time and effort in learning. Then they must build some substance behind their efforts. Only then should they start communicating about those efforts.

That includes welcoming accountability. Real brands with authentic purpose must accept – and even seek out – external validation by independent reviewers. People who really believe in their mission will care about true impact. They'll want to be transparent in their journey of learning, disseminating what they've found, creating allies and taking consumers along.

Brands also need to do something of a hygiene check. They will not get far if the brand, or even the parent company, offers products or messaging that seem to many consumers to threaten long-term health and welfare. Products from tobacco and armaments to infant formula may clash with the mission. Companies ultimately depend on a social licence to operate and maintain their legitimacy to do business.

Otherwise, as Ukonwa Ojo says, consumers will see through the purpose:

> Where there's a disconnect between what the brand is pushing, and what the brand actually stands for, you see a lot of missteps. People scratch the surface and find nothing there, other than the fact that marketers wanted to create a communication.[30]

Brand Say and Brand Do

Brands on a mission go beyond talk; they work for a direct impact. I like to distinguish between "Brand Say" and "Brand Do", terms coined in 2016 by Steve Miles and now used widely in Unilever and its agencies. Brand Say involves communicating to consumers about the social purpose; Brand Do is about translating this purpose into actually addressing social problems. Every brand communicates what it is about. The Brand Say for Lifebuoy, for example, is about helping parents to ensure that their kids fall ill less often by staying one step ahead of infections. Its main Brand Do is about developing handwashing behaviour change programmes to mothers and children, which just reached a billion people (see Chapter 6).

Brand Do is usually a long-term process, where the investment is about business development more than short-term sales results. And when the brand does Brand Say, it should offer not just one example, but several. It takes time and humility to build credibility. As Andy Last, CEO MullenLowe salt and author of *Business on a Mission* says, "It's important to balance the say and the do, what you are talking about needs to be proportionate to what you are actually doing."[31]

We judge people by their actions, not by their words. Miles points out that:

> A purpose isn't worth much unless it cost you money. You don't find out if people have principles until they have to pay to maintain that principle. And we are becoming less tolerant of the gap that exists between words and deeds.[32]

This book offers an operational framework to develop the Brand Do and feed it back meaningfully into the Brand Say. This practical framework focuses on addressing public health challenges through brand-led programmes. Through general chapters and case studies, it delves into the five key areas of work – the "Purpose Tree". I have chosen the tree of life (the baobab tree) as an analogy of what brands with purpose need and can create.

Figure 1.1 A baobab tree, Senegal 2019 (copyright Alan Jope).

The Purpose Tree has five deep roots that bring the purpose to life with benefits to the business, society, and the environment.

The baobab grows in my part of Africa and stays alive for over 1000 years (the oldest one is 6000 years). It keeps the water underground and is the strongest tree in Africa. The baobab tree is known as the tree of life, with good reason. It provides shelter, clothing, food and water for the animal and human inhabitants of the African savannah. The cork-like bark and huge trunk are fire resistant and are used for making cloth and rope. It is the place where major decisions are made.

Here are the five roots of the Purpose Tree:

1   Behaviour Change – using marketing expertise to change individuals' habits and wider social norms. Marketers and their agencies know how to do this; they just have to focus on problems differently and in a more collaborative way than they are used to.
2   Partnerships – working with public and private partners to create a multiplier effect for greater efficiency and breadth of impact. Brands must not be so arrogant as to think that they can solve problems alone. Without

partnerships they cannot get the moral authority, the scale or the learning they need to make a difference.

3   Brand Advocacy – of two kinds. One is to lobby governments and groups around the mission, whether through new funding or new policies. The other is to more generally communicate your purpose so your consumers understand how you make a difference to the world, and your stakeholders understand how to contribute.

4   Measurement – often the hardest part of the work, but essential to achieve real impact. Marketers have got much better at data collection and analytics, but they may need to adopt new metrics and standards of evidence for external accountability. Committing to academic validation and external accountability is crucial.

THE PURPOSE TREE

The baobab tree with its five deep roots brings the purpose to life with benefits to the business, society and the environment.

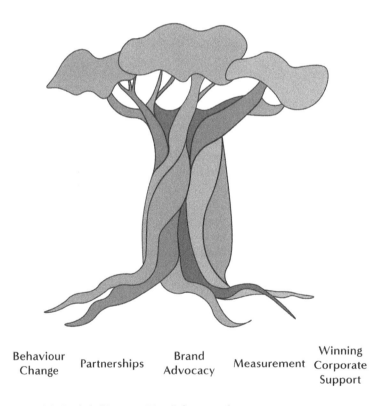

Behaviour Change   Partnerships   Brand Advocacy   Measurement   Winning Corporate Support

Figure 1.2 Baobab "Purpose Tree" framework.

5   Winning Corporate Support – success requires not just permission from
    the corporation to make these long-term investments by brands, but also
    strong leadership. Headquarters can also provide training, set up
    company-wide strategic partnerships, and even help create the marketing
    competencies of the future.

This framework bridges the gap between Brand Do and Brand Say and
brings real accountability. Brands can use it to make progress on delivering
the Sustainable Development Goals jointly with the public sector. It is
important to activate all of these pillars to follow through on your purpose.
Brands excel in creative and powerful communication, but that's not enough
to make a real dent in the world.

Challenges today

Whilst it's become much easier to embrace a social purpose within large
companies, there are still three big challenges: resourcing the mission, overcoming distrust and resisting purpose washing.

At Unilever, in the past, my team and I had to fight colleagues in brands
over budget for social mission activities. They wanted to put nearly all the
spending into core advertising focused on the products and their functional
benefits. Their short-term thinking was understandable when their job
depended on last month's sales report.

With a world of enlightened consumers, things are changing. Nowadays
brand managers, with the backing of corporate leaders, are much more likely
to accept purpose-based advertising. But this tension may always be a challenge, especially for brands at companies like Unilever with central and
regional marketing groups. How do you account for these expenditures in a
tight profit and loss game?

A second challenge, distrust from the public sector and NGOs, is also
getting easier. I'm seeing fewer people who think all the company is trying to
do is to sell products and therefore it must be up to something evil – as if
there was something wrong with ultimately making money. Not all profit is
bad. It often takes extended conversations for people to see the authenticity
and understand the benefits of a social purpose in brands.

The third challenge is newer, and it's getting harder. More and more
brands are jumping on the bandwagon of social purpose without authentic
commitment. They've seen the fluffy advertising from earlier attempts at corporate social responsibility advertising. Consumer distrust could hurt the
brands that are truly on a mission.

Marketers need to do the intellectual work of crafting a purpose that serves
both vulnerable people and the business. Only with profits can companies
make the long-term commitments necessary for real impact.

One solution that is getting some traction is to set up a "Benefit", or B
Corporation. Most companies are registered as C corporations, but a growing

number of US states and other countries are recognising this other status. Unlike their counterparts in C corporations, the directors of B Corporations (B Corps) have some legal protection for including social benefits among their goals, besides following the interests of investors.

For Emmanuel Faber, CEO of Danone, choosing to be a B Corp has been a strategic decision about helping to inspire people to engage with a brand:

> People no longer trust institutions, but they will trust each other. We need to deconstruct the company around a tribe of people that support an idea, with a brand of a product or a service that improves the life of people using it. We are a B Corp now for 30% of our sales, as it is a declaration to the world, to our employees, that we are serious about measuring our impact and going for goals that are broader than investor value creation or my bonus.[33]

Others are calling for deeper structural change. In *The Future of Capitalism*, economist Paul Collier calls for turning stakeholders into shareholders. So does Colin Mayer in *Prosperity: Better Business Makes the Greater Good*. They urge companies such as Unilever to become mutuals, owned by employees rather than outside investors.[34] Such a move would have employees take more ownership over the brand's purpose, while still ensuring a satisfactory long-term return on assets, and with a more people-focused angle at all levels.

Still, we need to distinguish ownership change from organisational change. As the case studies here show, brands on a mission can blossom under conventional ownership.

In a world that still has plenty of suffering, we need purpose-driven brands to join NGOs and governments in making things better. Brands can bring their special expertise and resources to bear, while actually improving their long-term prospects. The rest of this book goes through the five roots of the purpose tree and offers several case studies of brands on a mission. All of the chapters except for the case studies offer exercises at the end for brand managers looking to get started on social purpose.

Exercise

Visualising social purpose – what's your mission going to be?

Is your brand trying to identify or expand its social focus? Here are some tips to help you do that.

First, go back to the brand's founding principles. For many brands, the earliest impulse *was* a social purpose – the aim was to help a group of people by solving a problem they faced. What was your brand's original reason for being? Could that be adjusted to embrace an issue that is current today?

If that does not yield a workable concept, try to identify a social problem that is related to or resonates with the brand. To do this, consider the United Nations' Sustainable Development Goals. There are 17 of them, which identify some of the world's most pressing needs, including alleviation of poverty and hunger; improvements in health and well-being, and education; gender equality; improved water and sanitation; affordable and clean energy; improvement of work conditions; greater economic growth and innovation; reduction of inequality; sustainable cities; responsible consumption and production; action to address climate change; protection of the environment and living creatures; and peace and justice through strengthened institutions.[35]

Within these SDGs there are many additional worthwhile goals and sub-goals, ranging from combating the objectification of women, to helping people with disabilities access services, to contributing to lower child mortality, to driving gender equality, to alleviating loneliness. What is distinctive about your brand? Is there an educational role it could fill? Could it help connect providers of social solutions with people in need? What is the role that your product could play in contributing to solving the issue? The possibilities are limitless. It is important to remember that reducing food waste and decreasing reliance on plastic, and working on superior quality products, is a pre-requisite before thinking about a social purpose (see Chapter 12 on winning corporate support).

You should be able to complete this sentence: Brand Y is going to work on X social issue by contributing Z. (Example: Domestos is winning the war on poor sanitation by supporting a janitor programme in schools and offering cheaper affordable formats for toilet cleaning.)

It's important to consider the caveats, of course. For those, see the assessments "Gauging potential impact" and "Gauging readiness".

Assessment: Gauging potential impact

Once your brand has identified a social purpose to consider, there are questions that will need to be addressed. To clarify your thinking, I suggest scoring each of these statements on a simple 1–5 scale. For example, if the purpose you've identified is highly aligned with the brand's core promise, score it a 5.

The social goal we've identified:

   … needs our brand's involvement, even if other brands are focused on the same goal
   … is aligned with the brand's core promise
   … is likely to have a significant impact, for example affecting a large number of lives
   … is achievable, if not in whole then in discrete stages that the brand can be part of

… will yield results that are likely to be visible to the company's stakeholders

… will be considered *worthwhile* by stakeholders

… will cost an amount within what the company wants to spend

… will boost innovations on product lines

… is aligned to the company's wider strategic interests

… is already the target of Governments, NGOs and foundations that could be valuable partners

… could open up future markets for the brand.

If you get a score of 30 or more, you're onto something. If lower, it may be time to go back to the drawing board.

Assessment: Gauging readiness

Now for the really uncomfortable questions. Be ruthlessly honest in scoring these, again on a 1–5 scale. For example, if you agree that the brand would spend the time, money and other resources to thoughtfully craft a solution to the social goal, score that statement a 5.

The brand:

… would really spend the time, money and other resources to thought-fully craft a solution to the social goal

… would succeed in this goal at least as well as, if not better than, other companies that might take an interest in this area

… would be consistently accountable and transparent about the goal

… would always *do* as well as *say*

… sees the goal as more than just an exploitative quick hit (will help the brand in 5–10 years)

… would not be just jumping on a bandwagon

… is not currently doing or selling something harmful that would cast doubt on the social goal.

If you get a score of 25 or more, the brand may be well-positioned to forge ahead. If the score is lower, it probably isn't ready – there is more work to be done in moving the company towards making the necessary adjustments and commitments required for successful social-purpose campaign. See Chapter 12: Winning support within the corporation.

Notes

1 Mayer, C. (2018). *Prosperity: better business makes the greater good*. Oxford, New York: Oxford University Press.

2 WBCSD (2017). "Achieving the Sustainable Development Goals can unlock in new market value", *World Business Council for Sustainable Development (WBCSD)*. Available at: www.wbcsd.org/kuenx (Accessed: 5 January 2020).

3 United Nations (2015). *Sustainable Development Goals.* https://sustainabledevelopment. un.org/sdgs (Accessed:18 December 2019).

4 Weaver, M. A., Joanis, C., Toroitich-Ruto, C., Parker, W., Gyamenah, N. A., Rinaldi, A., Omungo, Z. and Steiner, M. J. (2011). "The effects of condom choice on self-reported condom use among men in Ghana, Kenya and South Africa: a randomized trial". *Contraception*, 84(3), pp. 291–298. doi: 10.1016/j. contraception.2011.01.010.

5 Moscibrodzki, P., Dobelle, M., Stone, J., Kalumuna, C., Chiu, Y. M. and Hennig, N. (2018). "Free versus purchased mosquito net ownership and use in Budondo sub-county, Uganda". *Malaria Journal*, 17, 363. doi: 10.1186/s12936-018-2515-y.

6 Harris, J. (2010). "Mosquito nets can't conquer malaria". *Guardian*, 8 July. Available at: www.theguardian.com/commentisfree/2010/jul/08/mosquito-nets-cant-cure-malaria (Accessed: 2 January 2020).

7 Smith, L. A. and Foxcroft, D. R. (2009) "The effect of alcohol advertising, marketing and portrayal on drinking behaviour in young people: systematic review of prospective cohort studies", *BMC Public Health*, 9, 51. doi: 10.1186/ 1471-2458-9-51.

8 Beevor, C. (2019) Personal interview.

9 Beevor, C. (2019) Personal interview.

10 UNICEF/WHO (2009). *Diarrhoea: why children are still dying and what can be done.* www.who.int/maternal_child_adolescent/documents/9789241598415/en/ (Accessed:18 December 2019).

11 Global Nutrition Report (2018). https://globalnutritionreport.org/reports/global-nutrition-report-2018/introduction/ (Accessed:18 December 2019).

12 Jackson, S. L., Vann, W. F., Kotch, J. B., Pahel, B. T. and Lee, J. Y. (2011). "Impact of poor oral health on children's school attendance and performance". *American Journal of Public Health*, October; 101(10), pp. 1900–1906. www.ncbi. nlm.nih.gov/pmc/articles/PMC3222359/ (Accessed:18 December 2019).

13 World Health Organization (2018). *HIV/AIDS, Global Health Observatory Data.* www.who.int/gho/hiv/en/ (Accessed:18 December 2019).

14 Akos, P. and Levitt, D. H. (2002). "Promoting healthy body image in middle school". *Professional School Counseling*, 6(2), pp.138–144.: www.thefreelibrary.com/ Promoting+healthy+body+image+in+middle+school.-a096194764 (Accessed:18 December 2019).

15 Yager, Z., Diedrichs, P. C., Ricciardelli, L. A. and Halliwell, E. (2013). "What works in secondary schools? A systematic review of classroom-based body image programmes". *Body Image*, 10(3), pp.271–181. https://uwe-repository.worktribe. com/output/931625 (Accessed:18 December 2019).

16 Willis, O. (2019). "The limits of 'traditional masculinity': experts call for gendered approach to men's mental health". *ABC News*. Available at: www.abc.net.au/ news/health/2019-02-05/mens-mental-health-masculinity-gendered-psychology-guidelines/10768294 (Accessed: 2 January 2020).

17 Govender, D. (2019). Interviewed by Sidibe, M., Tidworth, B. and Anani-Isaac, M., 15 February 2019.

18 Cooper, N. (2012). "Great brands and the role of ideals". *Market Leader,* Quarter 2 2012, 28–31. www.marketingsociety.com/sites/default/files/thelibrary/march-2012_13.pdf (Accessed:18 December 2019)

19 Unilever (2018). *Unilever's Sustainable Living Plan continues to fuel growth.* 20 May. www.unilever.com/news/press-releases/2018/unilevers-sustainable-living-plan-continues-to-fuel-growth.html (Accessed:18 December 2019).

20 Jope, A. (2019). Personal interview.

21 Kramer, M. R. and Porter, M. (2011). "Creating shared value". *Harvard Business Review,* 89, no. 1/2, 62–77.

22 Ghiridharadas, A (2018). *Winners take all: the elite charade of changing the world*, New York: Knopf.
23 Porter, M. (2019). Personal interview.
24 Moss, M. (2013). *Salt sugar and fat: how the food giants hooked us*. London: Random House.
25 Freudenberg, N., 2014. Lethal But Legal: Corporations, Consumption, and Protecting Public Health. Oxford, New York: Oxford University Press.
26 Business Roundtable (2019). "Business Roundtable redefines the purpose of a corporation to promote 'An Economy That Serves All Americans'". Available at: www. businessroundtable.org/business-roundtable-redefines-the-purpose-of-a-corporation-to-promote-an-economy-that-serves-all-americans (Accessed: 2 January 2020).
27 Fink, L. (2019). *Larry Fink's 2019 letter to CEOs: purpose & profit, BlackRock*. Available at: www.blackrock.com/corporate/investor-relations/larry-fink-ceo-letter (Accessed: 2 January 2020).
28 Ojo, U. (2019). Personal interview.
29 Paranjpe, N. (2019). Personal interview.
30 Porter, M. (2019). Personal interview.
31 Last, A. (2019). Personal interview.
32 Miles, S. (2019). Personal interview.
33 Faber, E. (2019). Personal interview.
34 Collier, P. (2018). *The future of capitalism: facing the new anxieties*. New York; HarperCollins. Mayer, C (2019). *Prosperity: better business makes the greater good*. Oxford, New York: Oxford University Press.
35 United Nations (2015). *Sustainable Development Goals*. Available at: www.un.org/sustainabledevelopment/ (Accessed: 2 January 2020).

2 Dove and the impact of body image

All the girls in my class want to get plastic surgery done because of the amazing results they see on Instagram. Plastic surgeons create fake profiles on Insta, with before and after pictures, and lure girls as young as 13 years to change their bodies. How do we know those pictures are real? That these surgeons are certified? The girls are taking the risk because they are not comfortable with their own bodies. They are constantly being bombarded with certain images and told their own body is inadequate. This needs to change. My campaign will expose these unscrupulous practices and force platforms like Instagram to ensure that the content being published on their website is more responsible.

(Julieta Ramirez Lopez, Girl Guide, Mexico[1])

Dressed in stylishly scruffy jeans with a "Free Being Me" T-shirt and spectacles, 18-year-old Julieta (see Figure 2.1) was one of dozens of girl guides and girl scouts attending the conference. Each brimming with ideas. Each determined to change the relationship that their friends, relatives and community members have with their own bodies. Their activism had been awakened in part by the efforts of one of the largest companies in the beauty industry: Unilever.

This is the story of how a corporation is changing conversations, attitudes and behaviours, as well as the social and media environment, by putting the might of its marketing behind a social purpose. Unilever's Dove, a multi-product brand best known for its non-soap beauty bar, has worked to redefine beauty and help millions of girls and women, and those who identify with women, become comfortable with their own bodies. This is an ongoing effort, with many partners, but so far Dove has created not just substantial social value, but also a solid return on investments.

Dove's experience demonstrates the power of brands on a mission. It also highlights the challenges of getting there. I've placed it here, early in the book, because it brings out many of the key learnings I'll address in the chapters to come. It also shows how you can make a genuine difference even when the product is not at the centre of the social mission.

Figure 2.1 Julieta Ramirez Lopez, Mexico 2019.

How Dove got a mission

Unilever, a large Anglo-Dutch multinational consumer goods company, has been in the soap business since the 1880s. In 1957 it launched Dove in North America as a "non-soap" cleansing bar. Dove included a patented moisturising solution that cleaned skin without drying it out – based on wartime research into non-irritant cleansers for battlefield wounds. Dove quickly became a household name with its "one-quarter cleansing cream" tagline.

The initial advertisements featured thin, glamorous models purring about how Dove made them feel pampered like the "girliest girl in the world". But with the feminist movement in the 1960s, the brand switched to testimonials from "real" women about the comparative benefits of the bar. This "realness" became a defining feature of the product's identity.

Still, the focus continued on the product itself. In the 1980s, after an independent university study found Dove to be milder than other leading soaps, Unilever marketed it extensively to physicians, paediatricians and dermatologists. The company also sent thousands of litmus strips to households so they could test the alkalinity of Dove against other soaps. Sales took off, and by 1986 Dove had become the highest revenue soap in the United States. It soon expanded into Europe and beyond.

In the early 1990s, however, the cleansing market became increasingly competitive. In particular, the new liquid body wash segment challenged the established bar market, with rival Olay introducing a popular moisturising product. Dove's market share flattened and sales stagnated. Its managers responded by expanding the product range to several new areas, including deodorants and hair care. They also expanded the brand to 80 countries.

This new approach worked so well that in 2000, Unilever designated Dove as one of its 40 "Masterbrands". Dove could now use a single brand identity to encompass a diverse range of products. It was a strong vote of confidence, but one that forced Dove's marketers to clarify what the brand stood for. After all, moisturising was not a relevant feature for deodorants, styling aids and some other Dove products.

When Dove's marketers conducted consumer surveys to help develop a new brand identity, the responses startled them: it seemed that a uniform beauty ideal had become so powerful that it was driving even the most educated and aware women to seek to change their bodies. They turned for advice to Nancy Etcoff, assistant clinical professor in psychology at Harvard Medical School, and Susie Orbach, a psychotherapist and leading feminist at the London School of Economics.

Orbach, who wrote *Fat Is a Feminist Issue* in 1978, points out that the West has:

> exported body hatred as a way of entering modernity. You're supposed to be engaged in your body to make it a certain way, not just for movie stars or prospective brides. It's a preoccupation from the age of six, which is when we start marketing cosmetic surgery to girls.[2]

In 2004, under the guidance of Etcoff and Orbach, Dove launched a ten-country "Real Beauty" study of 3200 women, aged 18 to 64. The study found that, although people in Western cultures rate themselves as better than average on everything from kindness to intelligence and popularity, only 12 per cent of the women surveyed described themselves as above average in appearance, and only 2 per cent saw themselves as beautiful. Almost half the women believed that their body weight was "too high". Sixty per cent believed that beauty was socially mandated and rewarded, such that if you meet the beauty ideal, you get ahead faster, with a higher chance at success.[3]

Other research showed that the media blitzkrieg of digitally altered and airbrushed images of models with blonde hair and size zero bodies undermined the self-confidence of women and girls. People have little understanding of the weight, shape and size of a healthy body. Instead they work from the artificial ideal projected by music videos, films, social media and magazines — fuelling a widespread perception of being "fat". Many women pursue this media-driven beauty ideal even as they recognise its absurdity.[4] Children become aware of their own appearance and society's bias against certain body types by age six.[5] Two-thirds of adolescent girls and nearly half of boys want to change their body weight or shape.[6, 7]

The Real Beauty study reflected these dynamics and confirmed a growing frustration with the media's narrow definitions and depictions of beauty. Three-quarters of the respondents wanted to see more diversity in images of beauty.[8]

The marketers had found a new identity for Dove – "Real Beauty". It also resonated with the brand's heritage. John Stuart, who managed the Dove advertising account at Ogilvy from 2005 to 2019, recalled that "Beginning in 1963, Dove was about the experience of its users, about realness and granularity."[9]

Still, this approach was so radical and so different from the advertising landscape at that time that the marketers, including Alessandro Manfredi, then Brand Director and today Executive Vice-President for Dove, needed to convince Unilever executives. "First we gained permission to conduct video interviews with the executives' children", recalled Manfredi. "Then we played a videotape of those interviews at an executive meeting".[10] The kids talked about wanting to change their bodies. Patrick Cescau, then CEO of Unilever, recalled,

> It suddenly becomes personal. You realise your own children are impacted by the beauty industry, how stressed they are by this image of unattainable beauty which is imposed on them every day – and the loss of self-esteem and other trouble going with it, anorexia and all of that.[11]

He and executives unanimously approved the team's approach.

The campaign for Real Beauty

The first campaign to follow this new approach was launched in Europe. Shot by Rankin – a photographer already known for photographing real women – the "Curves" photographs featured six real women (not models) in white underwear proudly showing off their curves after using Dove's new firming cream. The US team embraced this idea as well, and it garnered attention in major newspapers.

Following the success of the Real Curves campaign, the Campaign for Real Beauty launched globally with "Tick Box" in September 2004, with Dove Canada leading the way (see Figure 2.2). On huge billboards in four high-traffic locations, they put up pictures of everyday women with such questions as "Fat or Fit?" and "Grey or Gorgeous?" People were invited to text responses to the Real Beauty website, with a live ticker showing the results. Dove Canada funded the new campaign without any additional budgetary allocation, as the marketers convinced their category managers to contribute from their product marketing budgets. This was a radical change because thus far the categories within Dove Canada had operated in silos. And it was risky, because the contribution was substantial enough to limit product marketing for the rest of the year. Sharon MacLeod, a Dove Canada

campaignforrealbeauty.co.uk 🐦 | *Dove*

☐ fat?
☐ fit?

Does true beauty only squeeze into size 8?
Join the beauty debate

Figure 2.2 Dove Tickbox campaign, Canada 2004.

marketer, remembered, "What if people said the woman was fat or wrinkled? We had to be prepared to have that debate."[12]

But the response was largely positive. Dove US followed with billboards in New York's Times Square, and then in the UK and Asia. Over one million women visited the Dove website to cast their vote. And Dove's revenue in the US rose 6 per cent over the previous year.[13, 14]

Nancy Etcoff found the campaign striking.

I went to Times Square and saw those huge advertisements asking wrinkled or wonderful, fat or fit, and I thought: I could write for journals for the rest of my life and they wouldn't make all these people think about this issue in the same way that one visual from this brand can do. It's potentially very powerful, and very different from writing for your fellow academics.

MacLeod recalls,

> When we first launched the Campaign for Real Beauty (CFRB), we were shocked at the response. Tick Box quickly became the topic of watercooler and coffee break conversations. Our office was flooded with letters from women, girls, fathers who were raising young daughters, everyone wanted to get involved and show support. We had to hire a temp just to respond to all the mail. Having sparked a debate, we had to do something about it.[15]

The Dove team realised that this was a critical moment. It's not enough for brands to call attention to a social problem. To have a true mission, they have to do something about it. Dove had to move beyond "Brand Say" – what the brand communicated through advertising campaigns – to "Brand Do" – substantial actions to fulfil this social purpose. Experts were clear that in order to make a big impact, they needed to take action to prevent the issues at the age the issues first start: puberty.

Dove responded by starting what became the Dove Self-Esteem Project (DSEP).[16] They launched workshops for girls and created a toolbox for teachers and mentors.

To attract girls to the workshops, Dove Canada spent US$150,000 to create "Evolution", a 75-second film showing how the beauty industry digitally altered the images of women in ads. The clip gathered 170 million YouTube views in a month, the equivalent of US$150 million in advertising exposure.[17, 18] It became the first double Grand Prix winner in the history of the International Advertising Festival at Cannes.[19] Meanwhile Dove US officially launched DSEP at the Super Bowl in 2006 by adapting "Daughters", the film that had persuaded Unilever's executives, to create a new ad called "Little Girls". Set to the soundtrack of Cyndi Lauper's song "True Colours", similar to the original Daughters film, the ad showed a diverse range of girls stating what they disliked about their bodies, ending with the message "Let's make peace with beauty".

Scaling up through partnerships

All of these successes, however, didn't gain enough traction to make social purpose core to the brand's marketing strategy. In 2008, when Steve Miles took over as the Executive Vice President for Dove, he found that "The CFRB was becoming just a tagline attached to every advertisement. There was no real connection between the films being made and the educational workshops under the DSEP."[20] Investing in purpose was not mandatory, and many of Dove's country managers saw little benefit in doing so when they were focused on short-term profit targets. They thought the CFRB tagline was enough.

Part of the problem was that the campaign had gone overboard. Its third film, "Onslaught", told mothers to "talk to their daughter before the beauty industry does", even though Dove was part of the same beauty industry that the ad condemned. As Miles recalled, "We had slipped from being a celebratory, optimistic brand to a strident, militant one that was alien to the Dove heritage."[21] In reaction, many marketers had reverted to functional, product-based advertising, and paid only lip service to social purpose.

Previously in charge of Lifebuoy soap (see Chapter 6), Miles realised that Dove could gain that traction only by scaling up the self-esteem work. To do that, they needed outside help. The workshops were just too limited to make much difference. Only by convincing other organisations to contribute could Dove deliver measurable social impact. Changing mindsets and societal attitudes required concerted efforts on many fronts. With that, Dove could match Brand Say with Brand Do. The Brand Do had to inform the Brand Say.

To get the necessary traction, Dove needed to form large-scale partnerships for content, evidence and dissemination, and it needed to advocate with governments and international organisations to recognise self-esteem and body confidence as a social, gender and public health issue. Along the way it needed to continually engage its employees to ensure that they remain committed to the purpose.

Help came in the form of Unilever's new CEO Paul Polman. In 2010, under Polman, the company embraced the Unilever Sustainable Living Plan (USLP). The plan had the goal of improving health and well-being for one billion people. The corporate CSR department was dropped in favour of each masterbrand taking responsibility for part of this commitment. Polman made an external commitment that Dove would reach 15 million girls by 2015, up from eight million in 2010.

Investing in purpose was no longer voluntary. Each manager needed to accept his or her share of the target and earmark funds to meet it. "With USLP behind me," recalled Miles, "I was able to transform purpose from being this fragile coalition of the willing into a firm, mandatory part of country plans."[22] Armed with his personal conviction and a mandate from the CEO, Miles began to line up the pieces.

Dove had always recognised the importance of partnering with experts. These partnerships had begun around content and dissemination, but Miles now connected with additional experts to help on measurement. The Centre for Appearance Research (CAR), at the University of the West of England, was a leader in this area. Decades of research there, and elsewhere, were showing that people with body-image concerns are more likely to have low self-esteem, depression, stress and anxiety, whilst a positive body-image helps people to fulfil their potential and opt into life. People with body-image concerns are also more likely to engage in substance misuse, risky sexual practices and disordered eating. The detrimental impact extends to diminished relationships, civic engagement, education, career aspirations and work performance, throughout people's lives.[23]

Dove partnered with CAR psychologist professor Phillippa Diedrichs to review the scholarship on interventions for this age group, and to begin to systematically evaluate the impact of the DSEP programmes and improve their design. Following Diedrichs' advice, Dove adopted the pyramid for behaviour change for public health interventions (see Figure 2.3), aiming to retain the impact and quality of tools while reaching more young people directly.[24]

As Stacie June, Global Head of Education and Advocacy, Dove Self-Esteem Project, recalls:

> The pyramid was created to find ways to retain the impact and quality of our tools, while reaching more young people directly with them. We were previously dependent on teachers, parents and youth leaders to deliver the workshops, but began to develop innovative models harnessing media as a delivery mechanism to extend the reach of the body image messages.[25]

For Dove, the apex of this pyramid includes direct interventions such as "Confident Me" for teachers in schools, and "Uniquely Me" for parents, both in-depth tools with one to five hours of content.

A key partner for Dove has been the World Association of Girl Guides and Girl Scouts (WAGGGS), which represents 10 million girls across 150 countries, including Julieta who we met at the beginning of this chapter. In forming its partnership with WAGGGS, it helped that Dove had worked with academics on the content of the DSEP. "For us the fact that the programme was developed by experts was absolutely vital because we could have confidence in the content. It also kept the cynical this-is-just-another-corporate-ploy perspective at bay", admitted Sarah Nancollas, CEO of WAGGGS.[26]

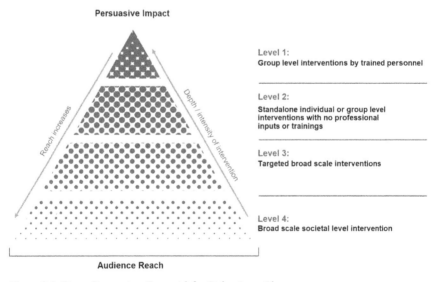

Figure 2.3 Dove Persuasion Pyramid for Behaviour Change.

In 2013 with WAGGGS Dove launched the Free Being Me programme, which educated girls and their troop leaders on body confidence. By 2018, this programme had reached 4.6 million girls worldwide.

"The programme with Dove has the biggest uptake of any we've ever done", said Nancollas.

> It was originally intended for a handful of countries. But body confidence is such an important issue that girls from 128 of our 150 countries decided to opt for it. The availability of expert-designed content through an activity pack that can be used in so many different ways and in so many different countries has been vital to the success of this programme.[27]

For Julieta:

> The programme changed how I view things. I was 15 when I followed in my mother's footsteps and became a girl guide. I enrolled in the Free Being Me programme, and liked it so much that I became a peer educator. The first change I saw was in myself. I used to tell my friends "you look beautiful" instead of commenting on their intelligence or kindness. We called people "fat". I began to understand this was not okay.[28]

Dove also learned about the effectiveness of the workshops. Diedrich found that:

> The single session programme has an immediate benefit that's not sustained, which is a common pattern that we see. You need to do multiple sessions to have a longer lasting impact, but we know that at some schools, one is all they will do. With the five-session version we are getting effects up to six months later.[29]

The next level in the pyramid consisted of e-books and games such as the 90-second Self-Esteem Squad. These standalone interventions require no staff and therefore reach a wide audience at a much lower cost. They are followed by broad-based entertainment and educational interventions on the DSEP website. In 2018, for example, Dove worked with Steven Universe, a popular series on Cartoon Network. The series ran six 60-second animations on body image, supplemented by downloadable comic books and workshops for 7 to 10-year-olds. The cartoon content was tested and proven to make an immediate positive impact on body satisfaction and other key body image indicators – a huge finding for the body image and mental health field of study. And significantly, in two years this series has reached over 20 million young people – a reach that took Dove ten years to achieve previously.

Figure 2.4 Dove collaboration with Steven Universe, 2018.

The last, lowest, rung of the pyramid involved broad-scale interventions, such as government legislation and industry-specific regulations, as well as social initiatives. In the UK, for example, Dove worked with the YMCA and the All-Party Parliamentary Group on Body Image to develop the "Be Real" programme.[30] This programme encourages schools, healthcare providers, and the fashion and media industries to promote more diverse and realistic body images. Dove is also supporting the Crown Act in the US, which seeks to end racial hair discrimination,[31] and other legislation to encourage more businesses and brands not to digitally distort the images.[32]

Miles and his colleagues made social purpose, boosting young peoples' self-esteem, into Dove's core proposition. Dove differentiated itself in the marketplace with its larger mission, going beyond the products themselves. But they also made sure that the various Dove products were themselves socially responsible. They made it easier for consumers to see product ingredients, and took on public commitments on plastic, including moving to 100 per cent recycled plastic bottles. They also enacted a policy prohibiting all animal tests, anywhere in the world, with all Dove products, and were certified "Cruelty-Free" by animal rights organisation PETA in 2018.

Seeking consistency across the corporation

Even as Dove was winning praise for its efforts, critics were pointing out a problem. Other Unilever brands went in a different direction. The most notable was Axe (Lynx in certain countries), the masterbrand for young men's personal care. Men who used its products, some advertisements claimed, would help win over women with the very "unreal" beauty disparaged in the Dove campaigns.

It was a major challenge for Miles and his team. Miles said:

> Historically companies were relaxed about owning brands with very different viewpoints, if each targeted a different consumer base – and that is what a portfolio strategy often requires. Yet the modern age requires that the consumer knows what a company stands for.[33]

Fortunately for Dove, broader social mores against toxic masculinity led Axe to drop its sex-based advertising strategy. As Alan Jope, the current Unilever CEO, recounted in an interview for Brands on a Mission, "Axe was guilty as charged of presenting an out-of-date representation of modern masculinity and an unacceptable portrayal of women."[34]

Another challenge came from Fair & Lovely, a skin-lightening cream sold mainly in South Asia, which ran ads praising light-coloured women over dark. WAGGGS pointed to "colourism" as a major issue for many girls around the world. At a Dove-sponsored event in 2018, several girl guides called on Dove to influence Fair & Lovely to take a different approach.

This was a tougher call because the desire for lighter skin in South Asia had been strong for centuries, long before Western colonialism. Unilever argued that if Fair & Lovely pulled out, women might resort to bleaches with more dangerous ingredients. However, they stopped explicit appeals to colourism. As Jope said, "We were wrong to equate skin colour with social or economic advancement."[35] Instead the marketing switched to promote women's freedom to get an education and gain financial independence. The Fair & Lovely brand signed on early to the corporate USLP and set up a foundation to provide college scholarships and online education courses for women in its markets.

Even so, the Fair & Lovely brand continues to be raised by consumers and DSEP participants as a problem for the Campaign for Real Beauty, and frequently comes up at Dove events.

Reaping dividends

Still another challenge had to do with target audiences. Dove's self-esteem programmes are aimed at 11–14 year-old girls, as researchers have found this is when body image interventions are most effective for prevention. But Dove products are aimed at young women aged 25 plus. Furthermore, since the programmes do not promote products or give out product samples, Dove managers might wonder how the brand really benefits from these investments. After all, brands on a mission still need to make money commercially. They aren't charities.

It turns out that far from hurting revenues, the CFRB has coincided with rapid growth. From 2004, with the launch of the campaign, to 2018, Dove's revenues increased from US$2.5 billion to US$6 billion,[36, 37] with accompanying growth in market share and profits. This growth occurred even as the brand sustained its price premium in a commoditising Personal Care market. Back in 2004 Dove was the third largest masterbrand within Unilever, and by 2017 it was number one.

While it is impossible to measure the relative contribution of social purpose, a recent study found that intent-to-purchase rose by between 10 and 25 percentage points when people were aware of the self-esteem activities. An internal Dove study argued that CFRB had driven US$280 million in global incremental revenue, and that every US$1 spent on communications returned US$3 in revenue. Further, three Dove campaigns – Sketches, Patches and Choose Beautiful – together earned 13.9 billion global impressions and an ROI of US$4.42 per US$1 spent, three times the average ROI of US$1.27 in the fast-moving-consumer-goods sector.[38]

An econometric study by Nielsen, taking three years of data from Dove across 20 markets worldwide, tested the hypothesis that the markets that spend a higher proportion of funds on social purpose outperformed those that had spent little or nothing on purpose. The study concluded that purpose markets had double the growth in share value compared to those without.[39]

"My experience on multiple brands, even allowing for all the other variables, is clear: Purpose is not a distraction from 'selling more' but the most powerful way to do so", concluded Miles.[40]

Julieta pointed out that:

> The Free Being Me programme really made me aware of Dove as a brand. Earlier it was just another soap company, but now it is like a partner. I am currently advocating for publishing more responsible

content on Instagram. The people from WAGGGS and Dove are helping me to work through my idea. We are in this together.[41]

These good financial results went along with the substantial social impact of Dove. By 2018, 35 million girls had participated in the self-esteem work-shops, along with thousands of teachers and parents. Going down the pyramid, hundreds of millions more were exposed to messages to counteract distorted notions of body image.

Dove had also supported advocacy, far beyond Julieta and other girl guides at the Women Deliver conference. The brand had lent its support to legis-lation against retouching advertising images. It also co-sponsored a series of TED talks in 2014, including one by Meaghan Ramsey, former director of DSEP, on "Why Thinking You're Ugly is Bad for You", that garnered four million views.[42]

More generally, Dove has helped to create an evidence-based model for changing attitudes and behaviours about body image. It is now available for any organisation to take on, with or without Dove.

Looking ahead

With a continuously increasing percentage of Dove's marketing spend now going towards social purpose, rather than simply functional product ads, Dove is setting its ambitions high. The brand is going beyond body image to promote inclusion generally, supporting discussions on gender fluidity and transgender. Its 2019 promotion, #ShowUs Campaign, with a ground-breaking library of 5000+ photographs devoted to shattering beauty stereo-types, responded to findings that 70 per cent of women do not find themselves represented in the media.[43]

The larger challenge is to expand the workshop approach and figure out how to bring about a sustained change in people's empowerment around their bodies. Only then will young people feel comfortable negotiating for safe sex and equal relationships. They'll have fewer eating problems and better mental health generally.

So far Dove's results have helped to convince Alan Jope to double down on mission-based brands. The Unilever CEO said,

> I want 100% of brands' efforts and resources to go behind purposeful marketing. Within the next few years, any brand that does not have an authentic purpose will not have a role in Unilever's portfolio. We believe this is our only way to grow our business.[44]

Notes

1 Ramirez Lopez, J. (2019). Women Deliver Conference in Vancouver, Canada.
2 Orbach, S. (2019). Personal interview.

3 Etcoff, N., Orbach, S., Scott, J. and D'Agostino, H. (2004). "The real truth about beauty: a global report. Findings of the global study on women, beauty and well-being". Commissioned by Dove, a Unilever brand.

4 Deliovsky, K. (2008). "Normative white femininity: race, gender and the politics of beauty". *Atlantis: Critical Studies in Gender, Culture & Social Justice* 33(1). Available at: http://journals.msvu.ca/index.php/atlantis/issue/view/59 (Accessed: 4 January 2020).

5 Smolak, L. and Thompson, J. K. (2009). *Body image, eating disorders, and obesity in youth: assessment, prevention, and treatment.* Washington DC: American Psychological Association. pp. 41–66.

6 Akos, P. and Levitt, D. H. (2002). "Promoting healthy body image in middle school". *Professional School Counselling Vol 6, no. 2;* 138–144. Available at: www.thefreelibrary.com/Promoting+healthy+body+image+in+middle+school.-a096194764 (Accessed: 4 January 2020).

7 Diedrichs, P. C., Ricciardelli, L. A. and Halliwell, E. (2013). "What works in secondary schools? A systematic review of classroom-based body image programs". *Body Image*, 10(3). doi: 10.1016/j.bodyim.2013.04.001.

8 Etcoff, N., Orbach, S., Scott, J. and D'Agostino, H. (2004). "The real truth about beauty: a global report. Findings of the global study on women, beauty and well-being". Commissioned by Dove, a Unilever brand.

9 Stuart, John. (2019). Personal interview.

10 Manfredo, A. (2019). Personal interview.

11 Financial Times (2008). "Taking a hardline on a soft soap". 7 July. Available at: www.ft.com/content/ca8b9882-4a0b-11dd-891a-000077b07658 (Accessed: 4 January 2020).

12 Macleod, S. (2019). Personal interview.

13 Jeffers, M. (2005). "Behind Dove's 'Real Beauty'". *Adweek.* 46(35) 34–35. Available at: www.adweek.com/brand-marketing/behind-doves-real-beauty-81469/ (Accessed: 4 January 2020).

14 Ibid.

15 Macleod, S. (2019). Personal interview.

16 It was originally called the Dove Self-Esteem Fund.

17 Neff, J. (2006). "Better ROI from YouTube video than Super Bowl spot. Dove's viral hit 'Evolution' is a real beauty". *AdAge.* 29 October 2006. Available at: https://adage.com/article/news/roi-youtube-video-super-bowl-spot/112835 (Accessed: 4 January 2020).

18 Ogilvy Toronto (2006). "Dove – Evolution". *Meanwhile.* 11 October 2006. Available at: https://meanwhile.wordpress.com/2006/10/11/dove-evolution-2/ (Accessed: 4 January 2020).

19 Neff, J. (2014). "Ten years in, Dove's 'Real Beauty' seems to be aging well". *AdAge.* 22 January 2014. Available at: https://adage.com/article/news/ten-years-dove-s-real-beauty-aging/291216 (Accessed: 4 January 2020).

20 Miles, S. (2019). Personal interview.

21 Ibid.

22 Ibid.

23 Diedrichs, P. (2019). Personal interview.

24 Adapted from Centre for Appearance Research (CAR) Intervention Model. CAR, UWE Bristol.

25 June, S. (2019). Personal interview.

26 Nancollas, Sarah. (2019). Personal interview.

27 Ibid.

28 Ramirez Lopez, J. (2019).

29 Diedrichs, P. (2019). Personal interview.

30 YMCA (2017). "Be Real campaign research highlights body image anxiety in schools". *YMCA England & Wales*. Available at: www.ymca.org.uk/latest-news/be-real-schools-research-toolkit-launched (Accessed: 4 January 2020).

31 Dove USA (no date). "The crown coalition". *Unilever, USA*. Available at: www.dove.com/us/en/stories/campaigns/the-crown-act.html (Accessed: 4 January 2020).

32 Dove USA (no date). "100% real beauty: introducing the Dove 'No Digital Distortion' mark". *Unilever USA*. Available at: www.dove.com/us/en/stories/about-dove/introducing-the-no-digital-distortion-mark-dove.html (Accessed: 4 January 2020).

33 Miles, S. (2019). Personal interview.

34 Jope, A. (2019). Personal interview.

35 Ibid.

36 Neff, J. (2014). "Ten years in, Dove's 'Real Beauty' seems to be aging well". *AdAge*. 22 January 2014. Available at: https://adage.com/article/news/ten-years-dove-s-real-beauty-aging/291216 (Accessed: 4 January 2020).

37 Miles, S. (2019). Personal interview.

38 IPA (2016). "Dove: beautifully effective: how Dove turned cultural resonance into ROI". *IPA*. Available at: https://ipa.co.uk/knowledge/case-studies/dove-beautifully-effective-how-dove-turned-cultural-resonance-into-roi/ (Accessed: 4 January 2020).

39 Ibid.

40 Miles, S. (2019). Personal interview.

41 Ramirez Lopez, J. (2019).

42 Ramsey, M. (2014). "Why thinking you're ugly is bad for you". *TED Institute*. September 2014. Available at: www.ted.com/talks/meaghan_ramsey_why_thinking_you_re_ugly_is_bad_for_you (Accessed: 4 January 2020).

43 Dove (2019). "Project #ShowUs". *Unilever UK*. Available at: www.dove.com/uk/stories/campaigns/showus.html

44 Jope, A. (2019). Personal interview.

3   Driving mass behavioural change

As we saw in Chapter 1, most poor health stems from lifestyle choices that can be altered and changed. At the heart of public health is prevention, which means that altering behaviour needs to be the focus of intervention. Take the problem of poor sanitation and the underuse of toilets in Burundi: had we done some formative research, we would have found that the toilets were either too far from people's homes, or not offering enough privacy because local cultural rules meant that mothers-in-law and husbands could not share the same toilet. Another important element was that a smelly toilet with visual faeces can hardly compete with an open-air defecation field. Finding solutions to these issues with behavioural approaches become key.

That's true even without massive investments in drugs or infrastructure. Some of the most common and damaging diseases in the world can be prevented by people adopting some simple, low-cost behaviours. From diarrhoea to HIV-AIDS, behaviour change is often the most important part of the solution. In *Gaining Control*,[1] the top 20 global causes of lost disability-adjusted life years (DALY), from undernutrition to lack of contraception and physical inactivity, can be improved with better behaviours.[2]

But it's very difficult to convince people to change their long-established behaviours. As well as listening to people, incentives and rewards are needed. That's where for-profit corporations can help, as they have incentives for people to buy their products. They have decades of experience in convincing consumers to buy different products, so they know how to influence behaviour. They bring extensive resources, capabilities and creative heft to think about solutions. Of course, for-profit corporations have been alleged to have acted to change people's behaviours for the worse (as with obesity from over consumption of fast foods or infant formula marketing), so we need to get the public sector and the private sector to partner effectively (see Chapter 5). We could make enormous progress in boosting the health of vulnerable people around the world if more of the resources of marketing were targeted at healthy behaviour.

As for the companies, they stand to benefit directly from promoting healthier behaviour. As explained in Chapter 1, many brands are losing out to commoditisation. If they embrace a mission of public health, they can regain their brand momentum and boost their margins, grow the pie in the long term and, of course, make their employees proud to work for them. They can even change the narrative about how terrible corporations are. While marketers may not always use a lot of behavioural theory, this is changing, with sciences like neuro-marketing on the rise.[3] They know how to use emotions to appeal to their consumers. They also more in tune with what works because they receive much more immediate feedback through metrics like sales. Obviously they have more resources and can take more risks in their communications approaches.

This chapter explains how and why commercial brands can contribute to public health. And we will see how successful behaviour change campaigns can use the best of the marketing resources, whilst appealing to NGOs, governments and solid science.

Changing behaviour with brands

Of course, governments and non-profit organisations are well aware of the need for behaviour change to improve public health, and they have a lot of experience with it. However they tend to approach the problem from a functional/health perspective, where products are marketed by focusing on health benefits. The public sector has made huge progress over the years, especially in social marketing. In my doctorate, which was meant to inform public health programmes, I looked at motivations like peer-pressure, disgust and using play to create a routine as an attempt to find better solutions to hand-washing and sanitation promotion for children in schools.

Public health academics, policy makers, marketers and behavioural economists have studied the challenge and advanced our knowledge. But, as I found in Burundi, we struggled to move beyond the paradigm that the free giving of resources determines uptake. Something about placing a value to the product was missing. While public health practitioners find it challenging to know if their messages are having an impact at the population level, marketers can see the effect of their messages on the everyday sales figures for their brands, and this feedback yields unique insights into consumer demand.

Marketing in its pure form is the science of persuading customers to choose a certain product over the alternatives. Much of marketing in normal circumstances is about persuading consumers to buy a company's product rather than that of a competitor. For new products, categories or product uses, marketing is about changing behaviour. First you identify a cue for the desired behaviour, something concrete that cues people to do something. Then you identify a desirable, tangible and visible reward for doing that behaviour. If you can link a trigger close in time and space to the reward, then you have a good chance of driving mass behaviour change. The process of Cue – Behaviour – Reward is simple and borne out in our biological systems for learning (see Figure 3.1),[4] yet also aligns well to the product development process that marketers have been thinking about for centuries.

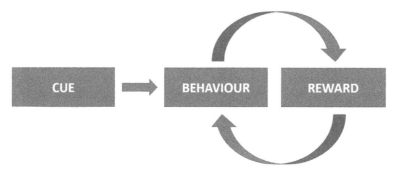

Figure 3.1 Cue Behaviour Reward process.

Marketers also excel at creating nudges with the products themselves, such as packaging that attracts your attention on the shelf or making the product easier to use (like pre-washed lettuce). But the nature of their work means that they have not worked as much on local environment nudges, changes to settings where behaviour is regularly carried out, which are required to transform the behaviours into habits.[5] This is where partnerships with the public sector will be essential (we will talk about this in Chapter 5).

Those concrete steps of Cues – Behaviours – Rewards are essential in motivating people to change their behaviour in a sustainable way. After all, some behaviour change comes at an immediate personal cost for the individual. The rewards for many public health behaviours (handwashing, toothbrushing, using a condom) are usually variable (you do not get sick "every" time you do not wash your hands), come only in the future, so are discounted, and often can feel time-consuming. Where preventive behaviours do not provide immediate rewards or something that you can see, the products can make a huge difference, giving you the right fragrance, the nice smelling breath or helping you perform the ideal behaviour better, such as the Quip toothbrush that automatically turns on for four 30-second intervals to promote brushing for two minutes.

A century ago, Americans were consuming more sugary foods, and their oral health was declining. Toothbrushing had been around since ancient times, but few people were actually cleaning their teeth. Public health officials saw the problem but struggled to address it.

In 1915 a new company launched Pepsodent, a toothpaste that included pepsin to better break down food left on the teeth. Initial sales were disappointing, so the company reached out to Claude Hopkins, a marketing executive. He had a model of changing behaviour by providing a clear trigger with an immediate reward. After reading through the oral health research, Hopkins discovered that food left a thin bacterial film on teeth, something people could feel, and that brushing with toothpaste would remove this film. This was the Cue. Hopkins triggered the Cue with ads making people aware of the film and telling them it dulled their teeth. By brushing with Pepsodent, the Behaviour, they would remove the film and get brighter teeth – the Reward.

The ads raised awareness of the film and linked its removal with brushing with Pepsodent. The sales of Pepsodent exploded. People noticed the film and were happy to remove it. And it turned out Pepsodent had an added advantage that Hopkins didn't realise, a third factor that further boosted the impact. Mostly to improve shelf life, the company had also added citric acid, mint oil and a few other exotic chemicals. Those chemicals left a mild tingling sensation on the teeth and gums. Not only did this sensation make people feel they had cleaned their teeth, but they grew to desire that sensation at the times of day they normally brushed their teeth. By creating these cravings, Pepsodent ensured that people would miss toothbrushing if they forgot.[6]

As other toothpaste makers saw Pepsodent's success, they imitated its ingredients, especially mint. By 1925, two-thirds of Americans were brushing with toothpaste with enormous benefits for public health. What made the difference was not adding pepsin, or urging people to prevent tooth decay, which was the information-based approach that public health professionals tended to use. What worked was the marketer's ability to link the use of Pepsodent with physically perceivable aspects of the experience. This included both the generic effects of toothbrushing and specific sensory properties of Pepsodent.

Now let's move to the present. More than three billion people still do not brush their teeth twice a day, and more than one billion do not ever use a fluoride toothpaste. The poor oral health that results is a primary reason for school absenteeism and loss of productivity at work.[7] In Ethiopia, as of 2015, over half of the population had never even used a toothbrush and toothpaste. The challenge in the United States and Ethiopia were obviously very different, but the task to get a population brushing their teeth is the same.

Ethiopia has a population of 103 million people with low population density and 84 per cent residing in rural areas. A major challenge in Ethiopia is the low penetration of toothpaste and toothbrushes: 58 per cent of the population had never used one in 2015. People do take care of their teeth but prefer a traditional method: 85 per cent of Ethiopians use a *miswak* (a stick used as a cleaning brush), with 36 per cent of people using it daily (Cue). The miswak (Salvadora Persica) inhibits the growth of bacteria, while also providing mechanical cleaning and has been proven to be an effective oral aid.[8] I have thought in the past that maybe we should just promote Miswak use more, but with a changing diet, including more sugar, increasing rates of cavities, halitosis and also just a jump into modernity, whilst we do not discourage using a Miswak in our programmes we do not openly promote it either. There is no consistency in how Miswak is used across the world, or when it is used and the frequency of use. (In Mali as a child I used it with charcoal on days where I had forgotten my toothbrush). It is hard to quantify how many individuals require access to dental care but one thing is for sure the needs are there and are increasing, as there were only 120 dentists and 1200 dental professionals (dentists and ancillary dental workers) in all of Ethiopia as of 2013.

One of the challenges that marketers face in the Ethiopian market is that 32 per cent of the population believes that using toothpaste is not necessary. Second, most of the population lives in rural locations where it is hard to reach, both logistically as well as through education and promotional messages. The media reach is poor, so a conventional campaign reaches few people. Most people do not realise that fluoride toothpaste also provides extended protection and can solve the problem of halitosis, which is common in Ethiopia. Therefore, marketers decided to focus on fresh breath and chose unconventional media to reach people with these messages.

Unilever's Signal brand of toothpaste embraced the challenge in Ethiopia and responded with a mix of television commercials, radio programmes, mobile phone apps and rural outreach programmes.[9] The "Little Brush Big Brush" app, for example, consisted of 21 two-minute episodes about quirky animal characters who had to complete brushing challenges.[10] Signal's marketers paired the app with a Facebook chatbot that offered personalised engagement. They made a special effort in schools, targeting 6- to 14-year-olds with a 21-day brushing challenge. And they offered special price discounts on Signal toothpaste tied to the campaign.

Signal's marketers did not do this alone. They partnered with the World Dental Federation (FDI) and participated in advocacy such as World Oral Health Day. The FDI evaluated the school programme, which Signal conducted in nine other countries including Ethiopia, and found an average 25 per cent improvement in the number of kids brushing twice-daily six months after completion of the programme.[11]

It isn't enough to give people a simple rational instruction. People find it cumbersome to brush their teeth twice a day – but they might do so if you offer them a clean mouth, a way to do this together with your kids, and more affordable products (Rewards). Marketing works by focusing on triggers and rewards – it adds immediate value to an action that may not seem so rewarding. This value can be virtual, rather than material, as long as the people experience this virtual reward with some intensity.

Brands on a mission do not simply react to consumers' existing behaviours and desires. They use their expertise to drive healthier, positive behaviours, acting as trendsetters, which can be positive and negative. This book is about rethinking what enlightened marketing is about. The crucial step is to go beyond focusing on the functional benefits of products, tapping into the more immediate and vivid sensorial and emotional benefits too. Marketers could help to bring about major public health gains by inspiring individuals to change their behaviour.

The brand advantage

Brands have several advantages in supporting public health campaigns. Some public health campaigns ignore behaviour change theory and focus on long-term benefits rather than short-term rewards. I have seen campaigns almost blaming the poor mother for her child's diarrhoea and stigmatising her for not washing her hands. Equally, I have been in partnerships where we were being asked to promote ash for handwashing. And yes, the evidence says it works but in the twenty first century soap is not exactly a luxury product and ash does not feel very dignified. A soap brand, by contrast, has an incentive to tell mothers that handwashing gives them nice-smelling hands. It offers them a choice of soap products in various formats and fragrances to pick from. Brands can thus promote benefits in ways that consumers understand and want.

Some government-run health campaigns have adopted this marketing approach. However, the budgets of public health institutions will never match the budgets of corporations (US$9 billion for Hershey and General Mills in 2016 compared to US$50 millions in comparison to a health agency).[12] Just imagine if we could make the marketing messages of commercial products more positive for health!

Public health behaviour change experts have long been thinking about how to motivate people to change their behaviours. Robert Aunger and Val Curtis at the London School of Hygiene and Tropical Medicine have identified 14 universal motives[13] that drive behaviour, with most shared between humans and other animals, and they have worked on how to connect the product and behaviour to those elemental drives of behaviour (from justice and nurture to status, affiliation and fear). To encourage handwashing after toilets, Lifebuoy drew on extensive research on handwashing motives[14] by tapping into the motive of disgust, with advertisements that showed germs glowing. Finding creative ways to use these motivations and applying them to product development linked to the public health programmes is essential. The major differences between private and public sector approaches is that the private sector is mostly guided by what people "want" whilst the public sector tend to focus on what they feel people "need" to do. Marketers may therefore be more creative in how they engage their consumers. They may also be able to target consumers better – they can focus on a particular segment rather than try to please everyone. Also with the product itself, marketers can alter a product's fragrance, design, packaging, pricing and even distribution network to drive the desired behaviour.[15]

General brand marketing, and the simple presence of the branded product, can reinforce behaviour change. With multiple exposures to the ads and equity of a brand built over centuries, consumers are more likely to take up that behaviour, which Lifebuoy demonstrated through a study.[16] Every time you see the product, you will be reminded to perform the behaviour. If you see a Lifebuoy bar coming out of the toilet, you're more likely to wash with soap. This is a cue that government and NGOs cannot bring to the table. Their job is rather to work with corporations to improve accessibility and reach, while focusing on ensuring that there are places to wash your hands, with running water (see Chapter 6) and corporations can contribute in creating smart partnership there.

Brands have another advantage over generic promotion: consumers' preferences. Iron deficiency, or anaemia, is a big problem in many developing countries. It affects as many as half of all Nigerian women of reproductive age – with serious developmental consequences for the children they bear. Public health organisations can urge Nigerians to eat more leafy green vegetables, but people often resist these appeals in part because they think their stews will become tasteless.

By contrast, Knorr, a €3 billion Unilever brand, has millions of consumers convinced of flavour of bouillon cubes for many years. Knorr responded to the anaemia problem with "Follow My Green Food Steps". It first developed iron-fortified bouillon cubes, then it launched a marketing campaign in Nigeria to encourage consumers to add green vegetables to popular stews made with the bouillon. The combination of greens and iron cubes would bring an increase up to the amount of daily iron required. The advertisements reassured consumers that they would get delicious food with those healthy ingredients. In addition, once consumers take a chance with vegetables in stews, they are more likely to try vegetables in other dishes – their attitude towards those foods are likely to change.

Knorr targeted those most at risk from anaemia (mothers and teenage daughters). The ads promoted mother-daughter bonding over the cooking of a remixed favourite meal (beef stew). In that positive moment, the ads mentioned the simple steps mums could take to increase iron content in the meal: toss vegetables into stews, stir them in, crumble in the new iron-fortified Knorr cube. Supporting the campaign were a series of testimonials from celebrities, government ministers and universities. A great song and dance was developed by Yemi Alade to accompany the movement (rewards). In a randomised community study there was a 41 per cent increase in the percentage of mothers who added leafy green vegetables as compared to a control group.[17]

In a similar way, brands can get away with controversial campaigns that governments or non-profits could never try. In 2013 Durex, a UK company that sells condoms, launched in Dubai with a video advertisement on social media. It offered an SOS pizza service, where instead of getting a pizza, Durex would discretely deliver a condom. The video went viral and was seen by millions of people across the Arab world. However, the United Arab Emirates government shut down the service after only a week, deeming it culturally inappropriate and likely to promote sexual promiscuity.

Volker Sydow, former head of the Durex brand, emphasised the freedom of brands:

> The messaging of condoms with ordering food was edgy for such a conservative country, but we decided it was the right thing to do nonetheless, because fundamentally we were promoting protection and better sexual health. Whilst in cultural terms this campaign may have been provocative to some degree it was just as clear that Durex was doing the

right thing when it came to sexual health: standing up for the right thing the brand is all about, pushing the envelope for people to live a better and more healthy life.[18]

Major global brands can be pretty cheeky in other ways. Levi's jeans have a mini-pocket within the right front pocket of the pants. Initially people used it to hold pocket watches. Levi's found out that some men were using the pocket to hold a condom. So, the brand created a marketing campaign, "Misused Ever Since", to encourage people to have condoms available. Marketers understand consumers best and are always open to consumer voices and changing trends. Now the question is how best to turn these skill sets to serve the world's poorest.

The behaviour change journey in the marketing process

Conventional brand marketing that switches people from one competitive brand to another can end up driving no incremental behaviour change and can confuse consumers. The challenge here is how to maximise marketing effort towards a defined jointly agreed positive behaviour change. Today in public health, we have a better understanding of the impact of behaviours on human health, not to mention on environmental degradation and climate change. The problem can seem overwhelming. It may be unclear exactly what behaviours need to change, and which elements of the environment (be it social or physical) are driving problematic behaviours. Moreover, it is often difficult to identify the immediate reward that a behaviour change will bring, and sometimes the behaviour change can seem less rewarding. All these challenges mean that motivating individuals to change is far from easy.[19]

On the plus side, brands can reap large gains if they are at the forefront of changing these behaviours. In cases where the product can play a role in healthy behaviours (such as Lifebuoy soap or Knorr bouillon cubes), then a successful public health-oriented campaign will also boost sales and open doors for collaborations. The brand will also gain familiarity and reputational benefits in the minds of generations of consumers.

I propose a three-step approach to integrate behaviour change into the marketing process:

Step 1: Disruption–Solution
Step 2: Trigger–Reward
Step 3: Norm–Reinforcement

In Step 1, Disruption–Solution, the brand has to become aware of a specific social issue connected to their product and its associated behaviours. There might be a need to bring awareness as to why the existing behaviour is bad or needs to be altered. To disrupt and create a handwashing habit, we have used demonstrations such as the Glow Germ, which reveals invisible germs on your hands to drive people to reconsider bad habits of not removing them.

Step 2: Trigger–reward. Once the brand commits to a behaviour to change, it needs a two-pronged effort: to trigger both individual and social rewards. The individual benefit can be healthier teeth or the feel of a clean mouth, but the social benefit is to be seen by one's peers as someone who cares for themselves or trains their children to have good manners, since reputation is a key driver of behaviour (see Erez Yoeli's TED talk[20]). The "Little Brush, Big Brush" app highlights both the trigger (it's night time, so a story appears) and the reward (brush your teeth with an animal), and thus gives children a great story about going to brush their teeth. It also gives parents a story to share with their children. Soap ads, for example, might emphasise that handwashing makes women feel good about themselves. But equally important are the indirect messages. Those same ads for soap can show images of handwashing before dinner. Equally, toothpaste ads can show kids brushing their teeth before bed. It is often difficult to identify the immediate individual reward that a behaviour change will bring, and so adding additional individual or social motives can drive change in these challenging behaviours to promote.

Step 3: Norm–Reinforce. In cases where the benefits of new behaviours are uncertain, people look to social proofs of what they should do. They look to norms to direct their behaviour and guide them to do the right thing. Creating norms makes the target behaviours socially desirable, either because they are commonly practiced, or because the failure to practice them will bring some kind of punishment. Failure to practice the behaviours will make others around you think less of you. The key to creating strong social norms is to make sure the expected behaviour is clear and observable, and that there are no excuses to avoid performing it.[21]

Brands can drive social norms in three ways:

1. clearly show the desirable behaviour
2. increase its observability
3. eliminate excuses.

Let's take these in turn.

It becomes critical to specify when and how to do the desirable behaviour and make that visible in programmes and advertising. Many preventive health behaviours are routine, to be done at regular intervals and are less effective if not done in a particular way (e.g. toothbrushing at night). The best audiences are those who are in a transitional stage when new habits are being formed, such as a new mother nurturing her infant, or during a pregnancy.

Increasing observability. This is about making the consumer's choice more observable to others, so it's good to show others' progress and even foster competition. Discovery Limited[22] is a South African diversified financial group that lowers insurance premiums for customers with healthy behaviours.

The group's Vitality programme has partnered with manufacturers such as Garmin, Suunto and Apple to monitor customer behaviour and provides a platform for members to track their fitness outcomes and their vitality status (gold, silver, bronze, platinum) is clearly showed and shared to all. The programme also tracks nutrition by recording purchases of vegetables, sugary and salty foods. By making these daily decisions visible, Discovery has encouraged people to change their behaviours (see Chapter 8).

Eliminating the opportunity for excuses helps in driving norms. Humans are very good at generating excuses for behaviours they do not want to perform, so social norms help to ensure compliance. To minimise excuses, brands can make the behaviour easy to do, such as conveniently putting a recycling bin just outside of the office with big signs on it.

Environmental nudges

To change routine behaviours, marketers must understand the situation and context – what marketers call the consumer journey. Suppose you want to induce people to reduce their salt intake. You might start with cooking behaviour. The routine of making a meal involves shopping, preparing ingredients and cooking, i.e. many actions in sequence. What are the motivations of cooks in that context? How can a marketer disrupt those habits to get cooks to consider using less salt? What are the available items, or props, that reinforce, or might disrupt, those bad habits?

It's not enough to study how people act in a general way; marketers have to understand them in the relevant context. The idea of behaviour settings came from Roger Barker in the 1950s,[23] who found that in the tavern, people "behave tavern" but when they are at church, they "behave church". The setting was a far stronger predictor of behaviour than anything about the person's individual characteristics or personality. You didn't need to know anything about the individual; they simply play a given role in the given setting. Of course a brand/product is just one element in this environment, but it is a powerful element, especially for repetitive behaviours. That is why the product matters so much – it's something that activates those repeated behaviours. How a product can influence the setting of a consumer's home is a key question, as we cannot change people's homes. Many product ideas are possible, such as a light that blinks on water bottles every 30 mins if you haven't drunk water, or a toothbrush that rings at bedtime.

So much of behaviour is unconscious and this is why the environment is important and why partnerships that complement products become critical – such as the environment for handwashing in schools with a toilet and handwashing sink. Drawing on work by Daniel Kahneman, we can distinguish between System 1 and System 2 behaviours.[24] System 1 is fast, automatic and often unconscious – it makes such decisions as how to walk through a crowd, what food sounds good when looking at a menu, or quickly assessing whether a product offered at a certain price is a good deal. It requires little attention, which is important given how many decisions we have to make on a daily basis (imagine having to reflect on all other possible uses of the money you are spending whenever you make the smallest purchase), but may involve actions that are bad for health.

For example, the System 1 self may choose a big, greasy hamburger, even if upon reflection you know it is not a healthy option. System 2 is slower and requires more effort. We draw upon it when we stop ourselves to reflect on big decisions, unfamiliar situations or difficult tasks. System 2 can also be biased, but it does serve us well in situations ranging from choosing whether to share what is likely fake news on social media,[25] and what kinds of food to buy at the grocery store when thinking with a longer-term mindset about health. System 2 is why ordering lunch earlier in the day when you are less hungry makes you more likely to order a salad.[26]

Another example comes from the situation where it is much easier to get people to recycle their waste in a fast food restaurant if there's a brightly col-oured bin, with simple wording, right next to the trash bin. Outside of that System 1 setting, though, people have to make a conscious decision to recycle. In that case, marketers need educational and persuasive messages (System 2) to get consumers to stop, take in new information and alter the value they ascribe to the relevant behaviours. Obviously the best approach is to combine these approaches, using both System 2 messages to get people to reflect on their priorities and beliefs with a supportive System 1 situational context.

Amplifying your impact: choices of media and cost

The choice of media channels will end up being crucial to translating your behaviour change programme into reality. The choices of media and channel depend on the intensity and repetition of the message required to drive the change. To encourage a new social norm, a broad reach is better, using tele-vision, radio and social media.

As we heard in Chapter 2, the pyramid model (see Figure 3.2) was created for Dove with the Centre of Appearance Research to find ways to retain the impact and quality of Dove's tools while reaching more young people directly. A behaviour change programme is similar to a pyramid, reaching fewer people with greater intensity at the top and many people with less intensity at the bottom.

At the top of the pyramid are face-to-face programmes and direct educa-tional programmes led by trained personnel, with carefully designed and tested audio-visual materials. These high intensity efforts come at a high cost per contact. At the bottom of the pyramid are broad-scale interventions, such as mass advertising campaigns or lobbying for supportive legislation. These efforts reach many more people, but with less impact per individual.

For brands to affect large enough numbers of people with relatively small behavioural changes, the best strategy is likely to focus on the middle of the pyramid. Here is where marketers can transform proven content (from the top of the pyramid) into messaging consumed by target audiences. An increasingly popular approach is to work with social media companies or creative media producers. For instance, Dove partnered with Steven Universe to improve body self-image (see Chapter 2). In this middle area, the impact can be quite strong, with a manageable cost. And in this mid-tier you can bring in influencers.

For maximum impact, programmes need to work with multiple channels. In rural areas where channels like television might not reach the whole population, a brand could start with a programme in schools, complemented by a radio or mobile phone programme.

It is often too expensive to run school- or clinic-based behaviour change programmes, but marketers can start with advertising to raise awareness or disrupt, and use social media and digitalisation to prompt new behaviours.

Television commercials and mobile phone advertising can be a powerful combination for behaviour change. We know a great deal about evaluating the results from the former, but many people in developing countries lack access to television. Nearly everyone has a mobile phone (in 2017 the world surpassed five billion unique mobile subscribers) so audio messages delivered by phone can reach a broad audience. This advertising can be cheaper than on-ground programmes, but more expensive than television or radio, yet it is a highly scalable intervention to encourage behaviour change across large segments of a population. Mobile also has limitations in terms of scalability because of IVR (Interactive Voice Response) being very expensive, and mobile networks are not always available in deep rural areas. As Richard Wright, a behavioural scientist at Unilever, points out, "People will now

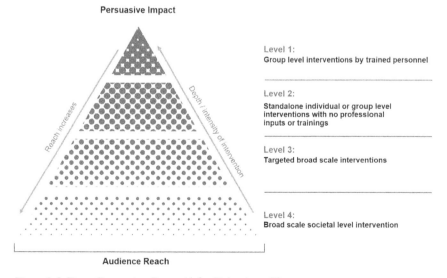

Figure 3.2 Dove Persuasion Pyramid for Behaviour Change.

engage with new technologies, but you've got to make them attractive and engaging, and pre-test them".[27]

Marketers can couple this awareness-raising with mobile phone apps – and use the latest frontier in beviour change: digital disruption. Ideally we need to develop new ways to use SMS that does not require downloading data, but can deliver exciting behaviour-oriented messages in a timely manner.

Even when brand campaigns fail to change behaviours in the short term, they can still make a difference. These branded campaigns can give people a sense of urgency and self-efficacy, which may ultimately lead to better behaviours in the long run. That's especially important for brands with missions that do not connect directly with the product, such as Dove's efforts to give teenage girls better body self-image. For brands whose products are at the core of the conversation, such as toothpaste and condoms, then the behaviour has to be the end point.

From campaigns to sustained behaviour change

To make a long-term difference, brands need to think beyond short-term campaigns with sparks. They must plan a behaviour change programme with the potential to scale and be the foundation to negotiate external partnerships with assurance that they will genuinely contribute something. It might take several different programmes over many years to earn a right to Say, and that's a significant investment. It starts with a pilot phase. A team of committed people at the brand work with others who know a lot about the target behaviour to jointly develop the theory of change. The team then trials their specific approach on a small population, as has been done both with Green Food Steps on Knorr and with School of Five on Lifebuoy. The key once again is to agree that the desired behaviour change is valuable.

Once the team has enough evidence of what works and what does not, they adapt the programme to minimise cost and maximise impact, and then scale it up to a full programme. Qualifying what works is always difficult to answer. Whilst brands use mainly market research agencies, their data measurement may not stand the scrutiny of peer-reviewed journals. This needs to be considered if academic validation becomes important for a brand.

Getting marketers to utilise behavioural theory is essential – especially agreeing the desired behaviour that is being instilled. Marketers may resist theories and follow their own instincts in devising specific campaigns. So, the team that spearheads the programme must clarify the essential (non-negotiable) aspects that must be kept, across all communication channels. These essential aspects can also form the basis for measuring results. By measuring results, brands can make it easier to learn from experience. Internal measures, such as key performance indicators, will keep people accountable in the short term, and will enable the team to show the business benefits of the approach.

Sometimes the core team must deal with conflicting goals. Suppose a soap brand is trying to position itself as the premium product in its market segment. The team may resist talking about handwashing after using the toilet, which might feel down-market. The solution can be found in the difference between the Brand Say, seen in mass communications, and the Brand Do, such as on-ground programmes. One campaign may focus on the Brand Say about how the brand is a superior way to wash hands. A separate campaign as a part of the Brand Do, pitched to different segments, could involve talking about using soap in specific moments at the individual level (see Chapter 6).

The brand will likely want outside help, especially for large programmes. The academics who helped with the pilot may point the way to and even help facilitate partnerships with non-profits or governments. It is also useful to bring in various experiences with the target audience and sensitivities around the social purpose. It can help think about demographics, cultural and social context, and understand who buys, who influences, who consumes, all related to the daily schedules of the target audience.

From there, brands will want to seek out ambassadors or key influencers, such as teachers and community health workers, devising detailed implementation plans.

Concluding thoughts

To make a difference to public health – to become a true brand on a mission – brands must go beyond their standard advertising and promotion/sampling programmes. They have to think about behaviour change at the core of their purpose journey. This has to be a pre-requisite before entering into partnerships with a meaningful contribution besides just giving cash, and instead give a chance to get your employees involved in seeing the difference they make with their advertising resources.

The good news here is that brands are already showing they can make a difference. This chapter, and this book, explain why public health initiatives can benefit enormously from the involvement of brands if they stay committed. As public health leaders recognise the genuine contribution of brands, marketers will have an easier time building processes and partnerships to change behaviour for the better and over the long term.

Exercises

Building your mission

Exercise 1: Visualising strategies for behavioural change

Too often, when brand teams start brainstorming about how to influence behavioural changes that relate to their brands' overall social goals, they go off in all directions at once. That can be time- and resource-consuming, not to mention frustrating for all concerned.

To choose the behaviour changes thoughtfully, brand teams should discuss and find answers to the following questions:

- What are the behaviour changes that will effectively contribute to the brand's social goal? For example, if the social goal is improving children's health, the desired changes might include getting mothers of young children to practice handwashing before meals or after the toilet, or getting children to brush their teeth at night, or teaching young girls body confidence to raise their self-esteem.
- Which of these changes are the most important, and why are they important?
- What role could my product play in delivering this change? Is there a role? Does this behaviour change help fuel innovative ideas?
- What would the public sector need to do in order to support these changes?
- Are the changes practical? Could the brand take ownership of this? Could you, for example, become the world's leading provider of handwashing programmes or self-esteem education to girls?
- Would it be practical/possible to measure the changes?

Once these questions have been answered, the next step is to consider the trade-offs between impact and use of resources. To do that, look at the next exercise: What is your impact pyramid?

Exercise 2: What is your impact pyramid?

The persuasion pyramid concept shown can be extended to a brand's plans for launching a behaviour-change programme. The pyramid can help companies think about which consumer behaviours they could change, in what ways, through what means and at what cost.

Let's say you're a consumer-products brand whose target audience consists primarily of women, and the social goal you've identified is reducing gender-based violence. To figure this out, you could build a pyramid of impact strategies, ranging from broad and inexpensive at the bottom, to deep and more expensive at the top.

At the base of the pyramid you might put the idea of creating ads for digital platforms bringing attention to women supporting each other and listening to each other during tough times.

Further up the pyramid might be initiatives such as creating counselling lines that women could call for advice and support. At the top might be creation of safe spaces where women would teach each other about recognising signs of abusive relations.

As you go up the pyramid, there would be increases in the cost per person and the difficulty of succeeding with each strategy. The goal is the same across the pyramid, but the means for reaching the goal become progressively more challenging and the impact on each person would be increasingly profound.

When you create your own impact pyramid, the bottom should be a simple behaviour change that your brand could persuade large numbers of your target audience to make, at relatively low cost. Then place a "wouldn't it be amazing if we could get people to do this?" idea at the very pinnacle. Array a number of intermediate ideas in between.

For each idea on the pyramid, outline the steps, resources and time that would be required, ranging from creating advertising to devising pilot tests to measuring results. Estimate costs for each one.

Now you have your work cut out for you.

Notes

1 Aunger, R. and Curtis, V. (2015). *Gaining Control: how human behavior evolved.* Oxford, New York: Oxford University Press.
2 Lim, S. S. *et al.* (2012). "A comparative risk assessment of burden of disease and injury attributable to 67 risk factors and risk factor clusters in 21 regions, 1990–2010: a systematic analysis for the Global Burden of Disease Study 2010". *Lancet,* 380(9859), pp. 2224–2260.
3 Nelson, N., Malkoc, S. A. and Shiv, B. (2018). "Emotions know best: the advantage of emotional versus cognitive responses to failure". *Journal of Behavioral Decision Making* 31(1), pp. 40–51. doi: http://dx.doi.org.ezp-prod1.hul.harvard.edu/10.1002/bdm.2042.
4 Niv, Y. (2009). "Reinforcement learning in the brain". *Journal of Mathematical Psychology,* 53, pp. 139–154. doi: 10.1016/j.jmp.2008.12.005.
5 Curtis, V., Dreibelbis, R., Buxton, H., Izang, N., Adekunle, D. and Aunger, R. (2019). "Behaviour settings theory applied to domestic water use in Nigeria: a new conceptual tool for the study of routine behaviour". *Social Science & Medicine,* 235, p. 112398.
6 Duhigg, C. (2012). *The power of habit: why we do what we do in life and business.* London. Random House.
7 Petersen, P. E., Bourgeois, D., Ogawa, H., Estupinan-Day, S. and Ndiaye, C. (2005). "The global burden of oral diseases and risks to oral health", *Bulletin of the World Health Organization,* 83, pp. 661–669.
8 Dahiya, P., Kamal, R., Luthra, R. P., Mishra, R. and Saini, G. (2012). "Miswak: a periodontist's perspective". *Journal of Ayurveda and Integrative Medicine,* 3(4), pp. 184–187. doi: 10.4103/0975-9476.104431.
9 Unilever bought Pepsodent in 1942, but then sold its North American operations to Church and Dwight in 2003. It continues to sell Pepsodent elsewhere, including Ethiopia.
10 Hall, E. (2016). "Unilever gets personal with family chatbot to encourage tooth brushing". *AdAge.* Available at: https://adage.com/creativity/work/little-brush-big-brush/49569 (Accessed: 18 December 2019).
11 Melo, P., Fine, C., Malone, S., Frencken, J. E. and Horn, V. (2018). "The effectiveness of the Brush Day and Night programme in improving children's toothbrushing knowledge and behaviour". *International Dental Journal,* 68 Suppl 1, pp. 7–16. doi: 10.1111/idj.12410.

12 Haddad, L. (2018). "Reward food companies for improving nutrition". *Nature*, 556(7699), pp. 19–22. doi: 10.1038/d41586-018-03918-7.

13 Aunger, R. and Curtis, V. (2013). "The anatomy of motivation: an evolutionary-ecological approach". *Biological Theory*, 8(1), pp. 49–63.

14 Curtis, V. A., Danquah, L. O. and Aunger, R. V. (2009). "Planned, motivated and habitual hygiene behaviour: an eleven country review". *Health Education Research*, 24(4), pp. 655–673.

15 Aunger, R. and Curtis, V. (2016). "Behaviour centred design: towards an applied science of behaviour change". *Health Psychology Review*, 10(4), pp. 425–446. doi: 10.1080/17437199.2016.1219673.

16 Tidwell, J. B. *et al.* (2019). "Effect of two complementary mass-scale media interventions on handwashing with soap among mothers". *Journal of Health Communication*, 24(2), pp. 203–215. doi: 10.1080/10810730.2019.1593554.

17 Lion, R. *et al.* (2018). "The effect of the 'Follow in my Green Food Steps' programme on cooking behaviours for improved iron intake: a quasi-experimental randomized community study". *International Journal of Behavioral Nutrition and Physical Activity*, 15(1), p. 79.

18 Sydow, V. (2019). Personal interview.

19 Curtis, V. and Aunger, R. (2012). "Motivational mismatch: evolved motives as the source of – and solution to – global public health problems". In *Applied evolutionary psychology*, edited by Roberts, S. C. pp. 259–275. Oxford, New York: Oxford University Press.

20 Yoeli, E. (2018). "How to motivate people to do good for others". *TED Institute*. Available at: www.ted.com/talks/erez_yoeli_how_to_motivate_people_to_do_good_for_others (Accessed: 18 December 2019).

21 Yoeli, E. (2018). "Is the key to successful prosocial nudges reputation?". *The Behavioral Scientist*. Available at: https://behavioralscientist.org/is-reputation-the-key-to-prosocial-nudges/ (Accessed: 27 December 2019).

22 Porter, M. E., Kramer, M. R. and Sesia, A. (2014). "Discovery Limited". *Harvard Business School Case* 715–423. Available at: www.hbs.edu/faculty/Pages/item.aspx?num=48352 (Accessed: 2 January 2020).

23 Barker, R. G. and Wright, H. F. (1955). *Midwest and its children: the psychological ecology of an American town*. Evanston, IL: Row, Peterson & Co.

24 Kahneman, D. (2011). *Thinking, fast and slow*. New York: Farrar, Straus & Giroux.

25 Bago, B., Rand, D. G. and Pennycook, G. (2019). "Fake news, fast and slow: deliberation reduces belief in false (but not true) news headlines". *Journal of Experimental Psychology*, doi: 10.1037/xge0000729.

26 Stites, S. D. *et al.* (2015). "Pre-ordering lunch at work. Results of the what to eat for lunch study". *Appetite*, 84, pp. 88–97. doi: 10.1016/j.appet.2014.10.005.

27 Wright, R. (2019). Personal interview.

4 Durex

How a global condom brand helps reduce HIV infections

Ever since the AIDS epidemic began in the 1980s, public health authorities have worked to promote safer sexual practices. Condom promotion has been a key element in their campaigns, with interventions ranging from expanded channels of condom distribution to free or reduced-price condoms.[1] An estimated 50 million HIV infections have been averted since the onset of the HIV epidemic by the use of condoms.[2] In sub-Saharan Africa, at least 70 per cent of the condoms made available over the last 30 years were free.

Although condoms are now more available and affordable, acceptance of condoms and their consistent use remains a key issue and many risky sexual acts still go unprotected. Condom use is lowest among poor and uneducated women, and inequity in all its dimensions (gender, education, income, sexual identify, location, etc.) is a defining factor for access and use. We have seen (Chapter 2) how body confidence and low self-esteem inhibit girls from negotiating the use of condoms. With health funding levels stagnant or falling, it is important to redefine a new generation of condoms programme to address these inequities. This chapter focuses on how the largest global condom brand, Durex, helped in this effort.

The public health conundrum of condoms

With correct and consistent use, condoms have a 97 per cent efficacy in preventing HIV. Condoms are also very effective in preventing sexually transmitted infections (STI), as well as unwanted pregnancies. The rate falls to 86 per cent with "self-reported consistent use", but that's still an enormous improvement over unprotected sex, especially for a tool that costs little. Both latex and polyurethane condoms have thus become a primary tool for averting STIs.

Many public health experts have called on governmental and non-profit organisations worldwide to distribute free or heavily subsidised condoms.[3, 4, 5, 6] In fact the cost to provide condoms from 2015–2030 is estimated at a minimum of US$60 billion,[7] assuming the 2015 condom use levels are maintained. Over the past few years, however, "condom fatigue" has set in, especially in sub-Saharan Africa. Condoms have been deprioritised and a business-as-usual approach prevails in many countries. Donor support for condoms has flatlined, with the United States President's Emergency Plan for AIDS Relief (PEPFAR) and the Global Fund to Fight AIDS, Tuberculosis and Malaria (Global Fund) spending less than 1 per cent of their resources on condoms.

The distribution of free condoms, either widespread or targeted to key locations or populations, is repeatedly shown to be a key component of successful condom programmes. The South African government built the world's largest condom distribution programme by developing a free condom brand called "Choice". New York was the first city in the world to have its own municipally branded condom, and it currently maintains the largest free condom programme in the United States. Since its launch, more than 300 million NYC condoms have been distributed – helping to reverse the trend in new diagnoses of heterosexually transmitted HIV infection, with a reduction of 53 per cent between 2007 and 2014.[8]

In other countries a mix of donor funding and social marketing techniques have been used to reach population at risks. In the Ethiopian city of Gondar, known for its ancient ruins and home to the country's main faculty of medicine at the University of Gondar, 80 per cent of female sex workers are reached by condom promotion programmes, with each receiving on average 715 condoms in 2014. Every location with sex work hotspots has condom outlets, with the type of outlet depending on the sex workers' willingness and ability to pay. Free dispensers are available in some areas, while others have socially marketed (subsidised) and commercial condoms. In a study of condom choices and self-reported condom use among men in Ghana, Kenya and South Africa, with four types of condoms supplied free of charge for six months, the preference was for the private-sector "premium" product – though this did not translate into a higher proportion of reported protected acts or lower STI incidence.[9]

Free condoms are of uneven quality and may necessitate lubricants that are not always available. As with malaria bed nets that I discussed in Chapter 1, the rate of correct use was much lower for free bed nets than for those purchased,[10] and it's been claimed that free nets often end up as fishing nets or wedding dresses,[11] and perhaps people found alternative uses for free condoms.[12]

People may doubt the reliability of free condoms, especially the educated urban populations (what UNAIDS calls the Urban Advantage). They might take them but then not use them, even if, or especially if, they understand the need for protection, as they are looking for the status that branded condoms can give. Studies in Africa, Asia and South America have shown that people are willing to pay for branded condoms and that brand equity scale was positively correlated with willingness to pay and with condom use. This is consistent with other studies that show that higher brand equity is associated with targeted health behaviours such as using treated bed nets and using sanitation facilities.

With a topic as sensitive as sex, you need to address barriers ranging from religious to social taboos in order to overcome resistance to using condoms. Henk Van Renterghem from UNAIDS makes this clear:

> Good condom programming is as much about promoting and distributing or selling condoms as it is about reducing barriers and other obstacles for people at higher risk and left behind.

Many of the UN organisations and non-profits have turned for collaboration to commercial condom brands, including Durex. Bithia Deperthes, who runs CONDOMIZE!, a joint programme of the UNFPA and The Condom Project, that aims to destigmatise condom usage (and a major distributor of free condoms for the UN), has this perspective:

> There is a funding gap in condom programming today. And people have stopped performing studies on condoms. So we are left with the private sector, because this has always been part of their strategy – to do market research to decide the next group of people to be targeted. Who are they? What do they like? They do that naturally.[13]

The rise of the Durex brand

People have used condoms to prevent sexually transmitted diseases since ancient times, usually made of gallbladders or other animal materials. The modern latex condom, durable and elastic, emerged only after the invention of rubber vulcanisation in 1839.[14] Even then, consumption was small for decades.

Durex began as the London Rubber Company Ltd in 1915. It sold condoms and barber supplies imported from Germany. It began producing its own condoms in 1929, which it called Durex for *du*rability, *re*liability and *ex*cellence.[15]

Sales took off a few years later when the Church of England reversed its opinion on contraception and allowed family planning within marriage.[16] Durex also began selling overseas, using export routes from Britain's colonial past. The company went public in 1950. Three years later it introduced electronic testing for breakages, largely replacing the traditional water testing. Then in 1969 the company produced the world's first anatomically shaped condom.[17, 18, 19]

The firm merged with Seton Scholl Healthcare in 1999 to form a new company, SSL International, selling a diverse array of personal care and medical products. Then in 2010, the Reckitt Benckiser Group Plc (RB) bought SSL for £2.54 billion.[20] Headquartered in the UK, RB manufactures, markets and sells health, hygiene and home products. In 2019, it had 40,000 employees and a market capitalisation of £54 billion.[21]

Durex, one of RB's many brands, offers condoms in a variety of sizes, shapes, textures, colours, flavours and materials. It is the largest-selling condom brand worldwide, available in more than 150 countries. Durex is the market leader in many countries, but it is a lesser player in Africa and two major developed countries: USA and Japan, where it faces strong regional competition.[22, 23]

As of 2018, there were a dozen major global condom producers, including some non-premium makers that compete with Durex on volume.[24] Indeed, Durex is no longer the largest condom maker by volume. Karex, a Malaysian company, makes more than six billion condoms a year, accounting for 15 per cent of the world's market for export. Besides presenting its own brands, it supplies condoms for free distribution by aid organisations. It even manufactures some of Durex's condoms. It also recently bought European and American condom brands.[25]

As a for-profit venture, Durex marketers are already motivated to convince people to use condoms. However, as part of its parent's ambitions around health, they've taken on a social purpose to promote safer sex. Ben Wilson, RB's global category director for sexual well-being, points out that "Trusted brands can help achieve public health outcomes in a different way."[26]

Nearly two-thirds of RB's 2018 net revenue of £12.6 billion came from their main health brands such as Gaviscon, Mucinex, Nurofen, Scholl, Strepsils, Clearasil, Dettol and Veet, along with Durex.[27] The company is "inspired by a vision of a world where people are healthier and live better".[28] It wants to become a world leader in consumer health, with ambitions to expand in infant formula and child nutrition, health relief, health hygiene, wellness, as well as vitamins, minerals and supplements. The goal is to "help people put their health in their own hands"[29, 30]

We can chart Durex's efforts on all the roots of Brands on a Mission.

Tackling barriers to behaviour change

By offering a branded product, Durex could be better positioned to boost condom usage than the free condoms distributed by the public sector. As a large brand within a global consumer giant, Durex certainly has the resources to make credible commitments to a market. To change behaviour, Durex marketers address the barriers that have stymied public health organisations: consumer trust/preferences, and lack of interest and accessibility. To gain consumer trust, they emphasise the product's reliability and its continuing stream of innovations. The very fact that consumers have to pay for the condom makes them more likely to trust it and places more value to the sexual encounter.

Overcoming barriers to condom usage, of course, has been a much bigger challenge. Durex marketers worked on several avenues here. The first was simply availability. It's much easier for the brand to sell in urbanised countries such as China. Access to rural Africa has been much harder.

Partly because of its social purpose, Durex is working to make its condoms accessible everywhere. Adopting Coca-Cola's tagline, Durex aims to have condoms "at an arm's length of desire".[31]

The main approach here has been to create an affordable value brand separate from the premium offering. In 2016 Durex bought the condom division of Brazil's largest maker of generic drugs, Hypermarcas SA, for US$175 million.[32] Soon thereafter it introduced the condom label "Feels" to South Africa, sold at the low price of 9.99 rand (US$0.70) for a pack of three, compared to 42 rand (US$2.90) for the premium Durex equivalent. As of 2019 it was planning to launch Feels in other African countries.[33] Margins are a good deal lower than with the premium brand, but Durex's leaders are comfortable sacrificing some profits for its social purpose.

The second barrier involved the awkwardness that people feel about condoms. Durex is famous, or perhaps infamous, for running edgy, head-turning ads that normalise condoms, often with humour. The goal is to drive positive discussions about sex and protections. As the leading seller of condoms worldwide, Durex accepts an obligation to promote overall usage, beyond a specific brand, assuming that any increase in condom acceptability will include an increase in sales of their brand.

It also has the long-term experience in what works for pitching condoms. The brand deliberately moved away from preachy campaigns that created anxiety and also moved on from sexual ads that were no longer effective. Indeed, especially in conservative countries such as India, Durex avoids ads that are entirely serious. The goal, said Volker Sydow, formerly the vice-president for Durex at RB, is for Durex to "have a twinkle in the eye, to make fun of itself. That would carry the brand much further and it will be regarded much more positively by many."[34]

Even so, Durex campaigns have been struck down in a number of countries. The brand took a chance in Dubai in 2013 with videos and other advertisements promoting a service to discretely deliver condoms like a pizza after 4 pm.[35] The Middle East team halted the campaign after just a week, after UAE governments found it culturally inappropriate and encouraging of promiscuity.[36] A joint campaign with bubble tea shop, Haytea, in China used suggestive images and taglines such as "Tonight, not a drop left" with a creamy drop dripping out of a cup. The campaign ended quickly when the National Office Against Pornographic and Illegal Publications said this type of crude advertising could "ruin the Chinese".[37]

Beyond easing communication, the brand works to make people more comfortable with sex. They have also implemented several innovations when it comes to condoms, including texture, flavours, thickness and other qualities that change the users experience. Miguel Viega-Pestana, the senior vice-president for Corporate Affairs & Sustainability at RB, said:

> Essentially as a brand, what we're trying to do is help people have good sex. What that means is we're trying to help people overcome physical

problems or emotional anxieties because typically the barrier to having good sex is either a physical problem or emotional anxiety. We don't talk about "great sex" because that phrase is often full of misconceptions driven by pornography.[38]

Durex specifically targets women in many markets, as they are substantial buyers of condoms for their partners. It often focuses on women in their advertisements through recent campaigns such as #OrgasmInequality and #ComeTogether (see Figure 4.1). Partly to support that push, RB in 2014 bought K-Y Lubricants, a brand with a high rating of trust among female consumers. By appealing to both partners in a heterosexual relationship, Durex can make the use of condoms more acceptable.

Figure 4.1 Durex #OrgasmInequality campaign, India 2019.

Besides broadening advertising beyond men, Durex has pitched the product for a variety of relationships. They recognise that sex is not always between men and women. They present the brand to "help the world become a more inclusive place, and to help people explore what sex means to them".[39] Volker adds that the brand does not distinguish between him and her, and recognises that the role of women in proposing and choosing condoms is very important.

Durex also considers the age segmentation. For 15-to-24 year-olds, they are moving to make their communications 80 per cent internet-based. The goal is to start educating young people two years before they start having sex, or as early as 13 years of age, wherever it's possible to do that legally. In religiously conservative areas in Latin America, Middle East and the Far East, the brand adjusts its messaging. Many countries still oppose sexual education to adolescents even though we know they are becoming sexually active younger and younger.

The landscape for partnerships

Durex has high ambitions for partnerships with outside organisations and governments; it is considered vital for the brand to reach these organisations. One way that Durex partners with governments is through the brand's Global Sex Survey. This is perhaps the world's largest study of sexual habits, attitudes and behaviours, bigger than anything a non-profit organisation would likely commission. By offering governments access to survey findings to help improve their public health education, the brand then works with the government to improve sexual awareness and education. For example, in the conservative country of Malaysia, the study gave Durex the credibility to partner with key leaders whose interests matched Durex's.

Viega-Pestana says:

> These public-private partnerships can be tricky as non-corporate organisations have different incentives. In managing partnerships with civil society, NGO, or government entities, there's a particular set of skills needed because you're dealing with an audience where the current theme of working is different from the general business community. They aren't always the natural partners that we would work with in our usual day-to-day basis.[40]

But when the partners are in sync, Durex can create long-standing relationships for scalable results that make a real difference for public health. Adds Viega-Pestana, "The partnerships work is embedded in our purpose-led business."[41]

Besides ensuring compatibility, however, Durex must protect its brand equity. Durex's strong position in the market makes it an appealing partner for public sector organisations. Few NGOs would turn their back on the brand, as there is the potential to really achieve something through a partnership. The focus for Durex must be on choosing the most suitable partner for an activity, avoiding "boring" NGOs, because "if a 17 year-old does not think your brand is cool, he will go for competitive brands".[42]

While the NGO partner gains credibility and name recognition by working with the condom brand, Durex gets help in moving from product sales to the larger social purpose and a chance to better position its advocacy platforms.

Partnerships can also help Durex gain vital market information. Working with the UNAIDS programme gave the brand a presence in many smaller, remote markets. It helped Durex improve public health now, and foster some market penetration in the future.[43]

The brand also partners directly with major events such as the Olympics. Durex donated over 100,000 condoms and thousands of sachets of lubricant to the Athlete Villages at the 2004 games in Athens and the 2012 games in London.[44, 45] It sent 350,000 condoms (and an additional 100,000 female condoms) to Rio in 2016.[46] The logic is that Olympic athletes are young, fit, with lots of energy, with an exploratory nature in common.

Durex started working with MTV's Staying Alive Foundation in 2013 to help young people talk more openly about sex. They've developed a variety of creative ways to start conversations, including the online "Someone Like Me" campaign, with videos, social media posts and other digital content that promotes healthy conversations about sex. In five years, the campaigns on MTV reached four million young people in 33 countries.[47] During broadcasts, the campaign mentions the Durex brand, so the partnership has immediate business payoffs as well as the larger social purpose.

Advocacy

Durex has done little direct advocacy for new policies or laws at the governmental level. Instead it has focused on general campaigns to improve sexual health. As a corporate brand, Durex can advocate explicitly for sex as recreation. As Sydow explained, Durex is quite open in saying that:

> sex also brings pleasure, which is very difficult in many countries to do, as many countries believe sex is just for reproduction and we of course do not agree. We endorse that sex is there for pleasure, whatever gender, whatever sexual orientation.[48]

Adds Ben Wilson, "We're finding that there isn't anyone stepping into this sometimes taboo topic, and as a brand we need to do that."[49]

That makes Durex's public campaigns inevitably provocative, which is fine with the company, as part of their strategy is to start conversations. Wilson said:

There's a simple lens to look at anything that's provocative, and it's are you trying to drive the right discussions and the right behaviours? As long as your intent is good, you potentially have a licence to be provocative because you're trying to do some good in the world.[50]

Sometimes even Durex's involvement per se is a problem. The brand came under fire in 2010 when it conducted an online sex education survey in the UK. The survey found that 90 per cent of parents and 80 per cent of school leaders and governors agreed that it was "very important" for children to receive safe sex information. Yet pro-family activists found it inappropriate for Durex to conduct the survey because it has a "vested commercial interest in persuading more people to use their product".[51]

Durex's biggest, and most daring, advocacy effort was the 2018 "Give a F*ck" campaign to raise awareness of AIDS, tuberculosis and malaria. In conservative countries the title was "Have Sex, Save Lives" (see Figure 4.2). The ads had the secondary goal of empowering young women and girls to continue their education.[52] For this worldwide campaign, Durex used spokespeople such as Javier Munoz, an American Broadway actor who starred in "Hamilton" and is living with HIV, and Phoebe Robinson, a female rights activist and comedian. The spokespeople are not pushing Durex; but "they're pushing the same issues that we are, and we have a stronger voice together", said Viega-Pestana.[53]

Durex ran this campaign as a partnership with (RED), a fundraising and advocacy organisation focused on AIDS and related diseases. In honour of the

Figure 4.2 Durex campaign with Zara Larsson, World AIDS Day 2018.

partnership, the brand issued a special version of condoms, (DUREX)RED, a portion of whose profits would go to (RED). The overall campaign was estimated to reach a billion people worldwide.[54, 55]

Another advocacy effort involved the Unicode Consortium that decides on emojis. A Durex-commissioned study suggested that 80 per cent of people 18-to-25 years old prefer to express messages through using emojis, and more than half use emojis regularly to discuss sex.[56] In the build-up to World AIDS Day 2015, Durex led a campaign to add a condom emoji, and their Facebook-based campaign won several PR awards (see Figure 4.3). Unicode declined to introduce a safe sex emoji, but Durex still declared it a success. As Sydow pointed out:

> The objective was to have a campaign out there and have people talking about it, and we established the reach without any media money at all because it was being picked up by all the guys out there. Durex adds credibility. Durex has the authority, and it has a very positive image and if it comes from us, people do listen.[57]

Measurement

Durex can estimate the number of people exposed to their advertisements and those who can buy their products. But they share the same challenges as other organisations in that they cannot reliably estimate how many people have changed their behaviour based on their purpose-oriented efforts. As a result, Durex focuses on the volume of condom sales generally and in specific countries as its general metric.

As the largest branded provider, Durex does take some credit for the global reduction in annual new HIV infections over the past decade, with public

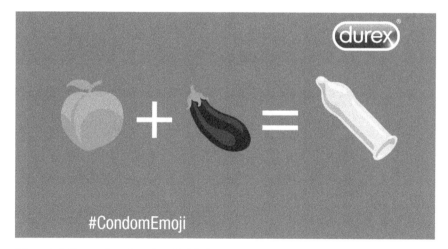

Figure 4.3 Durex Condom Emoji, 2015.

health researchers estimating that condoms have helped to prevent over 35 million infections since the epidemic began in 1981.[58] And Durex has found a correlation between its marketing efforts in a country, its volume of sales there and prevention of infections, although it can be difficult to make the link.

Remaining challenges

Most of the world's HIV infections have come about in sub-Saharan Africa, where Durex has little market penetration and where the rates of new infections are the highest.[59] Durex still needs to work out a business model and a distribution network that would work for Africa, taking into account the affordability component, and the fact of competing with many free and subsidised brands. Purchasing power is growing in many African countries, as is urbanisation, but for the time being partnerships with aid organisations that have established sales networks are vital. Segmenting the vulnerable population, such as targeting uneducated poor women or marginalised people (sex workers, migrants, uneducated, men having sex with men, people living with HIV) may become an important part of the private sector's model if it wants to be a brand on a mission.

Indeed, the CONDOMIZE! programme has worked to convince companies that a varying proportion of Africans depending on country income levels have substantial discretionary spending, and that they prefer branded condoms to free ones. The solution may be through online distribution, which can circumvent barriers in acquiring condoms. Deperthes points out that, "Africans have mobile money. They buy a lot online today. [This can overcome] the barriers we have seen with health workers judgmental about your young age and giving you just a few condoms."[60]

There are a lot of learnings from the private sector that have been shared with social marketing, and we probably need to move towards a total market approach that emphasises the strength of public sector distribution, social marketing and commercial sales to improve the overall efficiency and effectiveness of condom promotion.

Durex's experiences show the power and some of the pitfalls of brands on a mission. Sensitive issues such as sexuality can be easier to tackle when done by a brand. Its story also shows the journey of innovation in addressing demand issues. That's all the more reason for corporate marketers and public health organisations to learn about each other's strengths and weaknesses, and collaborate for long-term improvement.

Notes

1 Holmes, K. K., Levine, R. and Weaver, M. (2004). "Effectiveness of condoms in preventing sexually transmitted infections", Bulletin of the World Health Organization, 82(6), pp. 454–461. Available at: www.ncbi.nlm.nih.gov/pmc/articles/PMC2622864/ (Accessed: 4 January 2020).

2 UNAIDS (2015) "World Aids Day 2015 – Condom Chapter and Related Case Studies". Available at: https://www.hivpreventioncoalition.unaids.org/resource/unauds-wad-2015-report-condom-case-studies/. (Accessed: 18 December 2019).

3 UNFPA, WHO, UNAIDS (2015) "Position statement on condoms and the prevention of HIV, other sexually transmitted infections and unintended pregnancy". Available at: www.unaids.org/en/resources/presscentre/featurestories/2015/july/20150702_condoms_prevention (Accessed: 4 January 2020).

4 Centers for Disease Control and Prevention (2016) *Condom Effectiveness, CDC.* Available at: www.cdc.gov/condomeffectiveness/index.html (Accessed: 4 January 2020).

5 Mayo Clinic (2019) *Female condom.* Available at: www.mayoclinic.org/tests-procedures/female-condom/about/pac-20394129 (Accessed: 4 January 2020).

6 Centers for Disease Control and Prevention (2018) *Current Contraceptive Status Among Women Aged 15–49: United States 2015–2017, Data Brief 327.* (no date). Available at: www.cdc.gov/nchs/data/databriefs/db327_tables-508.pdf#page=2 (Accessed: 4 January 2020).

7 Stover, J. *et al.* (2017) "The case for investing in the male condom", *PLOS ONE,* 12(5), p. e0177108. doi: 10.1371/journal.pone.0177108.

8 UNAIDS (2016) "NYC Condom Reaching Key Populations with Targeted Distribution, Marketing and Mobile Phone App", *The Body.* Available at: www.thebody.com/article/nyc-condom-reaching-key-populations-with-targeted- (Accessed: 4 January 2020).

9 Holmes, K. K., Levine, R. and Weaver, M. (2004) "Effectiveness of condoms in preventing sexually transmitted infections", *Bulletin of the World Health Organization,* 82(6), pp. 454–461. Available at: www.ncbi.nlm.nih.gov/pmc/articles/PMC2622864/ (Accessed: 4 January 2020).

10 Moscibrodzki, P. *et al.* (2018) "Free versus purchased mosquito net ownership and use in Budondo sub-county, Uganda", *Malaria Journal,* 17. doi: 10.1186/s12936-018-2515-y.

11 Harris, J. (2010) "Mosquito nets can't conquer malaria | Julian Harris", *Guardian,* 8 July. Available at: www.theguardian.com/commentisfree/2010/jul/08/mosquito-nets-cant-cure-malaria (Accessed: 2 January 2020).

12 MEL Magazine (2017) "All the Things Condoms Have Been Used for Besides Birth Control", *MEL Magazine.* Available at: https://melmagazine.com/en-us/story/all-the-things-condoms-have-been-used-for-besides-birth-control(Accessed: 2 January 2020).

13 Deperthes, B. (2019) Personal interview.

14 Khan, F. *et al.* (2013) "The story of the condom", *Indian Journal of Urology,* 29(1), p. 12. doi: 10.4103/0970-1591.109976.

15 Smale, W. (2010) "New chapter in the long history of Durex", *BBC News,* 21 July. Available at: www.bbc.com/news/uk-10712088 (Accessed: 4 January 2020).

16 Bates, S. (2010) "Condoms and the Catholic church: a short history", *Guardian,* 21 November. Available at: www.theguardian.com/world/2010/nov/21/condoms-birth-control-catholic-church-short-history (Accessed: 4 January 2020).

17 Smale, W. (2010) "New chapter in the long history of Durex", *BBC News,* 21 July. Available at: www.bbc.com/news/uk-10712088 (Accessed: 4 January 2020).

18 Sydow, V. (2019) Personal interview.

19 Moran, J. S. *et al.* (1990) "Increase in condom sales following AIDS education and publicity, United States", *American Journal of Public Health,* 80(5), pp. 607–608. doi: 10.2105/AJPH.80.5.607.

20 Kennedy, S. (2010) "Reckitt Benckiser agrees $3.9 billion deal to buy SSL", *MarketWatch.* Available at: www.marketwatch.com/story/reckitt-benckiser-to-buy-ssl-for-39-billion-2010-07-21-42400 (Accessed: 4 January 2020).

21 RB (no date). *Healthier Lives, Happier Homes.* Available at: www.rb.com/us/ (Accessed: 4 January 2020).

22 RB (2019) *Durex – Changing sexual wellbeing*. Available at: www.rb.com/brands/durex/ (Accessed: 4 January 2020).
23 Credit Suisse (2016) "The global condom market, Equity Research: Credit Suisse", 13 September 2016. Available at: https://research-doc.credit-suisse.com/docView?language=ENG&format=PDF&source_id=csplusresearchcp&document_id=1064783631&serialid=0wDGIi%2FE2yNyPYP2XmhEP0I2jXV7E9uASb69BceitH8%3D (Accessed: 4 January 2020).
24 Mordor Intelligence (2018) "Condom Market Growth, Trends and Forecasts 2019–2024", *Mordor Intelligence*. Available at: www.mordorintelligence.com/industry-reports/condom-market (Accessed: 4 January 2020).
25 Chen (2016) "This Malaysian Company Is the World's Largest Condom-Maker", *Forbes*. Available at: www.forbes.com/sites/forbesasia/2016/08/03/malaysias-karex-buys-innovative-new-condom-brands-landing-it-on-asias-bub-list/ (Accessed: 4 January 2020).3
26 Wilson, B. and Viega-Pestana, M. (2019) Personal interview.
27 Reckitt Benckiser Group plc (2018) *Annual Report and Financial Statements 2018*. Available at: www.rb.com/media/4116/rb-ar2018.pdf.
28 Ibid.
29 Ibid.
30 Sydow, V. (2019) Personal interview.
31 Ibid.
32 Mano, A (2016) "Brazil's Hypermarcas receives $175 million balance on condom unit sale", *Reuters*, 4 October. Available at: www.reuters.com/article/us-hypermarcas-m-a-reckitt-benc-grp-idUSKCN1242KA (Accessed: 4 January 2020).
33 Buckley, K. (2018) "Durex Rolls Out Low-Cost Condoms in Africa", *Bloomberg*, 30 November. Available at: www.bloomberg.com/news/articles/2018-11-30/reckitt-benckiser-s-durex-adds-low-cost-condoms-in-south-africa (Accessed: 4 January 2020).
34 Kaiser Health News (2001) "Durex Condom Maker Using "Humor" Ads to Sell Condoms in Europe", *KHN Morning Briefing*. Available at: https://khn.org/morning-breakout/dr00006045/ (Accessed: 4 January 2020).
35 Stampler, L. (2013) "Durex Started A Condom Delivery Service in Dubai", *Business Insider*. 31 January 2013. Available at: www.businessinsider.com/durex-started-a-condom-delivery-service-in-dubai-2013-1 (Accessed: 4 January 2020).
36 Yahoo (2013) "Condom delivery service advert caused a stir". Available at: https://uk.news.yahoo.com/condom-delivery-service-advert-caused-a-stir-035013793.html (Accessed: 4 January 2020).
37 Zhang, P. (2019) "Durex ads 'more frightening than pornography,' online watchdog says", *South China Morning Post*. Available at: www.scmp.com/news/china/society/article/3007526/durex-ads-more-frightening-pornography-chinas-online-watchdog (Accessed: 4 January 2020).
38 Wilson, B. and Viega-Pestana, M. (2019) Personal interview.
39 Ibid.
40 Ibid.
41 Ibid.
42 Ibid.
43 Sydow, V. (2019) Personal interview.
44 Bee, P. (2004) "Olympics: Hopping, skipping and jumping into each others' beds", *Guardian*. Available at: www.theguardian.com/sport/2004/aug/02/athensolympics2004.olympicgames2 (Accessed: 4 January 2020).
45 Allen, H. and Varanasi, L. (2016) "A history of condoms in the Olympic Village, from 8,500 in Seoul to 450,000 in Rio", *Slate.com*. Available at: https://slate.com/culture/2016/05/a-history-of-condoms-in-the-olympic-village-from-8500-in-seoul-to-450000-in-rio.html (Accessed: 4 January 2020).

46 Ibid.
47 MTV Staying Alive (no date) "Someone like me", *MTV Staying Alive*. Available at: www.mtvstayingalive.org/campaign/someone-like-me/.
48 Sydow, V. (2019) Personal interview.
49 Wilson, B. and Viega-Pestana, M. (2019) Personal interview.
50 Ibid.
51 Harris, S. (2010) "Anger over sex education survey paid for by Durex", *Mail Online*. Available at: www.dailymail.co.uk/news/article-1324695/Anger-sex-education-survey-paid-Durex.html (Accessed: 4 January 2020).
52 Fleming, M. (2018) "Durex partners with (RED) to get people to "give a f★ck" about HIV", *Marketing Week*. Available at: www.marketingweek.com/durex-partners-red-give-a-fck-about-hiv/ (Accessed: 4 January 2020).
53 Wilson, B. and Viega-Pestana, M. (2019) Personal interview.
54 Red.org (2019) *Durex (RED) Campaign*. Available at: www.red.org/durex (Accessed: 4 January 2020).
55 Reckitt Benckiser Group plc (2018) *Annual Report and Financial Statements 2018*. Available at: www.rb.com/media/4116/rb-ar2018.pdf.
56 Maher, M. (2015) "Durex® Calls for the Creation of the World's First Official Safe Sex Emojis", *Business Wire*. Available at: www.businesswire.com/news/home/20151118005205/en/Durex%C2%AE-Calls-Creation-World%E2%80%99s-Official-Safe-Sex (Accessed: 4 January 2020).
57 Valinsky, J. (2016) "Durex writes a firm letter to the Unicode Consortium, pushing for a condom emoji", *Digiday*. Available at: https://digiday.com/marketing/durex-condom-emoji/ (Accessed: 4 January 2020).
58 Terris-Prestholt, F. and Windmeijer, F. (2016) "How to sell a condom? The impact of demand creation tools on male and female condom sales in resource limited settings", *Journal of Health Economics*, 48, pp. 107–120. doi: 10.1016/j.jhealeco.2016.04.001.
59 World Health Organization (2018) *HIV/AIDS Data and statistics 2018*. Available at: www.who.int/hiv/data/en/ (Accessed: 4 January 2020).
60 Deperthes, B. (2019) Personal interview.

5 Collaborating with outside partners

How do strange bedfellows get along?

Most brands on a mission aim to drive transformational change, at scale. But they cannot do it alone – they need partners to supply complementary skills, expertise, resources and networks. That gives rise to two kinds of challenges. First, brands must overcome the traditional resistance of non-profit organisations, governments and academics to working with for-profit companies. Second, they must select the partner carefully to ensure a good fit on goals, process, budgets and activities – so that the joint activities bring value to both the partner and the brand.

Partnerships are critical to bringing a brand's purpose to life. They can expand what the brand does well beyond what the brand could deliver on its own. They are also fragile and can flounder for many reasons. This chapter looks at why brands should partner, the types of partnerships and their benefits. Learning to manage partnerships is a key capability for any purpose-driven brand, and we will go through some of the pitfalls and advice on managing partnerships.

Overcoming resistance to working with corporations

The landscape for brands in 2020 is fundamentally different from when I joined Unilever. Non-profits and governments are open to working with companies in ways that would have been inconceivable before and way more inclusive. I spoke to Jane Nelson, who heads the Corporate Responsibility initiative at the Harvard Kennedy school and, together with Professor John Ruggie, has been documenting and pushing the agenda on cross sectoral partnerships for the last 30 years. Partnerships with the private sector have evolved from a less traditional relationship ranging from traditional procurement and consultative arrangements, which have been in place since for example the founding of the UN in 1945, to new types of cooperation at the global and operational level.[1] One important turning point was in 2015, when the UN's Sustainable Development Goals explicitly set out a role for the private sector in addressing those big challenges.[2]

That said, the non-profit and public sector still have little experience in partnering with companies, especially when it comes to being part of viable business models. What I am advocating for here is for partnerships with brands that are more inclusive of the need to generate profits than they have been in the past. Brands on a mission do more than just donate money; they get directly involved with making positive advances towards the social issue they believe they can impact through their core activities and competencies. At the same time, they need their businesses to benefit from those efforts, indirectly at the very least. Non-profit organisations have only recently begun to accept this calculus in theory, and many of them haven't yet worked it out in practice.

It is important to clarify that all non-profits organisations are not the same. UN agencies, NGOs, foundations are different legal entities with very different governance, policy and regulations (Table 5.1 clarifies simply the various roles). But for the purposes of this chapter, I will refer to the public sector when talking about non brands.

One important challenge is still the issues of misunderstanding and wrong expectations. I still remember the difficulty of explaining to UN agencies that the profits from selling soap would help to pay for handwashing programmes, and how we were made to feel guilty for wanting to sell our brand. The issues of misunderstandings and wrong expectations are real and still exist today. There is often little understanding of how business works and what is required to make it sustainable, and also exactly what brands want to benefit from, especially if it is not CSR. I've had to deal many times with frustrated brand managers coming out of partnerships meetings where they spent all their time justifying their existence as a business, or made to feel that they are trying to cheat the public sector in some way, which can be extremely demoralising. I say this all the time: I have yet to meet a brand manager

Table 5.1 Roles of organisations

Examples of types of partners	What to expect?
NGOs and Foundations	Social mobilisations, pooling resources, entry into difficult places and niche programmatic areas
Governments	Access to channels, permissions, lobbying for policy changes
Academia and think tanks	Latest thinking, evidence generation, advocacy and credibility
UN and its agencies	National programmes, expertise, convincing governments
Customers and retailers	Modern trade for cause-related marketing/joint funding and scaling up
Other likeminded private sector organisations	Create social coalitions, bundles in retailers (e.g. Global Handwashing Day/breakfast deals with fruit/bread)

(at least in Unilever) that wakes up in the morning and thinks about how they are going to mess up the world. On the contrary I have seen brand managers trying hard to find ways to fund these partnerships. On the other side, the brands cannot think that partners are an agency that they can pay and expect results from.

The other challenge is the expectation that the private sector will share lessons and programmes with rivals, or that a generic programme would grow the pie and we would all benefit. FMCG (Fast Moving Consumer Goods) Brands do not work like that. The competitive nature of companies makes it too difficult in practice. You can create a joint platform like Global Handwashing Day, but then individual brands will find ways to celebrate, and use the platform for their individual interests. This should be considered a good thing, because it means more resources in countries for handwashing with soap, so long as we are all talking about the same needed behaviours.

These difficulties are not surprising given the very different mandates of the partners. NGOs tend to oppose governments and fight for donor resources. The infant formula saga, involving Nestlé and others, saw UNICEF and other NGOs being seen as fighting against certain corporations. These groupings live in separate worlds and lack a common language and common metrics of success.

Still, the more companies clearly explain how they will benefit from partnerships, the better. Often the public sector needs to realise that partnerships do not yield financial outcomes immediately and that the private sector is not a bank – we must negotiate our budget, so any long-lasting initiative must be linked to performance.

Partnering with the public sector adds many advantages, such as legitimacy, support in entering white spaces, feet under the table at events that matter, innovation and learning. Partners can contribute different things: governments can offer scale, NGOs help with social mobilisation, academics with legitimacy. Lifebuoy has worked with Amref Health Africa (the largest African NGO for health) in Migori, one of the poorest counties in Kenya, to talk to new mothers about handwashing. They engaged with their health extension workers and trained women from the communities to deliver a message that Lifebuoy had developed with them. Desta Lakew, Global Director of Partnerships, saw value in this kind of work:

> With the SDG17 global partnership mandate, many NGOs and certainly Amref are seeking the right partnerships to advance key initiatives. We recognise that partnerships are critical to achieving universal health coverage and ensuring better health for Africans. Our journey into private sector engagement has been cautious in the beginning, but increasingly robust as we recognise that it takes all hands on board to really push the needle forward. This is a sentiment that we see growing among other NGOs. Our missions are too important and the stakes too high to leave the private sector out of the equation.[3]

Still, the public sector requires a good deal of explanation and reassurance along the way. They need to understand upfront how the company expects to benefit, so they aren't surprised later. It's important to be "painfully transparent" with these expectations on profits from social causes. Nitin Paranjpe, Chief Operating Officer at Unilever, elaborated:

> If you want trust, you need radical transparency. Too often in the past we have tried to hide things from people, because you think they look ugly and you want to avoid people getting to know them. But the truth is in today's world, you can't hide anything. And if they find out that you were trying to hide it, they will punish you. But if they find you to be honest and working toward the goal, then you can even be rewarded for your imperfection.[4]

The public sector benefits a great deal from these partnerships, from joint resources sharing to expertise in marketing to innovative products. And brands shouldn't feel obliged to commit a lot of resources upfront. At Lifebuoy, the policy was never to give cash to partners to start with (and to be fair the brand had a small budget in comparison to some of the billion dollar brands). Instead, a genuine collaboration was sought where both parties brought something to the table. But when dealing with NGOs and implementing partners you have to consider funding as an integral part of genuine collaboration. It is the implementing partners that lend technical capabilities and access to often unchartered "markets". A good example is Lifebuoy's work with Amref, as mentioned earlier, on neonatal mortality prevention in rural areas. Once the brand had demonstrated efficacy, Amref and Lifebuoy jointly sought further funding from external donors. It is done on a case-by-case basis and it is important to identify clearly the benefits to the business model and track the impact to the purpose.

A lot of progress is being done and Jane Nelson sums it up well by saying:

> Cross-sector partnerships are not an answer to every problem, nor are they easy to build. They require a difficult balance of idealism and pragmatism, passion and patience, action and reflection, creative vision and hard work, pooled resources and independent contributions, a strong commitment to principles and a willingness to compromise and adapt.

Think about scale

Early partnerships with various partners in brands placed the emphasis on pilots, with discussions on working at a large scale left for later phases. However, the result was too often never-ending pilots with little impact. Pilots have their role to fit initiatives to the local context, understand what's working and what needs improvement. Despite a great pilot with proven impact, scaling can be an issue if the brand is not doing well or the market opportunity is small.[5] For example, the neonatal programme in rural Kenya with soap was hard to expand, given the niche targeted population and the rural aspect of the programmes. So, brands need to think about scaling with partners from the get-go. That includes figuring out resources for scaling within the business model, without simply assuming that cash-strapped governments or NGOs will provide the main funding. The MOU should have the pilot as well as the scaling up built into it and clarity on the resources to keep aside for that.

Partnering with professional and academic organisations

Professional organisations aren't likely to help with programme investments, but they can give a brand credibility. Unilever's partnership with the Fédération Dentaire Internationale (FDI), which started in 2005, boosted Pepsodent and related brands (called Signal in some countries) in two ways. The first was the simple stamp of approval on the product. The second was the opportunity to study the efficacy of Pepsodent's Brush Day and Night programme. With its scientific lens, FDI can estimate the social impact of Unilever's work, and help to determine whether educational programmes are working.

Academic partnerships are becoming central to supporting brands on their purpose journey. As explained in Chapter 2, the Centre for Appearance Research improved Dove's programmes on body self-image with evaluations and advice. Yet the cultural gaps are enormous, and sometimes hard to bridge, as the job of professors is to objectively test hypotheses, while marketers often want to hear only good news because they fear damaging the brand.

Sometimes a company will help a university to establish a research centre aligned to its social mission. That allows like-minded academics to affiliate and pursue their research interests, while giving the brand early access to findings. Exposure to the researchers can also give marketers a greater appreciation of the wider context for social problems.

Unilever, for example, helped to create the Hygiene Centre with the London School of Hygiene and Tropical Medicine. This was the centre that paid for my dissertation field work in Senegal on understanding the motivations for school children to wash their hands with soap. Across the years since I moved over to Lifebuoy, the brand team benefitted from many of the centre's publications, as well as constructive criticism from director Val Curtis.

Indeed, any brand that collaborates with academics must be ready to receive negative evaluations and assessments. Lifebuoy had to deal with two such evaluations. The first happened soon after I joined the brand, when the Hygiene Centre found that Lifebuoy's Swasthya Chetna campaign in India had boosted overall hygiene awareness but not actual handwashing with soap. This was hard for the brand team to swallow, as the campaign had been publicised for years. But Lifebuoy remained committed to the mission, and the criticism forced the team to be more focused and creative in its efforts. It led to the ambitious goal of reaching one billion people with handwashing behaviour change programmes. Whilst brands can grow as a result of some of this negative experience, the biggest fear is the competitive advantage that other brands can gain from this knowledge.

The second setback involved the programme in Bihar state in India, discussed at length in Chapter 6. Lifebuoy's response to the bad news on behaviour change was to start a parallel track on learning from the experience and to improve the brand's programmes accordingly. The brand team also launched an internal publicity campaign to prevent the bad evaluation from ending the mission-driven business model. The biggest learning outcome was that if you are pursuing a social purpose, real impact is everything. If you're going to play in the "Do Gooders" field, then you need to be actually helping the world and to be able to prove it.

Academics are increasingly ready to partner with companies and see value in it. From developing joint research methods, to joint advocacy, Peter Piot, Director of the London School of Hygiene and Tropical Medicine, was clear on this point:

> I'm deeply convinced that we cannot improve health worldwide without involving all those who are playing a major role in society and people's health – from governments, to local communities, to NGOs, together with businesses. What's key is that the rules of engagement and of the game are clear on all sides of these public private academia partnerships. We should not have any illusion: a company is not an academic business or an NGO, and vice versa. Key is that we are transparent, so that we can capitalise on the strengths of each sector.[6]

Here is some advice on choosing your academic partner:

• Respect their independence: you cannot instruct them on what you want them to find.
• Seek a wider scope of interest than just your brand's purpose – you will benefit from understanding the wider landscape.
• Expect a three-year plus partnership with a scope of work that takes you from articulation of purpose through to implementation and evaluation.
• Agree upfront on what will and will not be published, what is a trial and what is not.
• Seek regular check-ins and involve those from your business who handle market insights, as they will likely understand study design and statistical complexities.

Corporate partnerships and the role of philanthropy

Partnerships need not focus on specific initiatives and often align to companies' wider strategic interests. For example, TRANSFORM is a partnership between business, government and civil society, founded by the UK's Department for International Development and Unilever in 2015, with the ambition to bring private sector creativity and commercial approaches, and combine with public sector resources, to solve persistent global development challenges.[7] The aim is to reach 100 million people in sub-Saharan Africa and South Asia by 2025. To date, it has supported more than 19 projects across nine countries, identifying and funding social entrepreneurs operating across improving livelihoods, environmental sustainability and health and well-being. Projects have included a mobile platform for shopkeepers in Kenya that encourages them to become change agents in their communities, and a portable handwashing station for low-income households in Bangladesh, all supporting a wider enabling environment.

Similarly, the Danone Ecosystem Fund empowers vulnerable stakeholders in Danone's value chain. So far it has invested over 185 million Euros, more than half of which has come from external partners, to address four areas:

- sustainability of water resources and other raw materials
- distribution to create logistical channels
- caring services to strengthen knowledge and access to nutrition and health services
- and recycling to reinforce the circular economy and improve sourcing of plastics.[8]

The Ecosystem Fund's projects have demonstrated the deep inter-dependency between these different areas across the value chain. The key element is linking the projects' innovation platforms to Danone's brands in order to integrate them into their business models and into what the company calls Manifesto brands.

The role of philanthropy and corporate partnerships can be important for social investments, product donations and employee volunteering.[9]

Global versus local partnerships

In the past, some partnerships arose when a company's CEO met his or her counterpart at a global charity, and then this was passed down to the businesses to ensure that a project came of it. A long series of meetings would follow and, if all went well, a pilot would happen where the two CEOs could show up, take pictures in front of smiling children and feel proud. Rarely did these partnerships move to scale, and rarely did they last unless the CEOs in question remained in charge for a long period and kept pushing the initiative.

A better approach is for companies to create a global team to nurture relationships with NGOs and ensure alignment with government priorities. The team can make sure that they are on the lookout for a company's strategic interests, bring in the brand teams quickly and build on the CEO's great networks. Most importantly, the global team can assess whether the proposed joint activities can help the business to grow, clarifying upfront what success would look like. Which means they need to understand what is a successful business model for the brands.

Brands must also understand the different contributions of global and local participants, and be ready to invest heavily in local relationships. Even initiatives conceived entirely at the global level must still be managed and implemented in specific areas. You can create a global framework of operation, but you're still limited to what works in specific locations. If your partner isn't operating in your key countries of future growth, then it's going to be hard to make a difference for your business.

When I joined Unilever in 2006 the company had partnerships for sanitation programmes in geographic areas where they had absolutely no business. That's not to say that there wasn't a need for sanitation, but Unilever couldn't contribute much beyond an injection of cash. That led to a substantial sanitation programme being conducted in Djibouti even though the company had no business there, and I remember questioning the sustainability of that model. Every year in Nigeria, World Food Day was celebrated and money would be raised to send to the World Food Programme partnership in another country as the World Food Programme did not have a presence in Nigeria. Yet it was a globally negotiated partnership. This raises the question of global and local partnerships.

Brands are also paying greater attention to locally-shaped initiatives and local implementing partners who understand the context in which initiatives are being implemented. When Lifebuoy and Global Alliance for Vaccination Immunisation (GAVI) piloted a campaign to promote vaccines in Uttar Pradesh, India, the brand team learned how much parenting differed from European and African norms. Fathers here were seen to have had little responsibility for the health of their children and were not included in the messages. Also, the team's focus was on preventing diseases that people in the villages saw as the will of the gods. The messages had to be adjusted accordingly with a part of the programme including the men, and most of it to both parents.

Building these local relationships takes time yet is essential. Agreements with governments will go nowhere without the frontline workers and their networks. In Ethiopia, the country's Women Development Army, a large mass of volunteer community health workers, is a great opportunity to partner if you can manufacture locally. In Indonesia, approval from the national government just wasn't enough; programmes still had to be negotiated with teachers in the various school districts.

In some cases you might want to skip trying to form partnerships with global organisations altogether and go straight to governments or local arrangements. This will avoid the overhead costs of global organisations. The transactional costs can be outrageous and if you are a small brand trying to grow, spending a lot of money at headquarter levels when you can spend that money doing a hygiene or sanitation programme directly with local authorities is something to think about and that I have challenged global headquarters on regularly. It all depends on your business objectives. If you already know your model and just want to scale across markets, then seek local partners. Local or regional works best when you have clear implementation guidelines and are also clear what success looks like, such as taking an existing school programme across markets.

Global is best when you are still articulating your social purpose and seeking a model for your initiatives. For Lifebuoy's partnership with Sightsavers, the handwashing model was adapted and developed for trachoma prevention, led globally but deployed only in the markets with trachoma prevalence. The same thing with Domestos's global Janitor programme, developed globally, tested in the Philippines and then implemented in South Africa. The developmental work of a new programme is best handled at the global level, between your corporate headquarters and a global NGO or intergovernmental organisation. The technical knowledge is often held with the experts in these organisations and, combined with a brand's expertise, can be used to develop a great programme.

A global approach can also work well when your company already has a strong partnership with a global charity. It's much easier to add the social purpose of a specific brand to an ongoing collaboration, than to start a new relationship. The bottom line is that it should benefit the brand locally.

Keeping your partners and setting parameters of success

Successful partnerships start with an aligned vision to address a major social challenge. The partners have shared objectives and respect for each other's organisation. Real impact, of course, depends on scaling up pilot programmes. To ensure success, brands have three imperatives:

1   Get to know the landscape you're operating in. It's essential to attend events and forums with NGOs, governments and other companies. The simple act of listening helps you discern what is really out there and identify similar initiatives taking place in other organisations. That's how Lifebuoy learned about GAVI's work to reduce neonatal mortality. The brand team discovered people who had the same goals and complementary resources, and found that they could work together for maximum impact.
2   Think horizontally not vertically; avoid getting stuck in issue-based silos. For Unilever, but not for many of its partners, nutrition, handwashing and gender equity were all related, and the company's brands needed to make connections across the portfolio. For example, if Domestos is dealing with sanitation and Lifebuoy with handwashing, linking them makes sense, because consumers experience hygiene and sanitation together. Many partners do think and work in silos, so it's good to find one that can work across sectors, such as UNICEF and Amref.

3   Move out of your comfort zone. Strange bedfellows can be the best part-
    ners because you extend your reach in ways you didn't expect. Lifebuoy
    makes soap, yet the brand has had a great deal of success working with
    one promoting immunisation.

Dealing with failure

Nobody likes to see a programme fall short of its objectives. But development
work isn't easy, and academics and NGOs know that some efforts will fail.
Brands, however, feel very exposed if a partnership does not succeed. Marketers may have tied the brand to a specific initiative and now face a hit to its
reputation, and possibly even to the overall company's name. The damage to
brand equity is hard and sometimes impossible to recover from.

My only advice here is to learn to fail fast. Failure can actually benefit the
brand in the long run, but only with a culture of learning from setbacks and
putting the lessons back in the business. There will always be a publicity risk.
But if we want companies to take the lead in addressing social challenges, we
need to be able to take the hit, and accept and learn from failure.

Another important issue is with community ownership of the solutions.
Brands tend to focus narrowly on a specific solution, but often these solutions
depend on a wider enabling environment. Solutions should also be designed
with sustainability as a key and overarching element of success. The intervention or solution needs to be absorbed into the environment and "owned" by
the community in which it is implemented.

That's where the corporate team and the partnerships team need to get
involved to promote complementary investments. Lifebuoy can teach people
to wash their hands with soap, but if people lack wash basins or running
water, behaviours will not change. That is how Unilever lobbied for the creation of an SDG6 sub-indicator on handwashing facilities. This is a great
example of how companies can align their lobbying efforts with CSR and
marketing initiatives.[10] Cross-sectoral partnerships were created that addressed
government policy on infrastructure to complement handwashing facilities
and ones that would address infrastructure and water bills alongside the handwashing and oral health. A start has been made but progress hasn't reached as
far as I would like.

Partnering with governments

By 2050, Africa will have over two billion people. If they are healthy, educated and skilled, then the private sector will thrive, because they will have
the disposable incomes to buy the private sector's goods and services. This is
what African countries specifically should be aiming for, by ensuring that
products are manufactured locally but with economies of scale to enable low
prices. This is where the partnerships with government should focus – it's not
a separate issue.

Working with governments is often both essential – to mobilise resources for scaling up – and tricky. The advantages of working with governments include reduced cost, alignment to government policy, bigger impacts and access to channels which private sector otherwise cannot reach, such as teachers and community health workers.[11]

Yet government agencies are often focused narrowly on their immediate portfolio. Ministries of health focus on medical treatments, not food, while ministries of agriculture think about food, not health, and no education in school can happen without the ministry of education. So, this is a difficult area for brands to navigate, and sometimes needing to take the lead in raising awareness and developing a programme. The disadvantages can be many: federal alignment not always leading to provincial alignment; sometimes the scale cannot be afforded by brands; or it can be difficult to secure an exclusive MOU.

In securing buy-in from governments, brands should involve the corporate office rather than individual brands. In India, Unilever worked to become a partner of choice in the government's Swachh Bharat (cleanliness) and Mission Indradhanush (immunisation) campaigns. Domestos, Lifebuoy and other brands could not have secured this approval on their own.

At that point, the government is enabling companies to scale up their initiatives. They can get a return on investment in the higher volume of sales.[12] Over time, governments can create an environment of ease of doing business where it is cheaper to manufacture locally.

We need to shift away from the notion that public good comes only from the public sector. Governments are particularly important to reach the most vulnerable people. It's difficult for the private sector to offer brands at a cost for those furthest behind. Governments can fill the gaps in the most marginalised areas, where the human development indicators are the worst off, where people struggle daily with hunger and violence. They can also keep pushing brands to develop innovative solutions to get there.

Partnering with the United Nations

UN partnerships can facilitate help with working with governments. The UN has a mandate to support governments in tackling major social challenges, and increasingly that means fostering private sector efforts.[13]

The rules of the United Nations forbid programmes to associate, directly or indirectly, with commercial brands. It is understandable that the UN does not want to appear to endorse a particular product or brand, even more so UN agencies with the mandate to protect children like UNICEF. But in the new era of partnerships with business models reaching the most vulnerable, these rules need to be adjusted. The public sector, UN and other multi-lateral systems, and NGOs can accommodate brands without this implying an explicit endorsement. The UN has developed partnerships where the brand's logo is not explicitly shown but the colour/shape of the product is mentioned or joint public sector advertising brought by a brand is carried out.

Take Kenya, which has some of the seven of the poorest counties in Africa. Like many sub-Saharan countries, it is struggling with massive foreign debt. Sid Chatterjee, the UN resident coordinator there, is clear on the UN's role:

> Between USD 3.3–4.5 trillion per year needs to be mobilised if we hope to achieve the 2030 Agenda for Sustainable Development. At today's level of both public and private investment in SDG-related sectors, developing countries face an average annual funding gap of USD 2.5 trillion. This does not mean that official developmental assistance is irrelevant. Rather, it must be used strategically – as an instrument to secure other sources of finance: public and private, domestic and international.[14]

There is a need to unlock new financing to support a public good such as health, because the government does not have it. The money is with the private sector, in the market, so governments need to incentivise investment, in particular in under-financed areas such as preventative health. We also need the digital technologies that only the private sector can provide. Companies can get a return on investment by being the first mover, being persistent, patient and adaptable to the market, as Unilever was when entering the Indian market.

For example, the private sector could service remote clinics through drones and telemedicine. The UN can be the neutral broker bringing together the government with partners under the right conditions to help public and private sector co-create solutions fit-for-purpose and tailored to the local context. It can help to ensure that a range of providers offer these systems of packages and services, in the right way and at the right price point to create shared-value and deliver value for money. And it can work on different types of financing.

In my experience, the biggest challenge in working with the UN is that it tends to be locked into a bureaucracy that restricts working with commercial brands. It takes visionary country coordinators to unlock this system. That's why brands prefer to work with organisations such as GAVI, which was set up to be able to do work that UNICEF and WHO cannot do. They are not constrained by association with commercial brands and can operate directly with implementation NGOs like Amref, or often a combination of both. This is what Seth Berkley, the CEO of GAVI, thinks:

> We can work with a wider breadth of companies, and with substantial capital, because we have a more business-like model, flexibility, and ability to work with different groups to be more performance driven. Donors want their investments to be transparent, performance-based, and outcome oriented, with risk assurance built in. For a long time the UN hid behind a sense that "We are the UN", you can't audit us.[15]

Chatterjee adds that his greatest difficulties have come from within the UN:

> The UN has to be either more dynamic or it becomes a dinosaur and becomes irrelevant. The renewed power of the UN will not come from the money that we bring to the table, but the great ideas and our ability to convene, connect and catalyse in order to make sure great ideas are turned into transformative action. It is a battle of making great ideas happen today, making sure that small, catalytic financing can change the game.

Finding leaders willing to take risks together is critical. I talked to Dr Natalia Kanem, Executive Director UNFPA. The UNFPA is the United Nations sexual and reproductive health agency that has a vision for a world where every pregnancy is wanted, every childbirth is safe and every young person's potential is fulfilled. And she is pretty clear with the need to have more innovative and disruptive partnerships:

> The UNFPA mandate has never been more relevant. Our work and partnerships must therefore be even more innovative, ambitious and focused at country level to ensure that we leave no woman or adolescent girl behind.
>
> One example of our innovative partnership approach is our collaboration with leading art and design school, the Parsons School of Design, and undergarment manufacturer Hela, to produce a new undergarment for refugees in Africa. This clean and reusable undergarment will help emergency-effected women and girls better maintain their menstrual hygiene. By co-designing with women in refugee camps, they provided real time feedback about the garment.[16]

Here's some advice for brands wanting to work with the UN:

- Choose the agency that aligns with your values and can add value to your purpose. The UN has a daunting number of agencies, and brands may struggle to understand the practical difference between UNFPA, UNICEF, UNDP, UN Women and UNAIDS. First clarify where you think you can add value, then seek conversations to illuminate each agency's focus. Check first if your corporate team has contacts or existing conversations with agencies.
- Start with an overall Memorandum of Understanding, from which you can design a three-year plan in a joint country of interest. Specify how you expect to co-create a solution for a specific problem and how the programme might be implemented.
- Agree on the use of corporate and brand logos. Most UN agencies will not allow their agency logo next to a brand logo, but may allow it with the company's logo. You will find many details to be fleshed out.

- Be bold. Go beyond cause-related marketing programmes which can be great in developed markets but limiting when you are trying to reach populations with cheaper formats.

Funding to financing

While building relationships with outside partners, it's easy to put off hard questions about funding. Most brands, with various P&L budgets, cannot immediately fund programmes at scale, and especially not the infrastructure that many programmes need. Domestos can raise awareness on sanitation, but building toilets is not core to their competencies, but behaviour change is.

There are different models of funding in partnerships, but the goal is for a campaign to show results after a few years, and then to generate resources that sustain the work for the long term. It helps to split funding with each party so everyone has skin in the game, a vested interest in the work. You can also bring other private partners to contribute from different angles, such as a plumbing company to build toilets, or a tank company for water storage. A common approach is to have funding from the corporate office, funding from the brand and funding from the NGO or its donors.

How to manage partnerships

Both sides must understand the needs of their partners before holding formal discussions. What is the business need that the partnerships will address? Is it scale? Is it credibility? The best scalable partnerships match areas of alignment with each partners' capabilities. The shared-value engagement has to be fully transparent and endorsed at the highest levels of the partnership for it to succeed. Brands need to be fully aware of the needs for their business models and must be fully involved in all steps in the partnership. Once a brand has fully developed its purpose, it should work closely with the corporate team, which may have already nurtured many of these global contacts. However brands must drive the process; otherwise the partnership could devolve into a publicity effort little tied to what the brand actually needs. They must resist governance rules that give only Corporate Communications the right to talk to external partners and make long-term partnership impossible. They must clarify that there should be no exclusive communication that removes the brands from the conversations.

The starting point is the brand's role in addressing the social challenge. Can the brand make a difference, and is that role going to be credible with participants or the brand's larger market? If not, the brand is better off writing a cheque than attempting to run a programme directly. It should bring something valuable to the issue.

From there, it's important to assess the capabilities that each partner brings, internally and externally. Brands tend to be strong marketers; they know how to change behaviour. Corporate sustainability offices bring an understanding and sensitivity to the environment where partnerships work. They know, for example, what is happening in the government of India, their existing programmes and priorities. They can "bring the outside in".

At Unilever, brand teams have been educated about the UN's Sustainable Development Goals. The corporate office on partnerships offers a deep understanding of the SDG framework and how businesses can fit in.

A big issue is identifying the real decision-makers in the corporation. Partners can get frustrated not understanding how the organisation works and who holds the purse and the vision for promoting the partnership. Brands need to clarify with external partners that the person holding the P&L – thus the lead brand manager, not a corporate manager – is the key stakeholder if the partnership is to be sustainable. If brands do not take the lead, then the partnership probably will not become embedded in the business model. That in turn means the partnership probably will not serve the brand's growth, or connect well with consumers.

While brands need to take charge, the brand teams need people to offer public health/ environmental skills and values. Those people will be the bridge between the marketing team and the external partners. They can reassure the partners of the brands' genuine interest in driving common goals to fruition (Table 5.2 describes the different roles within corporations).

From there, the key to get to scale is first confidence that the programme works, and second that it is cost-effective. Partners need to agree on how to hold a pilot programme, or whether to hold one at all.

At Unilever, a clear process is used to select partners. First, potential partners are mapped out, looking at their infrastructure for running programmes and initiatives. Their financial solvency is looked at, to make sure Unilever isn't the only organisation funding them, and they have the credibility and proper leadership in place. Brands get involved early. Eric Ostern, Unilever's Director of Global Partnerships & Advocacy, has significant experience of understanding how to manoeuvre across the organisation:

Table 5.2 Roles within corporations

What brands do? Global and local levels	*What corporate teams facilitate?*
• Define the purpose and exact business, the job to be done • Identify the relevant business model and KPIs • Assess which partner would appeal to consumers • Identify key countries/markets of interest • Identify the resources that the brand would need to contribute	• Understanding the landscape • Amplifying advocacy efforts by bringing in industry thought leaders • Addressing contractual and legal issues with the external partner • Representing the wider interests of the corporation

At Unilever, we have clear criteria for selecting partners and it's critical to consider several variables. We want to ensure that the organisations we work with share our commitment on the social issue that our brands seek to positively impact. Additionally, we look to partner with organisations that are credible, have strong leadership, are financially solvent, and have the infrastructure needed – and a strong track record – for delivering high-quality, impactful initiatives. The combination of all these criteria is instrumental in contributing to successful collaboration.[17]

Here's additional advice for brand managers:

- Clarify what can be expected and what cannot be expected from public sector partners (NGOs, foundations, government): slow but thorough, expensive but engaged collaboration.
- Be open to co-creation of programmes, but not all the time. Sometimes you are better off layering multi-sectoral approaches.
- Be open to getting insights on marginalised groups outside of urban consumers.
- Be open to longer planning periods, building trust with patience, which can improve implementation.
- Respect your commitments – do not promise spending that falls through because of budget cuts. Secure budgets at the start of the year.
- Strengthen partnerships over time, including investments in learning.
- Seek out external resources, and welcome the accountability that comes with it.
- Do not get carried away with do-gooding, rose-tinted spectacles – your brand is not a charity!

The future of purpose-led partnerships

There has been so much progress and so much learning on partnerships. At the heart of future partnerships should be new business models to address social issues jointly. That's all the more reason for brands to enter partnerships with transparency in developing sustainable business models. There is a new wave of impact investing as a mode of growing local sustainable businesses with social issue at the heart, and brands' programmes should be considered there. Brands will not win the trust of partners if they hold back on what they need, even for "strategic" programmes.

In partnerships with government, ease of doing business is coming to the forefront of the conversation. Can a ministry actually give a tax holiday to brands developing a package of services on preventative health (such as toothbrushing, handwashing, condoms and bed nets) or at least manufacturing facilities that make local production easier? Imagine what would happen if we get this right, so pricing and availability is less of an issue. We could get a long way on making universal health coverage affordable and addressing the prevention crisis.

In 2011 I went to see the Ethiopian Minister of Health, Dr Tedros, who later went on to head the World Health Organisation. I was trying to launch large scale handwashing programmes in rural Ethiopia, with help from the Women's Development Army and the health extension workers. He said categorically there will be no government partnerships until there was local manufacturing. "Come invest in Ethiopia, produce the soaps and toothpaste cheaper, and then we can talk about our networks." I had all my arguments ready about the status of health and hygiene in Ethiopia, but he was so right. Partnerships have to be embedded in long term vision of the country and everyone will benefit. As Nitin Paranjpe said in Chapter 1 "If it is right for India then it is right for us." There is now a toothpaste factory in Addis Ababa, and Unilever is making progress in reaching the furthest behind.

Exercise

Decision pathway: making partnership choices

In thinking about potential partnerships, there is much to learn and much to consider. Here is a pathway that can help you reflect on the kind of help you are looking for, what organisations you might want to partner with and why, what your dream partnership might look like, and which tasks you face in making partnerships happen.

Early-stage thinking: review what other brands have learned from partners

Among the many ways a brand can benefit from partnerships is in learning how to reach, interact with and support consumers. Time and again, brands have learned things they didn't even know they didn't know, as partners shared deep local knowledge to help multinationals avoid missteps and improve impact in pursuing social goals.

To cite a few examples from Unilever's experience:

- A South African NGO, People Opposing Women Abuse or POWA, helped the Joko tea brand understand that to combat gender-based violence the brand must support shelter spaces to protect women not just raise awareness about the issue.
- The Ministry of Education of South Africa helped the Domestos brand see that it wouldn't work to give a year's worth of sanitation supplies to schools – the temptation for janitors to divert the materials to the black market would be too great. Domestos worked with the Ministry to establish monthly replenishments and to figure out how to monitor janitors.
- Amref Health Africa helped Lifebuoy understand that to promote hygiene to new mothers in rural Kenya, it was necessary to interact with great tact and to choose the right teachers (women, not men, for example).

- An African foundation, the Well Being Foundation, helped Knorr under-stand that the best way to succeed in teaching cooking skills would be to embed instruction into life-skills curricula for teenagers, rather than doing one-off cooking classes.

Middle-stage thinking: consider global partners

If the brand is still in the process of articulating its social purpose and seeking a model for its interventions, it should consider a global partnership that could help with basic formative research and identify a pilot programme that fits the brand's business goals and the contribution that the brand can do to the social issue it chose to impact.

Options:
Create a core global team to look into relationships with academic organisa-tions and corporate partnerships.

- Academic organisations can help provide the latest thinking on research-based evidence, advocacy, credibility and the impact of various social missions.
- Corporate partnerships need not focus on specific initiatives and often align to companies' wider strategic interests and might have a network of like-minded organisations interested in the purpose of the brands.

Later-stage thinking: consider local partners or global partners with local representation as well

If the brand is at a point where it has settled on a social mission and has proof of concept, it should consider local partnerships that could help it build cred-ibility and achieve scale.

Options:
The social-purpose team should consider relationships with NGOs, govern-ments and UN agencies and look into professional organisations.

- NGOs can help in many ways, such as with entry into difficult places and niche programmatic areas.
- Governments can help with permissions, lobbying for policy changes, alignment with government policy and access to channels such as teach-ers and community health workers.
- The UN and its agencies can open doors to government programmes and provide scale. You may consider cause-related marketing.
- Professional organisations aren't likely to help with programme invest-ments, but they can give a brand credibility.

Notes

1 Nelson, J. (2002). "Building Partnerships: Cooperation between the United Nations System and the Private Sector". *United Nations*, Department of Public Information, New York.
2 Nelson, J. and Gilbert, R. (2018). "Advocating together for the SDGs". *Harvard Kennedy School*, Business Fights Poverty. Available at: www.hks.harvard.edu/sites/default/files/centers/mrcbg/files/Advocacy_Collaboration_SDGs.pdf (Accessed: 18 December 2019).
3 Lakew, D. (2019). Personal Interview.
4 Paranjpe, N. (2019). Personal interview.
5 Chandy, L. *et al.* (2014). "Getting to Scale", *Brookings*. Available at: www.brookings.edu/book/getting-to-scale/ (Accessed: 29 December 2019)
6 Piot, P. (2019) Personal interview.
7 TRANSFORM (no date). Available at: www.transform.global/Intro.aspx (Accessed: 18 December 2019).
8 Danone (no date). "Danone Ecosystem Fund". Available at: http://ecosysteme.danone.com/.
9 Nelson, J. (2002). "Building Partnerships: Cooperation between the United Nations System and the Private Sector". *United Nations*, Department of Public Information, New York.
10 AccountAbility and United Nations Global Compact (2005). "Towards Responsible Lobbying". Available at: www.unglobalcompact.org/docs/news_events/8.1/rl_final.pdf (Accessed: 18 December 2019).
11 Nelson, J. (2014). "How Can Multinationals Engage with Governments to Support Economic Development". *Brookings Institution*. Available at: www.brookings.edu/wp-content/uploads/2016/08/session-1-nelson-final.pdf.
12 Nelson, J. (2006). "Business as A Partner in Strengthening Public Health Systems in Developing Countries: An Agenda for Action". *International Business Leaders Forum, Clinton Global Initiative*. Available at: www.hks.harvard.edu/sites/default/files/centers/mrcbg/programs/cri/files/report_13_HEALTH%2BFINAL.pdf (Accessed: 18 December 2019).
13 Ibid.
14 Chatterjee, S. (2019). Personal Interview.
15 Berkeley, S. (2019). Personal interview.
16 Kanem, N. (2019). Personal interview.
17 Ostern, E. (2019). Personal interview.

6 How Lifebuoy secured a seat at the table of lifesavers

Lifebuoy is a well-known brand in the countries where our interventions take place. And having this link with Lifebuoy was very helpful in facilitating building confidence with the community and having access, since they knew about the brand and were confident and comfortable with it. Back in the UK [where the NGO is based], the partnership with Unilever also helped increase the profile of Sightsavers and has been really helpful for us in leveraging resources and getting interest from philanthropists.

(Caroline Harper, CEO of Sightsavers, 2018[1])

In 2013 Sightsavers, the world's largest organisation fighting preventable blindness, received a sizeable grant from the Queen Elizabeth Diamond Jubilee Trust.[2] The money was awarded to help eliminate trachoma in the Commonwealth, an eye disease from ancient times that is still the main cause of infectious blindness globally. A key part of Sightsavers' intervention involved getting children to wash their faces with soap as a preventative behaviour. However, delivering the hygiene programme in schools at scale was extremely challenging. For help in making that happen, Sightsavers turned to Lifebuoy, a soap brand owned by Unilever.

A decade earlier, as recounted in my Introduction chapter, my Lifebuoy colleagues and I had tried to work with UNICEF to promote handwashing with soap. At that time, due to several challenges and mistrust of for-profit companies, the partnership did not get off the ground. But since then we have secured two partnerships with UNICEF.[3] How did Lifebuoy get to the point where NGOs began seeking them out for partnerships? The answer was a decade of work to build the brand's credibility and experience in public health programmes. It was work that the brand's leaders embraced, as they were convinced that partnerships were essential for making a big difference in public health and also a vital part of Lifebuoy's purpose-driven growth model.

Lifebuoy's roots – building a model for collaboration

William Lever, the founder of what became Unilever, began selling Lifebuoy soap back in 1894. He had developed an antibacterial combination to fight cholera, a water-borne disease in areas with poor sewage, and one that claimed tens of thousands of lives in Victorian England.[4] Over the next century the brand expanded to become the world's biggest selling germ protection soap, sold in more than 50 countries. Lifebuoy sells over a hundred bars of soap per second, mostly to parents concerned about hygiene.

With that legacy, Lifebuoy was well positioned to help public health organisations reduce infectious disease in communities that, like England in 1894, lacked modern sewage treatment. Not surprisingly, handwashing with soap became Lifebuoy's main theme for public health, and protection from illness has been in Lifebuoy's DNA for over a century now.

Building on that early work, in 2006 the leaders of the Lifebuoy brand began exploring ways to promote handwashing directly to the children most at risk from disease. That's when they sought a partnership with the United Nations Children's Fund, or UNICEF. As described in my Introduction, they hired me to manage that partnership. Even with my background as a public health researcher, I could not make that partnership work as I would have liked. However, I learned a lot and became even more determined to make my stint in the private sector count.

In response, I gained a broader job title. My boss, Steve Miles, then Global Brand Vice President of Unilever Health Brands, made me Lifebuoy's Social Mission Manager – Unilever's first social mission manager. I was to embed public health and other social needs into the brand's business model and promote efforts to help vulnerable populations, while respecting the overall needs of running a commercial operation.

In 2007, as part of the Public–Private Partnership for Handwashing, and under my leadership, Lifebuoy/Unilever co-founded Global Handwashing Day. Other important partners were UNICEF, USAID and our competitors: Procter & Gamble and Colgate-Palmolive.[5] This was one of the first times that a joint collaboration with competition was done at Unilever.

This annual event, celebrated on 15th October, centres on shining a spotlight on handwashing with soap as a means to prevent infectious diseases such as dysentery and diarrhoea. To put the first global day together, I secured a small budget and got all the Lifebuoy communication agencies to give their time pro-bono. After a year of debating logos and principles of collaboration that would be acceptable to both the soap companies and the public sector, Global Handwashing Day was launched in 2008. In that first year over 20 million children from more than 20 Lifebuoy markets participated, washing their hands together. The event won endorsements from a wide array of governments, international institutions, civil society organisations, NGOs, private companies and individuals.[6]

Lifebuoy uses Global Handwashing Day to amplify its public health campaigns and garner support from governments, media and influencers. The campaign engages tens of thousands of Unilever employees to volunteer in schools and local communities to spread the handwashing message.[7] It also promotes large-scale activations, such as a Lifebuoy Bangladesh team setting a

Figure 6.1 Global Handwashing Day activity, Indonesia 2009.

Guinness World Record for the "Largest Human Image of a Hand" with 11,000 students.[8]

The success of Global Handwashing Day helped to maintain our faith in partnerships, despite the previous experience of the partnership with UNICEF. I kept saying that if Unilever and UNICEF could not figure out how to work together on handwashing, then we would have failed the children of today. Instead it forced us to clarify and develop what we could offer to potential public sector partners. We learned the importance of being transparent about our mission and business objectives. That was the only way to win the trust of the public sector.

Steve Miles and then Samir Singh, the first Lifebuoy Global Vice President, also saw the business benefits behind the social mission. I talked earlier in this book how I was inspired by Samir's leadership. From the start, Samir believed that public health would differentiate the brand from its competitors. The work might also boost long-term demand for the product. Where the social mission interventions are most critical, its main competitor is not the other soap brands but the lack of handwashing with soap itself, whether for behavioural reasons or lack of infrastructure. The social mission would further the brand's long-term growth and for that he gave me resources, way before it was normalised for brands to drive purpose.

To establish urgency, we set an ambitious target: to reach one billion people with our handwashing behaviour change messages. We made it part of the Unilever Sustainable Living Programme announced in 2010.[9]

Public health organisations had been promoting handwashing long before this time. However, they had always struggled with scaling up pilot programmes to change behaviour on a mass scale. One of the most effective ways was known to be through programmes in schools, but these are expensive, and many governments and NGOs have limited resources and expertise in behaviour change. In addition, their programmes rarely offered rewards to reinforce a lifestyle change of regular handwashing with soap. Lifebuoy, by contrast, was able to adjust its product packaging and communication to reach consumers with lifesaving hygiene messages. With product development and creative marketing, a century-old reputation as a germ fighter, combined with a new determination to promote social purpose, we knew that Lifebuoy could make a huge difference.

Figure 6.2 Lifebuoy School of Five characters.

We developed the "School of Five", a school-based programme to teach kids the five key moments for using soap each day: after using the toilet, before each of three meals and in bathing.[10] Until today many teachers in rural areas will tell us that they had never taught in such non-traditional and non-didactic format and how engaged their pupils were by this programme.

We hired Craig Yoe, the creative director of the Muppets, to design five cartoon superheroes for the key washing times for hands. Hairyback encourages kids to wash their hands after using the toilet; triplets, Biff, Bam and Pow, encourage handwashing before breakfast, lunch and dinner; and Sparkle, the leader of the gang, reminds you to wash your hands, face and whole body during bath or shower time (see Figure 6.2). The gang has adventures fighting their arch-enemy, Nogood, a baddie who loves germs.

The School of Five comic book to date is the most distributed comic book in the world. Surpassing Superman – it has been translated into 19 languages, printed over 19 million times and reached more than 300 million people.[11, 12]

But we knew we could not go as far as we wanted with the School of Five programme by ourselves. We needed governmental and NGO partners to add their networks, resources and reach, especially when it came to vulnerable populations. Jointly our programmes would be more powerful if we could layer the communications of private sector and public sector reinforcement. Our brand marketing budgets would have limited impact, but by combining resources and expertise, we could get real results.

To make sustainable change for populations in most need, we recognised that we needed separate initiatives to invest in infrastructure, including functioning handwashing facilities, as well as toilets and water. As these were completely outside our usual remit, we signed on to the WASH agenda, developed in 2015 to ensure that everyone has access to water, sanitation and hygiene services.

Finally, we took a decentralised approach. While Unilever's executives and the Lifebuoy brand team looked for major international partnerships, they allowed each national brand manager to explore local partnerships and experiment with different means of collaborating. Combined, these efforts helped shape a new corporate culture, and a strong message to potential partners. Rebecca Marmot, the company's then Vice President for Partnerships and Advocacy, summed up the approach as follows:

> Unilever is an organisation based on purpose-led brands, and we are committed to creating a sustainable future. Our brands are focused on driving transformational change, but they can't do that alone. We need partnerships because we need to leverage not only our skills, resources and assets, but also the skills, resources, assets and networks of others. I think the most productive forms of partnerships are when the partners have an aligned vision and shared objectives.[13]

Even with this message, Lifebuoy faced scepticism. We continued to work and develop new models, channels and technology to promote handwashing at scale. The one-billion target had a galvanising effect. Rather than seen as merely aspirational, the leaders of Lifebuoy empowered teams to work collectively and creatively. Kartik Chandrasekhar, Lifebuoy's current Global Brand Vice President, remembers that "when you're inspired by a vision and committed to it, it makes you find ways to get there".[14]

We made a point of always talking about our brand and our company. And doing so unapologetically. As potential partners understood our business and strategy, they started to trust that we would deliver as promised. Gradually we started to change the public sector's perception of Lifebuoy's potential contribution to public health, and more important the commitment to genuinely wanting to make a positive difference in the markets where we were selling. The point is to do as much good as you can with every bar of soap that you sell.

Our partnerships rapidly increased after 2010, partnering with a wide array of governments and NGOs. We experimented with models of behaviour change, and learned which ones brought success. The partners helped Lifebuoy find the areas that could most benefit from the brand's efforts – especially where handwashing could be a matter of life and death. Over time, the work shifted from urban locations, the low-hanging fruit where distribution was easier, to rural areas in Ethiopia, Kenya and India where there is greater suffering from disease. We also expanded our programmes from schools to reaching new mothers and their newborns, who were the most affected by diseases, working closely with neonatal experts at USAID.[15]

Most of our partnerships have used co-investment and leverage-funding models, pooling together resources from Unilever/Lifebuoy and the partners. However diverse in practice, these partnerships have built a repeatable, sustainable model, integrated with government systems and infrastructure. The goal is to promote handwashing behaviour change while supporting proper infrastructure in both schools and households. As a partnership evolves, it often becomes both more sophisticated, in terms of governance arrangements and partner types, and more specialised, in terms of targeted results and crosscutting impact. We have also as a brand committed to making the on-ground programmes more cost-efficient whilst respecting the pillars required to drive behaviour change. But even with partnerships and cost efficiency, on-ground programmes remain expensive, hence the journey towards channels innovation. Mobile Doctarni (a digital handwashing message programme) is reaching mothers with mobile phones exactly when she needs it the most and through a relevant channel.[16] This keeps the brand edgy and not stagnated in its approach, making partnerships more diverse.

The more partnerships expand, the stronger Lifebuoy's programmes have become. As Anila Gopal, Lifebuoy's Social Mission Director, recalls, "What was previously simply a good thing to have, because it helped build some credibility and add rigour to the programmes, has now become the only way to do business. And that's a big shift."[17]

Blended financing and other new structures

Lifebuoy has explored blended financing initiatives with a variety of philanthropic and international development organisations in the past few years. One of the first major ones came in 2013 with a multi-year grant from the Children's Investment Fund Foundation (CIFF), the world's largest independent philanthropy centred on children. After two years of hard negotiations, we secured a grant of over US$7.7 million, which was combined with the brand's marketing resources. The ambition was to reach nine million school children in Bihar, one of the poorest states in India. The goal was for Lifebuoy to build on its success with its School of Five campaign to promote handwashing in this populous, rural state of 100 million people, where high rates of childhood diarrhoea and pneumonia continue.[18]

The programme primarily targeted schoolchildren, and through them aimed to reach children under five years of age and new mothers, with staff visiting them at schools and in the community to encourage handwashing with soap. Lifebuoy was to train 600 health workers to visit all rural primary schools to engage with nine million students.[19] The brand also developed project-specific mobile-based geotagging to monitor the work, which would give high levels of programme accountability and also provide valuable feedback on the schools to the government.

Yet the programme faced challenges in the field, including a mass teachers' strike disrupting the early work, together with elections and extreme weather events. The programme ended in 2017 reaching a cumulative total of just 560,000 children against a planned total of nine million. An external evaluation carried out by the London School of Hygiene and Tropical Medicine found little significant improvement in handwashing compared to the threshold set by the partnership, particularly for mothers and in that particular setting of Bihar. Such a finding accelerated the stopping of the partnership.[20]

This was the first major setback for a Lifebuoy blended financing partnership and managing this within the brand and Unilever was difficult. We framed the experience as a learning opportunity rather than a reason to pull back from the partnerships. It underlined how difficult it is to drive handwashing behaviour change in some of the most remote and poor areas in India. Whilst the deployment of the scaled-up programme was excellent, the evaluation identified that a sharper focus on reaching mothers, and ensuring classroom engagement, complemented with participatory learning, would have benefitted the programme. The limited access to water and sanitation also had a significant impact, indicating the necessity of intervening at both demand-side and supply-side. It became clear that we needed to evolve our behaviour change approach to address these challenges. Although it was difficult to swallow this particular disappointment, we did not shy away from sharing the results both internally and externally.

Innovative partnerships inevitably carry uncertainty and risk that a company must be ready to absorb. It helped that Lifebuoy's social purpose had become embedded in its business model, with full continuing support from Unilever headquarters. The experience pushed Lifebuoy to clarify the scope and vision for future partnerships and engage more strongly in its programmes.

Meanwhile in 2014, before the end of the Bihar programme, a cross-sectoral bid made by many NGOs and including Lifebuoy won funding from the UK Government's Department for International Development (DFID). The money was to launch the South Asia WASH Results Programme through a consortium including Plan International, WaterAid, Ipsos, Water and Sanitation for the Urban Poor, and Loughborough University's Water, Engineering and Development Centre. The programme promoted the use of hygienic household toilets and handwashing with soap in rural Pakistan and Bangladesh. Under a payment by results contract, the consortium received funds from DFID upon delivery of the agreed parameters for outputs (reach) and outcomes (impact).[21]

The four-year project had two phases: delivering the main behaviour change messages (2014–2015); and sustaining those changes with ongoing handwashing promotion and advocacy for better water infrastructure to opinion leaders (2016–2018). The initiative reached 17 million people, with direct delivery to over four million students across 57 districts. Six months after the second phase, reports indicated that handwashing increased by 43 per cent and knowledge of the importance of handwashing rose by 33 per cent.[22]

This successful partnership required complex governance with multiple stakeholders. With funding contingent on results, the partners were motivated to continually measure progress and decide on scaling elements only from objective indicators. The partnership taught NGOs about the private sector's results-driven way of operating and set a benchmark for future collaborations between government development agencies and companies.

The payment by results approach was a resounding success with the performance-driven brand team. Together with the implementation teams in Bangladesh and Pakistan, the brand team put in place clear process and midcourse indicators to ensure that success was being achieved.

Academic certification to build credibility

Lifebuoy has also built credibility with academics. It was the first brand accredited for handwashing campaigns by the UK's Royal Society for Public Health in 2015. The society certified the brand for its products as well as its educational aspects. It assessed the objectives, health priorities, mode of delivery and communications materials of Lifebuoy's previous campaigns. It stated that "during the accreditation assessment, Unilever clearly demonstrated that improving community health through sharing knowledge and encouraging behaviour change is central to both its business and social mission strategy". And the society continued: "Lifebuoy's evidence on the impact of changing hand washing behaviour and increasing the use of soap in the health and wellbeing of individuals (especially among children for under 5s) and communities is extremely impressive."[23]

Separately, Unilever has partnered with the London School of Hygiene and Tropical Medicine, my own alma mater, especially through funding on hygiene research. Lifebuoy thereby has gained access to experts including my doctorate supervisors Val Curtis and Robert Aunger. In my time working on the Lifebuoy brand, they have been both my best advisors and my biggest critics, consistently pushing me and the rest of the Lifebuoy team to improve our programmes.

Working with governments

Many of our programmes have been run directly with governments, through public–private partnerships. In 2018 Unilever partnered with the South African government's Department of Basic Education to run a programme in all 15,000 public primary schools, to reach all grade-one pupils. The goal was to promote healthy behaviours with three Unilever brands: Lifebuoy, for handwashing; Domestos, a toilet cleaning brand, responsible for toilet hygiene and Pepsodent (known in South Africa as Mentadent), a toothpaste brand, to help promote oral hygiene. Unilever designed the intervention in consultation with the Ministry of Education's Curriculum Directorate, as part of the existing curriculum of hygiene education and life skills.[24]

Each of the three brands already had behaviour change programmes happening independently elsewhere in South Africa. By integrating the programmes around common behaviour change principles, Unilever presented a coordinated and cohesive approach that was easier to scale up. Putting the local government at the centre also ensured it would take some ownership. The three-week programme included teacher training, an approach we adapted from Lifebuoy programmes run in Indonesia.

This multi-brand, integrated school hygiene programme improved the company's standing with the government and in public health circles. This type of partnership is very much give-and-take, and in this instance the government insisted on oral care. Although Mentadent did not have a strong presence in South Africa, we agreed and worked jointly to include practising teeth brushing daily in school as part of the programme. This in turn enabled Unilever to gain direct engagement with national government authorities, and was more likely to be included in future conversations on large-scale school programmes. Queen Mgobhozi, South Africa's Social Mission Manager for South Africa, pointed out how this ambitious approach boosted credibility: "Because we've put ourselves out there, we are now seen and known as a leader even by the other private sector companies, trusted for our programmes or just for having a truthful and proven track record of social purpose."[25]

These efforts also brought direct results. An independent assessor conducted a pilot study in 300 schools and found significant behaviour change linked to the individual SDG indicators. As for the business side, the individual brands saw higher sales as well as greater recognition from consumers who felt compelled to support their local schools across the country. Government leaders also saw how partnering with a private sector company improved their public health campaigns.

Nevertheless, hygiene behaviour change is limited by the lack of adequate infrastructure in South Africa – toilets, handwashing facilities and water availability. Unilever and the Government of South Africa, as a result of this joint partnership, are now extending their collaboration to more joint advocacy activities like World Oral Health Day, Global Handwashing Day and World Toilet Day. We even ran a cause-related marketing campaign to contribute to the running of the programme in some of the most remote schools. On the official curriculum, we shared the key messages of hygiene on the back of books. In addition, the relationship is allowing us to discuss other initiatives like the Dove Self-Esteem programme and the janitor programme extension.

Pairing up for other public health goals

Lifebuoy began the partnership with Sightsavers against trachoma in 2014. Trachoma is a neglected tropical disease found mainly in poor, rural communities with limited clean water and sanitation. The simple act of hand and face washing with soap can reduce the risk of trachoma in children by 60 per cent. The partnership started locally in Kenya and very rapidly took off, as Caroline Harper, Sightsavers' CEO, recalled:

> This was a unique opportunity for Unilever to be involved in a programme that is historic in that its aim is to eliminate an old disease that has been around since the beginning of time. It is something I think that people working for Unilever would be very proud to be part of and involved with. I do know that talking about the fact that Unilever was partnering with us on a programme has been helpful for us also, because of the fame of the brand and the company.[26]

Here the brand was applying its expertise to a public health challenge beyond handwashing, but it made sense because it still involved soap. Lifebuoy adapted its school-based handwashing programme to include face washing and created the "Super School of Five".

We launched the programme in Kenya in 2015 and soon expanded it to Ethiopia and Zambia. It reached 600,000 kids in over 300 schools, with hundreds of teachers trained to deliver it.

The payoff came quickly. Supported by other NGO and government efforts, the programme helped reduce the prevalence of trachoma by 30 per cent in those two years. Programme evaluators found a six-fold increase in the frequency of all washing events in intervention schools as compared to control schools. Hundreds of thousands of children now know to protect themselves, their families and others from the devastating experience of blindness.

Figure 6.3 Lifebuoy Sightsavers Super School of Five programme, Kenya 2016 (copyright Karel Prinsloo).

The programme helps form and reinforce good habits because it's fun, memorable and concretely rewarding. This is what motivates children to change their behaviour. Each child receives a diary in which they are expected to write every day for three weeks. Each day has the five superheroes with a bubble next to it. Every time a child washes their hands and face they can tick off a bubble. At the end of each day, then each week, teachers and parents sign off to show they have seen how many ticks have been entered. Sometimes teachers will encourage participants by giving little prizes to those who follow the activity most assiduously.

The students also take a pledge, committing to washing their hands and faces at the five critical times every day. They are encouraged to sing songs to their families and others to spread knowledge about staying trachoma-free. Ownership by students and teachers is important, because they find creative and innovative ways to take the message forward. I have seen kids create their own version of the pledge, and teachers give out awards for the most creative ones. Others have held intra-school competitions, encouraging pupils to devise new songs about hand and face washing.

In 2017, as part of the two-year evaluation team, I returned to several places where the intervention had taken place. There I found that the superheroes and their songs had become embedded in the fabric of the schools. Not only that, each school had added its own creative stamp on the programme, adapting the music and the pledge or creating plays about the characters. Also in the communities surrounding the schools, families and others had taken on the messages of the programme, greatly reducing their vulnerability to trachoma in the process.

Especially important was the expansion to Ethiopia, where 70 million people are at risk of trachoma. Because of the work with Sightsavers, we managed to secure another partnership co-funded with Lifebuoy and Big Win Philanthropy to support Ethiopia's Seqota Declaration of the Ministry of Health to end child stunting.[27] Within that we are working on improving hygiene.

Already the Lifebuoy team has adjusted the curriculum for those areas. The idea of breakfast, lunch and dinner does not work when one meal a day is the best that can be hoped for. We have also changed the superheroes' names to make them more relatable to the local culture and adapted the materials into small booklets for all children.

Success here led to another innovative partnership in 2017, with the Global Alliance for Vaccine (GAVI). This partnership sought to promote handwashing with soap and immunisation together in Utter Pradesh in India – two of the most cost-effective interventions to help children reach the age of five.[28]

Unlike previous public sector initiatives, this programme reframed the rationale to immunise and handwash. Instead of telling parents these steps would ensure their child's simple survival, they said it would help their children thrive under the umbrella of successful parenting. The programmes emphasised the number of times each day for handwashing, and the number of immunisations in a child's first five years. Discussions are underway to scale up the programme, to reach millions more children.

The work enabled Lifebuoy to spread its expertise on behaviour change to an NGO, and vice versa. Kartik Chandrasekhar pointed out:

> In the case of GAVI, they understand about vaccinations and educating people. Add that to our knowledge of handwashing behaviour change, and two plus two equals five! So, I think that for me this is the joy of having partners: we learn, they learn and together, joint pooled learnings help make a bigger health impact than if we were both going alone.[29]

The key however remains in the challenge of scaling up across geographies. Seth Berkley, CEO of GAVI says "It would take confidence and cost effectiveness so that both Gavi and Lifebuoy are convinced beyond the pilot."[30]

Lifebuoy has been at the forefront of humanitarian response as well, with a partnership with Oxfam. And a partnership with the Power of Nutrition merges Hygiene and Nutrition to make a more holistic impact.[31]

Following rigorous formative research, to bridge the gap in identifying the drivers and barriers of behaviour change specifically in emergencies,[32] the Lifebuoy Oxfam partnership developed and deployed Mum's Magic Hands, a programme designed to impact handwashing behaviours in communities affected by emergencies. Results showed a 45 per cent increase in handwashing with soap after toilet (along with hardware) and an 18 per cent increase in handwashing before eating. This has enabled Mum's Magic Hands to be the go-to handwashing behaviour change programme across more than ten emergencies in Asia, Africa and the Middle East. It has also expanded Lifebuoy's partnership to include global humanitarian organisations such as UNHCR and local partners such as Friendship Hospital.[33]

Thanks to these and other on-ground partnerships, Lifebuoy is gaining real-world knowledge on improving public health. Each project moves the brand towards devising leaner, more efficient models that can work at a national or supranational level.

Communication and advocacy

While most of its partnerships have focused on direct behaviour change, Lifebuoy has also worked on making people care about handwashing through a campaigning approach, leveraging powerful communications with celebrity influence and advocacy. These programmes are more targeted than Global Handwashing Day, but still involve general campaigns rather than direct messages in schools or health centres.

In 2013 Lifebuoy launched the "Help a Child Reach 5" campaign, which started in Thesgora, a village in the state of Madhya Pradesh in India that has one of the highest rates of child mortality from diarrhoea. We created short films with compelling stories on the individual tragedy of losing a child to preventable infections. We distributed it widely through online social media at low cost.

The first video, Gondappa, reached #2 on YouTube's Indian charts (over 19 million views). The Help a Child Reach Five campaign has won several major industry awards, including a Silver Lion at the Cannes Lions International Festival of Creativity in 2013.[34] The campaign importantly also had a positive effect in Thesgora, with more children washing their hands before meals.[35]

Building on that heightened awareness, Lifebuoy together with the Unilever Corporate team began promoting handwashing through events on the side-lines of the UN General Assembly (see Figure 6.4). The brand lobbied UN officials and member states for adding handwashing facilities availability to what became Sustainable Development Goal #6 (SDG 6), on clean water and sanitation, released in 2015.

SDG 6 is a landmark for handwashing in international development, as it includes specific targets that governments are to report on. Indicator 6.2.1 asks for the "proportion of the population using safely managed sanitation services, including a handwashing facility with soap and water". The component on hygiene tracks the percentage of population with basic handwashing facilities at home, a proxy for handwashing behaviour. These measures

Figure 6.4 Paul Polman and Kajol Devgan, Global Citizen Festival 2015.

can focus decision makers on where investment matters the most for health, gender and environmental outcomes.[36]

In this and other advocacy, Lifebuoy has enlisted the support of media celebrities. These include the Indian Bollywood star Kajol, who has represented Lifebuoy at the UN General Assembly, and Kenya TV news anchor Janet Mbugua. The brand also supports the Bangladesh national cricket team, the most popular sport in the country of 160 million people, to drive aspiration towards handwashing.

Measuring results

Lifebuoy's success in gaining credibility with the public sector has paid off materially. Since 2013 alone, the brand has raised millions of euros of co-investments from partnerships with 30 governments, NGOs and philanthropies. Those funds, along with expertise and connections, have expanded Lifebuoy's impact far more than it could have done alone. The brand hit its target of reaching one billion people with handwashing messages in 2019 (459 million people through on-ground programmes and 587 million people through television reach).[37]

Lifebuoy's partnership-driven programmes have also been good business. Lifebuoy has been one of the fastest growing brands in Unilever for the ten years since 2009 and is now sold in more than 35 countries.

Most important, we have seen a sizeable fall in child mortality due to diarrhoea and pneumonia, the two leading diseases preventable with handwashing with soap.[38] Most of that decline has taken place in the countries with Lifebuoy-deployed programmes. Though it is, of course, difficult to determine how much of this improvement came directly from the programmes, I believe that Lifebuoy and its partnerships have made some contribution to this progress.

Ways of measuring changes in a socially desirable behaviour such as handwashing is hard, and we have innovated to come up with less costly and less intrusive methods to track our progress. Most people know they should wash hands regularly with soap, so people may overclaim their rate of handwashing if asked directly. Similarly, direct observation may cause people to act differently from how they are alone; it also misses important handwashing occasions outside the home.

Lifebuoy and its partners have looked for ways to track what people actually do. The most innovative method is a motion-sensor soap logger that captures behaviour at points in time, and weighs the soap to objectively track actual use. The logger is embedded within the bar of soap. A small trial within an India schools-based handwashing programme placed those bars in households with children who had been through the programme, and a control group of households whose children had not. The former showed significantly more handwashing than the control group.[39] Similar technology monitored the impact of Lifebuoy programmes in Kenya and Ghana, as part of the Millennium Villages Project partnership with Unilever and the Earth Institute, yet here as well the trial involved small numbers, due to the high cost of the loggers, that it is hard to generalise results coming from loggers.[40]

Lifebuoy has since validated a measurement method that is more affordable with potentially less bias than conventional techniques. Sticker diaries (pictures) ask respondents to track a range of daily activities in pictorial form, without revealing which daily behaviour is being targeted. A recent academic study confirmed that this approach was less biased than conventional methods of self-reporting behaviour, which should encourage more researchers to assess this approach.[41]

Future opportunities

Every year Global Handwashing Day is celebrated by over 200 million people in 100 countries across the world.[42] That's far more than Lifebuoy markets alone. Children show up to sing handwashing songs and pledge their commitment to handwashing with soap. Lifebuoy's mission is far from complete: the brand is now working on reaching the next hundreds of millions with handwashing messages by 2025, a faster pace than with the first billion and infused with more learnings. It will continue to rely on partnerships, with hopes of attracting millions in additional funding – partly through innovative co-investment and governance approaches. But even this stepped-up financing will not be enough for these harder-to-reach populations. Therefore the brand is working on digital technologies and new channels and platforms to make scaling the programmes more cost-effective, and to work on multiple behaviours and wider collaborations (e.g. expanding its nutrition and immunisations partnerships). It is also finding ways to engage consumers and the millennial generation to be our ambassadors and spread the message further.

Mobile phone apps, for example, can reach remote populations with little access to mass media or on-ground programmes. Following the techniques of "sticky" video games, these apps could promote participation in handwashing campaigns at a fraction of the cost of conventional approaches. Digital platforms provide a variety of tools to reach people in the right place at the right time with relevant hygiene messages about latest disease outbreaks. The successful Infection Alert System,[43] used in all of Lifebuoy's markets, may be just the start of a major investment in hygiene-oriented apps.

Another promising model to engage consumers, and particularly millennials, is Heroes for Change. In this community programme, launched in Kenya, university students volunteer their time to teach children handwashing habits.[44] The brand has also worked with girl guides and scouts in schools to include a handwashing module and badge, and unleash the energy and passion of children to drive change in the community.[45]

Along the way, Lifebuoy is engaging in findings from public health research. Several studies in the past found that conventional antibacterial soaps using actives like Triclosan offered households no better protection from disease than plain soap,[46] while putting potentially harmful ingredients in the water supply. In 2016 the US Food and Drug Administration banned the incorporation of several commonly-used antibacterial ingredients from soaps, most notably triclosan.[47] Unilever had in fact already stopped manufacturing skin care and cleansing products – including Lifebuoy – with triclosan in 2015, before the ban, replacing it with a range of alternatives, including natural and nature-inspired antibacterial ingredients.[48]

The brand is also going beyond handwashing to help with infrastructure development. The partnership model is essential here as Lifebuoy has limited expertise and resources in this area. The focus will be on working with partners that address health systems, sanitation, water, immunisation and nutrition, to find solutions which will provide multiple benefits to health.

Lifebuoy has shown that it can be an effective partner to governments and non-profit organisations. Now the brand can build on this success by developing far-reaching initiatives for public health. In doing the hard work upfront to show its commitment and capabilities, Lifebuoy can be a model to other brands looking to raise their game in social purpose. Partnerships are essential for major impact, but brands have to earn a place at that table – the table of lifesavers.

Notes

1 Harper, C. (2019) Personal interview.
2 Sightsavers (no date) "The Queen Elizabeth Diamond Jubilee Trust", *Sightsavers.* Available at: www.sightsavers.org/donor-institutions/the-queen-elizabeth-diamond-jubilee-trust/ (Accessed: 3 January 2020).
3 Gopal, A. (2019) Personal interview.
4 Lemon, J. (no date) *Cholera in Westminster, Cholera and the Thames.* Available at: www.choleraandthethames.co.uk/cholera-in-london/cholera-in-westminster (Accessed: 3 January 2020).
5 Global Handwashing Partnership (no date) *Global Handwashing Day, Global Handwashing Day.* Available at: www.globalhandwashingday.org/about/ (Accessed: 3 January 2020).
6 Ibid.
7 Unilever (2019) "Lifebuoy Way of Life: Towards universal handwashing with soap 2019". *Lifebuoy.*, p. 7. Available at: www.unilever.com/Images/lifebuoy_way-of-life_2019_annual-report_tcm244-418692_1_en.pdf (Accessed: 3 January 2020).
8 Dhaka Tribune (2017) "Lifebuoy attempts Guinness World Record for Handwashing Day", *Dhaka Tribune.* Available at: www.dhakatribune.com/bangladesh/dhaka/2017/10/15/lifebuoy-attempts-guinness-world-record-handwashing-day (Accessed: 3 January 2020).
9 Unilever (no date) "Sustainable Living", *Unilever.* Available at: www.unilever.com/sustainable-living/ (Accessed: 3 January 2020).
10 Unilever (2019) "Lifebuoy Way of Life: Towards universal handwashing with soap 2019". *Lifebuoy.*, p. 9. Available at: www.unilever.com/Images/lifebuoy_way-of-life_2019_annual-report_tcm244-418692_1_en.pdf (Accessed: 3 January 2020).
11 Shannon, H. M. (2014) "The School Of 5 Superhero Comic Program Saves the Lives of Children In 23 Countries – Craig Yoe In The Bleeding Cool Interview", *Bleeding Cool.* Available at: www.bleedingcool.com/2014/07/21/the-school-of-5-superhero-comic-program-saves-the-lives-of-children-in-23-countries-craig-yoe-in-the-bleeding-cool-interview/ (Accessed: 3 January 2020).
12 Unilever (2019) "Lifebuoy Way of Life: Towards universal handwashing with soap 2019". *Lifebuoy.*, p. 9. Available at: www.unilever.com/Images/lifebuoy_way-of-life_2019_annual-report_tcm244-418692_1_en.pdf (Accessed: 3 January 2020).
13 Marmot, R. (2019) Personal interview.
14 Chandesekhar, K. (2019) Personal interview.
15 Unilever (2012) "Lifebuoy and USAID partnership for newborn health", *Unilever.* Available at: www.unilever.com/news/news-and-features/Feature-article/2012/lifebuoy-and-USAID-partnership-for-newborn-health.html (Accessed: 3 January 2020).
16 Unilever (2019) "Lifebuoy Way of Life: Towards universal handwashing with soap 2019". *Lifebuoy.* Available at: www.unilever.com/Images/lifebuoy_way-of-life_2019_annual-report_tcm244-418692_1_en.pdf (Accessed: 3 January 2020).
17 Gopal, A. (2019) Personal interview.
18 CIFF (no date) *Reducing child mortality in Bihar through improved hand washing. 2013–2017.* Available at: https://ciff.org/grant-portfolio/handwashing-lifebuoy-school-of-five/ (Accessed: 3 January 2020).
19 Ibid.
20 Lewis, H. E. *et al.* (2018) "Effect of a School-Based Hygiene Behavior Change Campaign on Handwashing with Soap in Bihar, India: Cluster-Randomized Trial", *The American Journal of Tropical Medicine and Hygiene*, 99(4), pp. 924–933. doi: 10.4269/ajtmh.18-0187.

21 Plan International UK (no date) "South Asia Wash Results Programme", *Plan International UK*. Available at: https://plan-uk.org/about/our-work/healthcare-and-clean-water/clean-water-and-sanitation/south-asia-wash-results (Accessed: 3 January 2020).
22 Ibid.
23 SPH (no date) *Lifebuoy – RSPH Campaign Accreditation*. Available at: www.rsph.org.uk/our-services/accreditation/case-studies/case-study-life-buoy.html (Accessed: 3 January 2020).
24 Unilever (2017) "Partnership gives 1 million learners a brighter future", *Unilever South Africa*. Available at: www.unilever.co.za/news/press-releases/2017/partnership-gives-one-million-learners-a-brighter-future.html (Accessed: 3 January 2020).
25 Mgobhozi, Q. (2019) Personal interview.
26 Harper, C. (2019) Personal interview.
27 Woods, G. (2019) "How soap and superheroes are changing lives", *Sightsavers*. Available at: www.sightsavers.org/from-the-field/2019/10/how-super-school-of-five-is-changing-lives/ (Accessed: 3 January 2020).
28 Gavi (2017) *Gavi and Unilever's Lifebuoy join forces to tackle preventable diseases and save children's lives*. Available at: www.gavi.org/news/media-room/gavi-and-unilevers-lifebuoy-join-forces-tackle-preventable-diseases-and-save (Accessed: 3 January 2020).
29 Chandesekhar, K. (2019) Personal interview.
30 Berkeley, S. (2019) Personal interview.
31 The Power of Nutrition (2019) "Mobile phones can save lives: An innovative partnership with Unilever, Lifebuoy and The Power of Nutrition to tackle hygiene and malnutrition", *Power of Nutrition*. Available at: www.powerofnutrition.org/mobile-phones-can-save-lives-an-innovative-partnership-with-unilever-lifebuoy-and-the-power-of-nutrition-to-tackle-hygiene-and-malnutrition/ (Accessed: 3 January 2020).
32 Sagan, S, *et al.* (2019) "Assessing emotional motivators for handwashing with soap in emergencies: results from three Asian countries", *Waterlines 2019* 38:1, 20–35. doi.org/10.3362/1756-3488.17-00024
33 Oxfam (no date) "Mum's Magic Hands", *Oxfam*. Available at: https://policy-practice.oxfam.org.uk/our-work/water-sanitation-and-hygiene/mums-magic-hands (Accessed: 3 January 2020).
34 Abraham, S., Chawda, V. and Dorsett, J. (no date) "Lifebuoy: Help a child reach 5 Case Study", *WARC*. Available at: www.warc.com/content/paywall/article/warc-prize/lifebuoy_help_a_child_reach_5/102862 (Accessed: 3 January 2020).
35 HUL (no date) "Help a child reach 5", *Hindustan Unilever Limited*. Available at: www.hul.co.in/sustainable-living/case-studies/help-a-child-reach-five.html (Accessed: 3 January 2020).
36 UN Water (2017) "Integrated Monitoring Guide for Sustainable Development Goal 6 on Water and Sanitation – Targets and global indicators", *UN Water*. Available at: www.unwater.org/publications/sdg-6-targets-indicators/ (Accessed: 3 January 2020).
37 Unilever (2019) "Healthy handwashing habits for life", *Unilever*. Available at: www.unilever.com/sustainable-living/improving-health-and-well-being/health-and-hygiene/healthy-handwashing-habits-for-life/ (Accessed: 4 January 2020).
38 UNICEF (2019) "Pneumonia in Children", *UNICEF*. Available at: https://data.UNICEF.org/topic/child-health/pneumonia/ (Accessed: 3 January 2020).
39 Wright, R. L. *et al.* (2015) "Use of Electronic Loggers to Measure Changes in the Rates of Hand Washing with Soap in Low-Income Urban Households in India", *PLOS ONE*, 10(6), p. e0131187. doi: 10.1371/journal.pone.0131187.
40 Unilever (no date) "Helping people get into healthy hygiene habits", *Unilever*. Available at: www.unilever.com/sustainable-living/improving-health-and-well-being/health-and-hygiene/healthy-handwashing-habits-for-life/helping-people-get-into-healthy-hygiene-habits/ (Accessed: 4 January 2020).

41 Schmidt, W. *et al.* (2019) "Comparison of structured observation and pictorial 24 h recall of household activities to measure the prevalence of handwashing with soap in the community", *International Journal of Environmental Health Research*, 29(1), pp. 71–81. doi: 10.1080/09603123.2018.1511772.
42 Global Handwashing Partnership (no date) *Global Handwashing Day, Global Handwashing Day*. Available at: www.globalhandwashingday.org/about/ (Accessed: 3 January 2020).
43 Lifebuoy (2019) *The Infection Alert System – Lifebuoy*. Available at: www.youtube.com/watch?v=MCYxclz_uh8 (Accessed: 3 January 2020).
44 Amref (2017) *Amref joins Unilever in Launching "Heroes for Change" Programme*. Available at: https://amref.org/news/amref-joins-unilever-in-launching-heroes-for-change-programme/ (Accessed: 3 January 2020).
45 Lifebuoy (2018) *Lifebuoy Empowers Guides to become Handwashing Heroes*. Available at: www.youtube.com/watch?v=D3I_lmqfK0A (Accessed: 3 January 2020).
46 Infection Control Today (2003) "National Institutes of Health-Funded Study Says Antibacterial Soap No Better Than Regular Soap", *Infection Control Today*. Available at: www.infectioncontroltoday.com/general-hais/nih-funded-study-says-antibacterial-soap-no-better-regular-soap (Accessed: 5 January 2020).
47 US Food and Drug Administration (2019) "5 Things to Know About Triclosan", *FDA*. Available at: www.fda.gov/consumers/consumer-updates/5-things-know-about-triclosan (Accessed: 5 January 2020).
48 Unilever (2020) "Triclosan and triclocarban", *Unilever UK & Ireland*. Available at: www.unilever.co.uk/brands/whats-in-our-products/your-ingredient-questions-answered/triclosan-and-triclocarban.html (Accessed: 5 January 2020).

7 Brand advocacy

Can brands drive social movements?

To carry out a social mission at scale, brands must operate on a level higher than simply focusing on consumer behaviour change linked to their products. They will advocate for broad-based efforts to support systemic change benefitting society at large. Here we are talking about the role of brands raising awareness for a social issue that brings greater value to society beyond increasing buy-in to the brand and the products manufactured. It entails talking to governments and cultural influencers, and bringing along citizens in the hope of sparking a groundswell of support and collaboration that lasts for years, not weeks, and beyond individual campaigns.

While brands can of course communicate with policymakers on a case-by-case basis, they often gain more traction when bringing to the table their creative expertise in advertising and engagement towards a higher purpose. Shifting public perception towards healthier outcomes can have a win-win-win for governments, brands and the public. But doing it well means approaching it with a different mindset than conventional brand communication.

Taking a stand in today's popular culture

Enlightened brands have realised that broadening out to shift public perceptions and general cultural narratives is key to educating consumers, not just focusing on policy. They have done this partly because of wider social trends in authority, as the public is less likely to trust the recommendations of governments and other major institutions. They are more likely to trust their peers or someone like them, which makes democratising channels such as social media increasingly powerful. As Emmanuel Faber, CEO of Danone, has pointed out, "Today we are able to connect, learn and share at a speed and scale never before possible."[1]

With traditional authority figures losing their influence, companies and brands have a greater opportunity, and indeed responsibility, to shape narratives and communities for the better. Social power is moving to looser arrangements, more networked, open source, collaborative, transparent, short-term and conditional.[2] Popular brands, whether national or global, can help fill the gap with their unrivalled reach and trust built over years with consumers, including a ready-made presence on media with television and digital advertising. They can tap into "tribal" communities of people who share a certain interest or commitment. And brands can and are starting to take a position on moral issues which they have previously not done (such as Walmart on gun control and the sale of certain types of ammunition).

In a study of global brands ("The Truth About Global Brands"), across 29 countries, 81 per cent of 30,000 consumers surveyed agreed that brands play a meaningful role in people's lives.[3] They tend to trust companies and brands to drive change quicker than politicians and multilateral organisations. But be careful: once trust is broken, it's hard to repair. As the author Seth Godin has said, "If you earn trust then you can do everything else, but if not, then you won't create any progress let alone a movement."

A key principle for creating a movement is attracting other partners to your cause. The word "advocacy" in fact comes from the Latin "advocare", – to call out for support.[4, 5] Purposeful brands do that by enlisting help from a wide range of partners and ordinary people to achieve their stated goal. They open up discussions with governments, community leaders, NGOs, and consumers, building trust and support around a mutual objective and prompting policymaking and funding to hasten transformational change.[6]

Advocacy is primarily for the benefit of society in general, and nowhere is this truer than with public health, so benefits to the brand must be secondary or long-term. This is why we are calling this *brand advocacy*, where brands will achieve far more by thinking and engaging broadly, using their iconic status and creative skills of their people to keep the key issue on the public agenda. Ambitious advocacy efforts often require rival brands to come together, as with Global Handwashing Day when Unilever's Lifebuoy worked with Procter & Gamble's Safeguard and Colgate Palmolive.

Setting roles with partners

Businesses have a role to play in influencing policy. If you get the right group of businesses together, then you have a higher chance of showing what the right policies could be, working with the governments.[7] Paul Polman says this on the role of businesses in setting policies:

> Businesses are not policy setters; you need to set policies in partnership with governments and others. The Modern Day Slavery Act in the UK, introduced when Kevin Hyland was the UK's Independent Anti-Slavery Commissioner, is a fine piece of legislation. Likewise the Foreign Corrupt Practices Act in the US. Of course some companies don't like these Acts, but today you have to ask these companies why don't they like it?[8]

The 2015 UK Slavery Act[9] introduces new requirements for organisations in regard to their business and supply chains. It's important to work in tandem with government, not just lobbying for market advantage but for wider policies.[10]

But here we are talking about creating social movements. While there is no universal consensus definition of a social movement,[11] academic definitions generally share three criteria: a network of informal interactions between a plurality of individuals, groups and/or organisations, engaged in a political or cultural conflict, on the basis of a shared collective identity.

For our purposes, we will define social movement as the following: "a group of people working together to advance their shared ideal".

This group creates change together; they DO something. Brands make that happen by tapping into universal emotions: Nike does not just sell training shoes, it promotes courage: "Just do it".[12] Domestos is not just a toilet cleaner, it combats poor sanitation.[13] Apple does not sell hardware and software, it sells creativity and innovation.[14]

Many public health issues already have national or global networks to support collaborative advocacy, from the World Toilet Board to the Global Alliance for Improved Nutrition. The Global Handwashing Partnership (previously the Public–Private Partnership for Handwashing), for example, helped the Lifebuoy brand to promote hygiene, getting handwashing higher on the agenda of international policy groups such as Sanitation and Water for All. The coalition is seen as a neutral convener, so its proposals get more respect than brands acting alone. When the pharmaceutical company Bayer proposed the World Contraception Day, it drew on a coalition of 17 NGOs, government organisations, multilateral bodies and medical societies.

Still, brands do best when they focus on mass awareness and engagement to drive social change, as that's the unique expertise they bring. After all, a brand works by evoking a series of connected feelings in people. Those feelings are not just about using or consuming a product; they can also mean working with the brand to accomplish broad goals.

Similarly, social movements depend on emotional appeals as much as reasoned arguments.[15] And even with those arguments, consumers – especially youth – are more likely to accept advice and education from a trusted brand that "gets" them (their behaviours online, media consumption, values etc.) than a traditional authority trying to communicate a broad-brush generic nationwide health message to millions. For example, the Edelman survey says 49 per cent of consumers believe brands can do more to address social ills than government.[16]

A successful movement has a few key characteristics. It has a positive vision for the future, not just a fear of the present.[17] It speaks to each individual's personal sense of justice through their connected identity. It uses symbols, language and culture that resonates.[18] It calls for tangible, repeatable and sustainable ways to act, both material and ritual. It gives people agency and makes them actors, not just beneficiaries.[19] Finally, it brings people and communities together on shared platforms and through partnerships.[20]

The strongest brands stand for something bigger than the products that they sell, as we have seen in the various case studies. They stand in unity with the public sector, the populations united against a COMMON ENEMY which is a social issue (such as child mortality, women's equality, trachoma elimination). Alinsky in his book *Rules for Radicals: A pragmatic primer for realistic radicals*[21] sets rules for a successful social movement and makes the common enemy identification the key to any successful social movement. Whilst this might be too much of a stretch to apply to brands, nevertheless it is an important element to reflect on: the ability to invite brands to join the fight against social injustice. Of course this can backfire and one needs to be careful about the misinterpretation of the fact that people are being manipulated by the "corporation" and this is something "that brands have created", but above all I believe that we need to move beyond ideology and unite for positive action.

Marianne Blamire is Global Chief Strategy Officer at MullenLowe salt, and she worked hand-in-hand with me creating the assets for Global Hand-washing Day. From her experience of supporting brand advocacy work, she sums up a list of what brands can do to help create a movement:

1   Go beyond the brand: focus on the social purpose itself and on a measurable outcome, ideally aligned to the Sustainable Development Goals. Not only will this inspire consumers, but it will also draw in rival brands and partners from the public and private sector.
2   Identify a specific issue and set a rallying cry: Picture a desired outcome in, say, ten years, such as "We have reduced child mortality from x to y in 5 years and mobilised z million people rallying behind that issue." Combine education with inspiration so people know what they can do, tangibly, as soon as you've made them aware of the issue.
3   Make the issue human and simple: strip out jargon, make the complex simple and the simple compelling. Make it relevant to ordinary lives. Inspire people to care about the issue as much as you do.
4   Identify participants and a plan for engagement: you need both broad grassroot support and high-profile supporters. To whom does your issue matter to, and how? Can you align with their values (if a celebrity), policies (if government) and existing programmes (if an NGO)? How will your brand educate and captivate each audience?
5   Provide multiple ways to participate: movements are emotional and communal, but people interact in different ways. For this reason, always provide a choice, such as watching and posting on social media, pledging donations, event attendance, volunteering and user-generated content. The act of jolting the public awake to a hidden issue, such as mental health, can break down social stigma and be of huge educative value if executed sensitively, so do not underestimate the power of online content views and TV. People can move up the steps as they deepen their interest and commitment (see Figure 7.1).

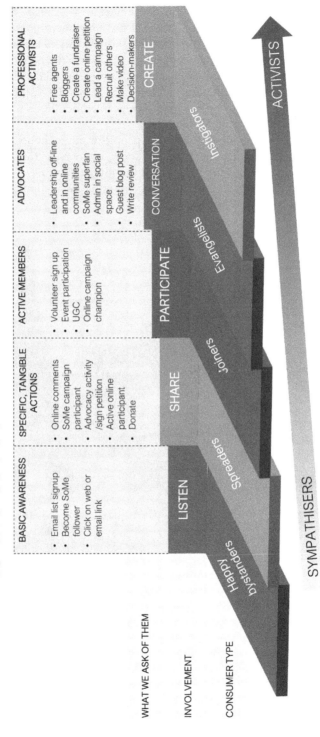

Figure 7.1 Ladder of consumer engagement to the cause (source: MullenLowe salt).

6   Devolve power to partners and consumers, so they share ownership. In the public health context, it's critical the movement goes beyond your brand as the issues are far too complex and systemic to be tackled in isolation. Not recognising this complexity can dent a brand's credibility and make worthy efforts unsustainable because of the budget and resources required to maintain it alone. Partners, such as NGOs, provide subject-matter expertise and behavioural change methodologies to add a depth that's harder for brands to deliver on.

7   Be transparent about the journey: people want to know if progress is happening and what the brand is doing to increase the pace. There's authenticity in explaining how hard the journey will be – that's why it's a mission. Be open to learning from consumer interaction as you go, and adjust the appeals accordingly.

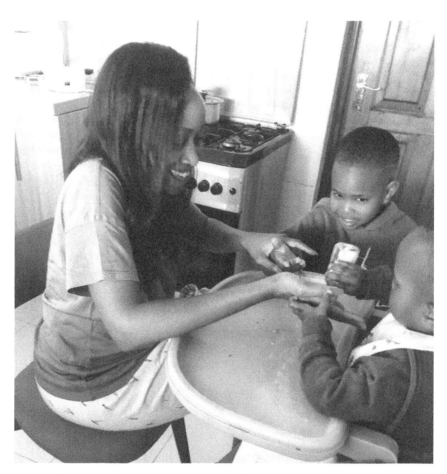

Figure 7.2 Janet Mbugua, promoting handwashing with her children on social media, Kenya 2019.

Working with influencers

Brands are used to working with celebrities and other influencers on regular campaigns, but the process is different for advocacy. The challenge here is to win over influencers so there's no paid sponsorship or only a small honorarium. That means educating the influencers so they voluntarily join in. Authenticity is key, so brands must stay true to the styles of their celebrities.

Janet Mbugua, a prominent Kenyan television news anchor and media personality, agreed to support Lifebuoy's "Help a Child Reach Five" campaign.[22] She talked about teaching her two toddlers to wash their hands (see Figure 7.2) with soap and the resulting video went viral. Mothers from all over the country, from nurses to rural mums, wrote about their struggles with handwashing. An earlier photo of Janet at the hospital with her newborn baby, using a hand sanitiser, also helped spread the word.

Celebrities are comfortable speaking to large groups, so brands can also invite them to major gatherings. Lifebuoy convinced Kajol Devgan, a major Bollywood actress, to present at the United Nations General Assembly about the Lifebuoy Help a Child Reach 5 campaign. She went on to speak alongside the Prime Minister Narendra Modi of India in support of his national campaign for sanitation, "Swachh Bharat". As she put it, "I would not stand up for something that I didn't believe in. It makes a difference that I can speak from experience. It was such an emotional moment for me when my son turned five."[23]

Opportunities with social media and millennials

New digital media has certainly made it easier for brands to advocate, especially on difficult or low-engagement issues. Toilet cleaning, for example, is not a natural subject for Facebook discussions. But when people discover that there are hundreds of millions of people still defecating in the streets or in fields, we can stir up their interest and ask their help. Particularly with younger generations, social media has enormous influence in tackling taboo subjects. They communicate without borders as "armchair activists" in many countries around the world.

Social media also gives people an easy way to self-identify with a cause. On World Aids Day or Breast Cancer Month, they just switch their profile picture on Facebook. It can take a long time for brands to get recognition for association with these global days. Brands need to be in it for the long haul, with consistency of investment and building trust. Success will not come over night or after a single media campaign.

Lifebuoy launched the campaign #JustOneHour to encourage college students to deliver a handwashing programme at a local school or clinic. The campaign was promoted on YouTube and radio in ten countries, from India and Pakistan to Singapore and South Africa. In Kenya, Unilever worked with several outside partners to establish the "Heroes for Change" programme, delivering a range of Unilever brands' social missions, cost-effectively, to difficult-to-reach low-income communities. Heroes for Change recruits and trains youth volunteers, giving them an opportunity to create impact in their communities.

Heroes for Change CEO Elsie Wandera-Odhiambo, who previously worked in Unilever and is now establishing the movement as a separate company, says:

> We want this to become its own entity where youth can engage and volunteer their time to drive social change. We found that they're asking themselves every day: how do we participate in this big picture stuff? They have the social currency and trust within their communities to deliver social impact programmes at no cost. It helps us scale up at a lower cost and with greater impact on the communities, as well as on the young people. We went on digital platforms such as Facebook and WhatsApp to mobilise them and spread the message and since worked with over 400 young people reaching 900,000 people in Kenya with the health and hygiene messages.[24]

Figure 7.3 Sally Ndwiga, Heroes for Change volunteer, Kenya 2019.

The volunteering also gives these students a connection to Unilever and other partners, which can lead to internships and employment.

Sally Ndwiga, who is a Hero for Change participant in Kenya, summarised her experience:

> After receiving my acceptance email into the Heroes for Change I was very excited and energised to bring change in my community. Upon successful training, I was deployed under the oral health programme to teach children below the age of thirteen the importance of brushing their teeth at least twice a day. Teaching young children was not easy, but at the same time it was not impossible, it was a new challenge I took on positively. After eight months of volunteering, I had reached 30,270 children from within my community and beyond. The greatest reward from this programme was the joy and fulfilment I felt every time I saw the children's eagerness and excitement to learn from me. Being among the top Heroes within the Nairobi region has opened doors of employment for me. Currently I am working full-time in the Heroes for Change company to use my passion and purpose to inspire other young people in Kenya.

Above all, social media reduces the cost of delivering messages. For Life-buoy's "Help a Child Reach Five" campaign, advertising agency MullenLowe created a series of three-minute videos distributed on social media. Each video was set in a country struggling with hygiene, such as India, Indonesia and Kenya. The first video gained 19 million views and won several industry awards, and some went on to run as TV commercials.

Because social media offers freedom of expression, it also gave brands instant feedback, especially negative comments, so they can adjust messages to avoid a broad backlash, and also allowing for testing before launch. Brands can use that same freedom to ride the wave of other campaigns or recognition days when objectives align. "Earth Hour", a global campaign led by the World Wildlife Fund, encourages people to turn off their lights one evening to raise awareness of the need to act on climate change. Durex, the condom manufacturer, piggy-backed Earth Hour in a brand-relevant way encouraging people to connect with their partner in the dark, while of course making sure to use Durex for protection. Durex did not work directly with WWF, but its alignment with their efforts helped increase the cultural relevance of Earth Hour.

Future brands may have little choice but to concentrate their efforts on social media. With 94 per cent of teens globally on a mobile device daily, younger people increasingly congregate on those channels, from YouTube and Instagram to TikTok. They are therefore harder to reach with conventional advertising on television or even websites.

Help from marketing and communication agencies

As advocacy shifts from the halls of government to mass media, brands must rely on the creativity and outside-in perspective of their communications agency pool. This is especially true for public health campaigns that require an understanding of behavioural change as well as an ability to use creativity to raise awareness of taboo issues. This combined expertise needs to be taken to the next level.

Agencies can get very creative and go far beyond conventional messaging. State Street Global Advisors in Boston, the world's third largest asset manager, wanted to encourage investment in funds that support women. It worked with the McCann agency in New York, and together they commissioned "Fearless Girl".[25] This is not a social media campaign, but a life-size bronze statue cleverly placed in front of the famed Charging Bull statue on Wall Street. It went up just before International Women's Day in 2017. Concerns from the sculptor of the bull statue led to its removal, but it went only a short distance and is now in front of the New York Stock Exchange. It has become a tourist attraction, with many parents taking their daughters there.

Close relationships are essential here; it takes time for agencies to produce material unique and bold enough to be amplified – and that supports your brand without showing your logo. Creative directors must understand that advocacy is not about selling something; instead, it's about communicating on an issue with real-world sensitivity. Andy Last, founder and CEO of MullenLowe salt, says brands:

> must co-create, rather than give a brief to an agency that goes away for weeks and come back with a Mad Men sort of magical campaign. We need a collaborative approach, not only between us and our clients, but between us and influencers, and experts, and NGOs and those partners.[26]

Agencies can also help in working with partners. For Global Handwashing Day, MullenLowe salt helped in the partnership led by Lifebuoy to write the brief and create the logo and planning kits to distribute to partners. Those materials showed the brand's commitment to the cause, not the brand, and helped convince other groups to join in. And they did this pro-bono.

Agencies can also help brands take on controversial issues. Ben & Jerry's ice cream brand boldly advocated for marriage equality in Australia, but in its usual witty way. During a push for parliamentary action in 2017, the brand's 26 stores no longer allowed customers to order two scoops of the same ice cream together – they had to choose two different flavours. It helped that public opinion polls showed a majority in favour of granting homosexuals the right to marry, but parliament was stuck debating a proposed referendum on the issue. As part of the campaign, the stores installed post boxes and encouraged customers to write to their member of parliament right there, something that the Body Shop did in the 1990s.

By contrast, the Gillette shaving brand mishandled its "We Believe" campaign against toxic masculinity. The campaign shifted the brand's usual tagline by asking "Is this the best a man can get" and then showing scenes of bullying, sexual harassment and even "mansplaining" – giving women condescending explanations. While praised by some observers, it led to a large backlash. Critics on social media called it preachy and inauthentic, and tied too closely to the brand.[27] No one likes to be told they are bad, and then asked to buy something.

Agencies can help brands be both brave and respectful of consumers. It helps to focus on the Brand Do, the concrete programmes from the brand, such as Ben & Jerry's letter-writing campaign. Agencies can also ensure that brand managers "do their cultural homework", as Jill Avery, a senior lecturer at Harvard Business School, calls it. Advocacy campaigns need to start from a solid understanding of the cultural phenomena to be featured in the communications. Without a grasp of the deep well of emotions, identity politics and ideologies likely to be triggered, they risk a backlash or worse.

That's what happened in 2019 when Unilever's Red Label tea brand in India ran a campaign encouraging families not to "abandon" their elderly relatives at the massive Kumbh Mela pilgrimage festivals. Online ads urged people to watch a "heart-warming video; an eye-opener to a harsh reality", but people saw the ad as a criticism of the festival and Hinduism generally – and called for boycotts of all of Unilever's products.[28] Better knowledge of the context might have kept this well-intentioned campaign from going awry.

Fearless Girl notwithstanding, agencies will also need overarching technical competence. Advocacy campaigns will increasingly work through social media and related digital connections. Since technology changes quickly, with new platforms gaining popularity often without much notice, agencies must be in tune with progress. Advertising awards are huge, the fact that we work with big advertising agencies give us access to these platforms and has potential to open a lot of doors if used correctly, especially for partners.

Working internally

Any social movement from a brand should start in its own offices with its people. It has to be simple and creative enough that employees want to be engaged, and to sustain that engagement. With Lifebuoy's handwashing campaign, there have been different themes each year. And as Unilever has launched new campaigns such as ones aligned with Oral Health Day and World Food Day, everyone has been encouraged to get involved as volunteers, from factories to tea plantations, and even suppliers and retailers (see the exhibit on participation). Employees now expect their brands to produce materials that they can show to their families about why they go to work. Competitions have also been run where the winning employees get to visit various Brand Do programmes keeping their favourite brands accountable to their promise.

Conclusion

The biggest challenge is still ensuring that the brand team understands how to work with partners to drive specific elements of a social movement, encompassing policies and consumer involvement. The key is ensuring that the consumers themselves become the debater and the champion of the issues. You need a bigger issue than one your brand can fully encompass. Marketers tend to resist that perspective and focus on a moment in time when they can attract consumers' attention whilst still giving all their creative might. The real brand advocacy happens with a big vision and an authentic commitment on the ground. It's not about just spending money. It's about putting all your power towards developing joint solutions.

Exercise

Assessment: gauging readiness to spark a social movement

The strongest brands stand for something bigger than the products they sell – they stand for social movements that benefit society. But is your brand ready to move up to that level? Is it able to inspire consumers, draw in rival brands, and engage partners from the public and private sector? In this assessment, score each of the following statements from 1 to 5; a score of 40 or higher shows that the brand may be well-positioned to help drive a social movement; a lower score suggests there is still much work to be done before the brand is ready.

The big picture

The social movement that the brand hopes to spark:

- … is a positive vision for the future rather than a fear of the present
- … speaks to individuals' sense of justice
- … brings people and communities together
- … gives people agency and makes them actors, not just beneficiaries
- … calls for tangible, repeatable, sustainable behaviours, so people know specifically what they can do to help
- … aligns with values of celebrities, governments and NGOs

Operational aspects

The operating plan for supporting the social movement:

> … includes a plan to educate and captivate audiences
> … specifies a simple, inspiring rallying cry and uses symbols, language, and culture that are relevant to people's lives and align with their values
> … provides multiple ways for people to participate, such as donating, attending events and volunteering
> … devolves power to partners and consumers so that they share ownership
> … specifies measurable outcomes
> … provides transparency about progress towards the goal
> … requires us to be open to learning from consumer interactions and adjust our appeals accordingly

Notes

1 Faber, E (2019). Personal interview.
2 Heimans, J. and Timms, H. (2018). *New Power: How Anyone Can Persuade, Mobilize and Succeed in Our Chaotic, Connected Age*. New York: Doubleday.
3 McCann Worldgroup (2018). "The Truth About Global Brands 2: powered by the streets". *McCann Worldgroup*. Available at: https://cms.mccannworldgroup.com/wp-content/uploads/2017/05/TAGB2_ExecSummary_WebsiteVersion.pdf.
4 Latin Definition for: advoco, advocare, advocavi, advocatus (ID: 1789) (no date). Latdict. Available at: https://latin-dictionary.net/definition/1789/advoco-advocare-advocavi-advocatus (Accessed: 28 December 2019).
5 Definition of Advocacy (no date). Merriam Webster. Available at: www.merriam-webster.com/dictionary/advocacy (Accessed: 28 December 2019).
6 Nelson, J. and Gilbert, R. (2018). "Advocating together for the SDGs". *Harvard Kennedy School*, Business Fights Poverty. Available at: www.hks.harvard.edu/sites/default/files/centers/mrcbg/files/Advocacy_Collaboration_SDGs.pdf (Accessed: 18 December 2019).
7 Ibid.
8 Polman, P. and Ruggie, J. (2019). "The Business Case of Sustainable Development: a roundtable discussion". Harvard Kennedy School, 11 April.
9 Panasar, R. *et al.* (2017). "The Modern Slavery Act 2015: Next Steps for Businesses", *Harvard Law School Forum on Corporate Governance*. Available at: https://corpgov.law.harvard.edu/2017/03/10/the-modern-slavery-act-2015-next-steps-for-businesses/ (Accessed: 28 December 2019).
10 Ibid.
11 Opp, K.-D. (2009). *Theories of political protest and social movements: A multidisciplinary introduction, critique, and synthesis*. Abingdon, Oxon: Routledge.
12 Ketel, J. (2018). "The one reason why Nike's Just Do it campaign was brilliant", *Medium*. Available at: https://medium.com/@jerryketel/the-one-reason-why-nikes-just-do-it-campaign-was-brilliant-e6006126864 (Accessed: 28 December 2019).
13 Unilever (2017). "Two Domestos innovations that will help tackle the sanitation crisis", *Unilever*. Available at: www.unilever.com/news/news-and-features/Feature-article/2017/two-domestos-innovations-that-will-help-tackle-the-sanitation-crisis.html (Accessed: 28 December 2019).

14 Safian, R., Safian, R. and Safian, R. (2018). "Why Apple is the World's Most Innovative Company", *Fast Company*. 21 February 2018. Available at: www.fastcompany.com/40525409/why-apple-is-the-worlds-most-innovative-company (Accessed: 28 December 2019).

15 Ganz, M. and McKenna, L. (2017). "The Practice of Social Movement Leadership", *Mobilizing Ideas*. 23 June 2017. Available at: https://mobilizingideas.wordpress.com/2017/06/23/the-practice-of-social-movement-leadership/ (Accessed: 28 December 2019).

16 "5 Key Takeaways from the 2019 Edelman Brand Trust Survey", 18 June 2019, https://adage.com/article/digital/5-key-takeaways-2019-edelman-brand-trust-survey/2178646.

17 Ganz, M. (2011). "The Power of Story in Social Movements". Available at: http://marshallganz.usmblogs.com/files/2012/08/Power_of_Story-in-Social-Movements.pdf.

18 Ibid.

19 Ganz, M. (2012). "We can be actors, not just spectators", *New Statesman*. Available at: www.newstatesman.com/politics/politics/2012/07/we-can-be-actors-not-just-spectators (Accessed: 28 December 2019).

20 "Public Narrative Worksheet Fall 2013 (2013)". (no date). Available at: http://marshallganz.usmblogs.com/files/2012/08/Public-Narrative-Worksheet-Fall-2013-.pdf (Accessed: 5 January 2020).

21 Alinsky, S. (1971). "Rules for Radicals", *Wikipedia*. Available at: https://en.wikipedia.org/w/index.php?title=Rules_for_Radicals&oldid=930269946 (Accessed: 5 January 2020).

22 Lifebuoy (2016). "Lifebuoy Help A Child Reach 5 'Sherry'", *YouTube*. Available at: www.youtube.com/watch?v=0v8qP4nCs2Y (Accessed: 28 December 2019).

23 Devgan, K. (2018). Personal interview.

24 Wandera-Odhiambo, E. (2019). Personal interview.

25 *Creation – Fearless Girl* (2017). Available at: www.fearlessgirl.us/creation/ (Accessed: 5 January 2020).

26 Last, A. (2019). Personal interview.

27 Boyd, H. and Kehler, M. (2019). "Did Gillette Miss the Mark with Its Toxic Masculinity Ad?", *Knowledge@Wharton*. Available at: https://knowledge.wharton.upenn.edu/article/gillette-toxic-masculinity-ad/ (Accessed: 31 December 2019).

28 Newsfeed (2019) *BoycottHindustanUnilever Trends After Red Label Tea Ad Faces Criticism*. Available at: https://newsfeed.co.in/india/boycotthindustanunilever-trends-after-red-label-tea-ad-faces-criticism/ (Accessed: 4 January 2020).

8 How Discovery Limited promotes health through its Vitality brand

"Health care is a human right", proclaimed the World Health Organization at its founding in 1948. Governments in dozens of countries have since launched programmes for universal access to medical treatment at no charge. Yet much of the world's population still lives in countries with limited coverage. They risk falling into poverty from the expense of caring for a catastrophic or chronic health problem, and in so many places poor people simply go without care because they are already in poverty. And that's likely to continue, as governments in most of those countries are too deeply in debt to consider a major expansion in medical spending.

To fill the fiscal gap, we need innovative brands on a mission to improve health and reduce the cost of medical care. One such brand is Vitality, part of the Discovery Group. Vitality's leaders have worked aggressively to promote preventive medicine and healthier behaviour. Their success and struggles can guide companies in every part of the health care sector, and beyond.

The challenge of universal health coverage

Achieving universal health coverage (UHC) is indicator 3.8 of the UN's Sustainable Development Goal 3. It includes protection against financial risks as well as access to essential medical care and vaccines. The absence of coverage means that 100 million people fall into poverty annually because of medical expenses. In Kenya alone, where I live, an estimated six million people suffer this fate every year. It's a problem of economic as well as human dimensions.

Providing full medical coverage is a daunting prospect for many governments. As an example, using 2012 figures, it would cost Nigeria US$51 billion simply to bring its number of physicians up to the OECD median. This sum equals a fifth of its GDP, and ten times the government's public health budget.

In countries without universal coverage, people rely on health insurance, charity or self-care, or they suffer through their afflictions. WHO estimates that over half of the world population does not have access to essential full services.[1] Not surprisingly, insurance makes a difference: studies of low and middle-income countries have found that people without insurance are more likely to go without treatment and to benefit less from preventive services, and to have a lower self-perception of their health. Yet they also pay more for care as a percentage of their disposable income, and are more likely to incur catastrophic financial loss. Over 930 million people (around 12 per cent of the world's population) spend at least 10 per cent of their household budgets to pay for health care.[2] Even so, most insurance plans are too expensive, or are simply unavailable, for the majority of people in countries without universal coverage.

There's no simple solution. Conventional public–private partnerships for healthcare in developing countries have mostly failed.[3] Most of the spending is wasted due to (1) treatments that lack evidence of efficacy, (2) inefficiencies in providing care, (3) frequent preventable medical errors, and (4) inflationary costs due to misaligned incentives in pricing and reimbursement.

A more promising idea is to use technology to promote prevention, better assess the efficacy of treatments, and boost the efficiency of health care delivery.[4] So far, health insurers, not governments, have taken the lead here. If, as seems likely, private health insurance expands in developing countries, then these companies have an opportunity to help improve health care in multiple ways.[5] They can help prepare the ground for future attempts at universal health coverage.

They can best pursue this opportunity with new kinds of partnerships with the health care sector and government. Insurers would gain as much as the health care providers. Insurance clients' perception of the value of health insurance is very much linked to the quality of the services around them. Collaborations that promote health care offerings and financial inclusion could boost purchases of health insurance. Enter Discovery.

Discovery Limited and the power of incentives

Discovery Limited[6] is a diversified financial services group founded in South Africa. Adrian Gore, an actuary, launched it in 1992. Within a decade, the company became South Africa's largest health insurer. The key to its growth was its Vitality programme, which attracted consumers and made them healthier through incentives.

Discovery also discouraged unnecessary medical spending by pioneering in South Africa the combination of insurance with a medical savings plan. The service covered nondiscretionary medical costs but applied a high deductible for discretionary medical spending, funded through a medical savings account. Buyers paid towards the savings account through regular contributions in addition to their insurance premiums. Premiums remained low, but the additional contributions were still affordable, as members on average reduced their discretionary spending.

Discovery listed on the Johannesburg Stock Exchange in 1999, with an initial market capitalisation of US$500 million. It has diversified into life insurance, property and casualty insurance, long term savings and banking, and now operates in 22 markets reaching 25 million customers. Gore continues to run the company as CEO.

The Vitality philosophy builds on the insight that 80 per cent of healthcare costs are driven by modifiable factors relating to lifestyle choices. The Global Burden of Disease data produced by the Institute for Health Metrics and Evaluation indicate that four risk factors (poor diet, physical inactivity, tobacco use and excessive alcohol consumption) lead to four chronic diseases (cardiovascular disease, type 2 diabetes, chronic lung disease and various cancers) that contribute to 60 per cent of deaths worldwide and 80 per cent of healthcare cost. Besides the direct suffering and strain on welfare systems, these maladies reduce workplace productivity and household spending.

Vitality aims to reward customers for positive behaviour changes in line with scientific findings. The model focuses on those modifiable lifestyle risk factors and encourages people to do assessments and preventive screenings. For example, customers with healthier behaviours benefit from rewards, lower premiums or get more cover (see Figure 8.1).

The process starts with the programme's Health Risk Assessment,[7] which determine a customer's "Vitality Age".[8] That's a risk-adjusted age determined by lifestyle indicators such as physical activity, nutrition and smoking, biometric indicators, such as blood pressure and cholesterol, as well as mental health. It quantifies the extra mortality risk caused by members' lifestyle choices. Working from their unique risks and demographic profiles, the programme prescribes customers a set of activities to reach recommended health goals.

Figure 8.1 Vitality Shared Value model.

To boost the motivation, Vitality customers can get rewarded through Active Rewards or gain discounts on purchases from a network of wellness companies and retailers. Some sellers offer products and services to boost health, while others offer fun and recreation.

Behavioural change at scale

Behavioural change is key to Vitality's business model. Vitality initially appealed to people who were already inclined to live healthier lives, because they got benefits from following their natural inclination. As a result, some critics called Vitality "a marketing gimmick designed to attract healthy people to the company while leaving the sick for someone else to cover".[9] Yet the Vitality programme actually rewards increases in healthy behaviour no matter the initial starting point.

In South Africa, all new members start out with "Blue" status, regardless of their health condition. They earn points through health activities and improvement from the baseline, bringing them to Bronze, Silver or Gold status. Members earn points in three ways:

- Understanding their health: Simply reporting their health status through online questionnaires and going to check-ups at locations such as Discovery Wellness Centres in drug and department stores.
- Getting more active: working out at a gym, or using wearable fitness devices to track physical behaviour.
- Making healthy choices: in nutrition by buying healthy foods and quitting smoking.

Vitality's business model flows from three tenets: societies require companies to fulfil a socially progressive core purpose; technology is an enabler; and health risks are largely behavioural so can be changed.

Vitality by necessity has had to pioneer its approach. As CEO of Discovery Vitality, Dinesh Govender points out, when it comes to behaviour-driven health, that "there aren't many evidence-based solutions".[10] The company's growth has centred around learning to collect health data and then establishing mechanisms to increase engagement and motivate new habits. The Vitality Health Check (VHC), for example, screens members for a wide variety of indicators, including body mass index (BMI), blood pressure, glucose, cholesterol, non-smoker status, HIV, dental and glaucoma screening.

The popularity of this test among members is illustrated by the rapid increase in administered tests in South Africa over a 3-year period between 2015 and 2018. 2015 saw 257,000 VHCs performed, which increased by 21 per cent to 312,000 in 2018.

Vitality members have access to gym facilities and running groups, and they can demonstrate their activity levels with tracking devices from manufacturers such as Apple, Garmin or Suunto. The *Active Rewards* programme shows their progress, and rewards, in a user-friendly way.

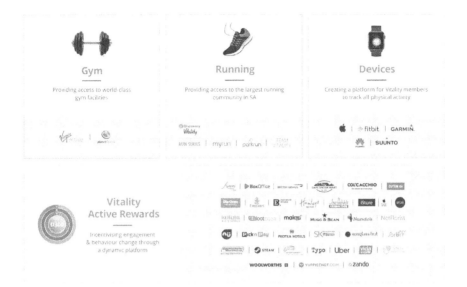

Figure 8.2 Vitality Active Rewards programme.

Two high level statistics that Vitality tracks are the percentage of members regularly exercising, and their average number of days per month with substantial exercise. The former measure grew from 34 per cent in 2015 to 43 per cent in 2018, while the latter jumped 84 per cent in that period, from 7.3 days to 13.4 days.

Vitality estimates its healthier insurance pool has saved Discovery the equivalent of US$121 million in 2018 alone, and US$1.2 billion from 2008 to 2018.

Rather than rely solely on self-reported activity, Vitality has worked to monitor fitness levels directly. In a joint study with RAND Europe and Apple Watch in 2018, Vitality data on 423,000 participants in three countries[11] contributed to the largest behaviour change study on physical activity based on verified data. A subset of the group, 91,000 people, each received an Apple Watch for a small upfront amount and were told that they would pay nothing more than the initial amount if they achieved their weekly physical activity goals over the 24 months. The watch users boosted their activity by an average of 34 per cent, or 4.8 days per month, over those not using the Active Rewards with Apple Watch benefit. Vitality based the model on learnings from behavioural economics that losing a benefit already received was a stronger motivator than being offered a future reward.

The same was true for nutrition. Vitality encouraged members to track their food purchases by offering Healthy Food cash backs at Pick 'n' Pay and Woolworths, South Africa's largest food retailers. Through direct integration with the grocers, the company then recorded the composition of the baskets as healthy, unhealthy or neutral, and rewarded the purchase of foods with high nutritional content through a cashback mechanism. Vegetable purchases by members increased by 29 per cent over the three-year period while sugar and salt purchases fell by 33 and 31 per cent, respectively. The programme offered Vitality members up to 25 per cent cash back on fresh fruit, vegetables and 6000 other selected products. The retailers embraced the concept, with some stores dedicating an entire section to Vitality-qualified foods.

With these programmes, Vitality is getting customers to change their behaviours towards a healthier life. Prevention is more cost effective than medical treatment, reducing the burden on the health care system.

Advocacy

Most of Discovery's engagement with the public sector to date has involved sharing the results of Vitality's findings on behaviour and health as well as implementing campaigns and programmes that drive public good. While Discovery and Vitality have done little direct work with governments, they have carried out several initiatives to promote wider public health.

Vitality introduced Vitality Open in South Africa towards the end of 2018, which allows non-members to download its app, engage in activity and receive rewards for a limited time. The initiative was highly successful in convincing 550,000 new customers to register for Vitality.[12]

Figure 8.3 Vitality Open app benefits.

Britain's Healthiest Workplace began in 2013 as a collaboration with Cambridge University, RAND Europe and recently the UK's Financial Times.[13] Many UK employers were doing little to invest in the health and wellbeing of their staff. Data from Britain's Healthiest Workplace estimated that health-related lost productivity costs the UK economy £91 billion in 2019, and argued that this cost would fall substantially with employers' greater investment. Shaun Subel, Director of Corporate Wellness Strategy at Vitality Health points out that:

> Many US employers are investing in health and well-being programmes because they are exposed to significant healthcare liabilities and chronic health conditions. But in the UK, you have the ultimate universal health-care system through the NHS, a free to use system at point of need. So you can't make the same argument. If an employee has a chronic health condition, they become a customer of the NHS; it's not a need to be served by employers.[14]

Accordingly, *Britain's Healthiest Workplace* aimed to show that even with a public universal health care system, employees were still suffering from preventable health conditions, and that employer-investment in wellbeing could pay off in greater productivity. It sought to establish that employers can influence the health of employees, and that employee health affects both absence levels and employee performance while at work.

The project survey involves 160 questions for employees covering lifestyle, clinical and mental health, work engagement and productivity, as well any health and wellbeing interventions that were offered by employers. The questionnaire also has a component for someone from the company's Human Resources department to fill out, focusing on work organisation and work environment.[15]

The project has an indirect marketing purpose. Subel says:

> We don't look to drive sales off the back of it. But it forms a key part of our shared value insurance model, trying to build the case for corporates to think more broadly about the prevention and health promotion agenda for their staff.[16]

Companies see a dashboard with trends among their workforce, such as the average Vitality age gaps, the distribution of health status levels and the main risk factors. Employers can track these over time and see if contracting with Vitality has delivered results.

The Vitality Institute-US[17] was founded in 2013 as part of Discovery's commitment to health promotion and wellbeing programmes. Its main purpose was to evaluate the barriers of and opportunities for health promotion, and the prevention of chronic disease in working age Americans. As part of its work, it urged the National Institute of Health (NIH) to increase spending on prevention-oriented research, and outlined ways for Discovery and other companies to help.

Francois Millard, a senior vice president at The Vitality Group, said "The recommendations were simple interventions that we all know yet still aren't ubiquitously followed. For example, only a very small segment of [NIH] funding goes to prevention, and we quantified how much of its budget that was."[18] Yet the report was strong enough to be picked up by the Harvard School of Public Health along with the Robert Wood Johnson Foundation. Those two organisations incorporated many of the recommendations into their *Culture of Health: A Business Leadership Imperative* programme.[19]

The South Africa ObeCity Index[20] ranks the country's large cities on obesity or overweight status. It highlights the growing problem of obesity, globally as well as in South Africa, draws attention to its causes and suggests what can be done to reduce this problem. The resulting index document that delves into detail on beneficial behavioural change serves as a pulse check for individuals and the government.

The Global Vitality Pledge (see Figure 8.4), announced in 2018, built on the Vitality Apple Study[21] described above. Vitality's Global Insurance Network is an alliance of large insurers worldwide who they have partnerships with. Vitality, along with its global network, committed to making 100 million people 20 per cent more active by 2025.[22] That number amounts to roughly a tenth of the global health and life insurance population. Insurers such as AIA, Generali, Manulife, Ping An, John Hancock and Sumitomo Life, who are otherwise competitors in some markets, committed towards this single goal.

Millard said, "What we want to do through Vitality and through this insurance network is give our partners the ability to help deliver a shared value insurance model in their local markets."[23] Added Andre Nepgen, head

Figure 8.4 Global Vitality Pledge, 2018.

of Vitality's Global Network, "It creates a pooling effect in that the insurance partners and everyone else who joins the pledge gets pulled into it – and find new ways of making people more active through Vitality."[24]

Partnerships

Vitality's success as a brand has depended heavily on partnerships. It has worked closely with research institutions, technology companies and retailers, as well as other insurers, to publicise its offering both for behaviour change and delivering on their core purpose of making people healthier.

The Vitality programme is adapted for each market by adjusting its incentives and rewards, to match the business and geographies of its partners. Today the network works across 24 markets with insurers representing more than 300 million customers.[25] This network is the platform for the Vitality Pledge mentioned above.

The Vitality and Apple Watch initiative, for example, arose from philosophical alignment between Apple and Discovery.[26] Apple had innovative technology, and Vitality had behaviour change know-how to use for that technology that could improve health outcomes across the Global Vitality Network. Vitality was able to monetise the behavioural change it drove, as healthier insurance clients, on average, result in lower claims.

Vitality Insured Persons 1, 2 and 3 was a series of South African studies ending in 2011 that linked engagement in the Vitality programme with lower medical costs and lower health insurance claims.[27] These studies were independently researched and published in peer-reviewed health and science policy journals. By partnering with the scientific and policy community, Vitality has received external verification for its ideas, thereby cementing its place as a leading developer of intellectual property on behavioural change.

Discovery partnered with Cambridge Telematics in 2014 to apply its shared value model to auto insurance. The Telematics app gave Discovery feedback on customers' driving when they had their mobile phone in their car. It showed the route driven and detailed driving behaviour measures such as whether the customer accelerated or braked hard in places, cornered aggressively or drove too fast.

Discovery aimed to reduce road car deaths by rewarding people for better driving. This partnership was thus part of Discovery's strategy to create an entire ecosystem based on promoting positive behaviours. In areas where most of the deaths involve pedestrians, Discovery has provided free fluorescent backpacks along with educational booklets on being a good pedestrian.

Measurement

Underlying Discovery's success is the value it places on measurement and independent verification of its results. Its mission of promoting healthy behaviours would be unachievable without quantifying its progress.

Otherwise Vitality would be no different from a loyalty rewards programme. By changing their behaviour or maintaining good behaviour members gain retail rewards, lower insurance premiums and lower interest on loans.

Vitality's measurements, at the individual and macro level, drive sales growth in two ways. Accountability on an individual level makes Vitality interactive and personalised, increasing its appeal over other health or wellness programmes. On the macro level, Vitality's wealth of data, and its comfort with the scientific community, makes it an appealing partner for other corporates, whether technology providers or other insurers. Over the past 15 years, Discovery has amassed more than 40 million life years of proprietary data linking lifestyle behaviour with mortality and morbidity – the world's largest and most comprehensive behavioural database for insurers. The company can do much to analyse the benefits of different health behaviours and their motivational influence.

On average, Vitality-Life insurance integrated policies have a 42 per cent improved mortality rate over other insured people, with highly engaged members having as much as a 76 per cent reduced mortality rate. Vitality members live on average 14 years longer than the average insured South African. Cardiovascular conditions decrease by up to 32 per cent, compared to non-Vitality clients. Academic research has shown that hospital costs for engaged Vitality members are 10–30 per cent lower than non-engaged members for chronic conditions, and admission rates are 10 per cent lower. The length of stay in hospitals is 25 per cent lower.

A major future opportunity is in improving the health of people who are not Vitality members. If governments cannot or will not take up the challenge, perhaps the company can figure out a way to do this.

Sidebar: AllLife Insurance

A quite different insurer, also founded in South Africa, is another brand on a mission. AllLife Insurance, founded in 2004, aims to deliver affordable life insurance to stigmatised groups, such as people with HIV and diabetes. Its products rely on robo-underwriting,[28] algorithmic pricing, technology platforms and continuous health management through data intelligence to keep costs low, and in 2019 it provided about US$580 million in coverage. It processes a life insurance application for a diabetic in less than a day, compared to an industry average of around a month.

The company plays an important role in South Africa, where 19 per cent of adults are HIV positive. To date it has served more than 100,000 customers, providing a safety net to families by preventing a decline back into poverty. Having life insurance transfers to other segments of financial inclusion – for example, by enabling policyholders to access mortgage financing.

Besides growing rapidly as a business, the company is enabling its customers to live longer, healthier lives. HIV-positive customers see an average of 15 per cent improvement in health, as measured by CD4+[29] count, within six months of being insured. AllLife is working with insurers elsewhere to deliver life insurance products to diabetics globally. In 2017 it announced a partnership with Royal London, the UK's largest mutual, life, pensions and insurance company, to provide coverage to some of the UK's 4.5 million diabetics, a demographic previously considered "uninsurable".[30] As with Vitality, AllLife combines business success with improvements to public health outcomes.

Future challenges

Vitality is undoubtedly an innovative and adaptive, socially-driven brand on a mission. Mass behavioural change is at the forefront of the company's mission to create a healthier world through lifestyle improvements. Advocacy through non-governmental organisations has played a key role in the development of the company's wellness programme. Partnerships have been integral to scaling its reach globally from its start in South Africa. Measurement has been essential for maintaining the latter three pillars.

Yet so far the company's success has rested almost entirely with middle to high income people. Looking ahead, Vitality's parent, Discovery, has been refining a product for lower income South Africans who cannot afford the company's main health insurance.

Over four million South Africans have no health insurance and rely entirely on the public system for their health care needs, or they pay for private health care out of pocket incurring huge expenses.

Discovery found that lower income populations had higher levels of stress, less regular exercise and less healthy diets than its conventional customer base. Discovery's product for this population, Primary Care, covers primary care, dentistry, optometry services and basic radiology services as well as medication for chronic and acute diseases, priced at US$11 per month (versus conventional plans of US$55–250 per month).[31] And in 2017, Discovery launched two new Vitality products designed for members enrolled in Primary Care: Vitality Move and Vitality Active. This plan also required a different set of grocery and gym partners that offered lower-costs services. It is too soon to know if this will be a success.

Another challenge is to better connect its marketing with its social purpose. Most customers have little awareness of Vitality's or Discovery's mission – they choose Discovery's offerings because of the high-status benefits of its offers. One way to raise awareness might be to explain how Vitality is promoting its behavioural incentives to non-members. If it can get traction here, it might make even more progress towards making universal health coverage affordable.

A company created with social mission at the core has shown that it is possible to make a real difference in lifestyles norms for all. It is clear that when customers, insurance companies and health systems all line up behind healthier lifestyles, it ends up being a sweet spot for them all.

Notes

1 World Health Organization (2019). "Universal health coverage (UHC)", *WHO*. Available at: www.who.int/news-room/fact-sheets/detail/universal-health-coverage-(uhc) (Accessed: 5 January 2020).
2 Ibid.
3 World Economic Forum, BCG (2016). "Health Systems Leapfrogging in Emerging Economies", WEF in collaboration with BCG. May 2016. Available at: www3.weforum.org/docs/WEF_Health_Systems_Leapfrogging_Emerging_Economies_report.pdf (Accessed: 13 November 2018).
4 Bitar, J. *et al.* (2016). "Leapfrogging: Value-Based Health Care Comes to Emerging Markets", *BCG*. Available at: www.bcg.com/en-us/publications/2016/health-care-payers-providers-leapfrogging-value-based-health-care-comes-to-emerging-markets.aspx (Accessed: 21 November 2018).
5 Sterlin, E. (2017). "Building up to Barcelona", *Private Healthcare in Emerging Markets: An Investor's Perspective* (4), p. 2. Available at: https://www.ifc.org/wps/wcm/connect/355fc329-ee12-4609-b852-da83bf42287d/HealthNewsletter_issue1_FINAL.pdf?MOD=AJPERES&CVID=16RX2uP (Accessed: 18 December 2019).
6 Porter, M. E., Kramer, M. R. and Sesia, A. (2014). "Discovery Limited". Available at: www.hbs.edu/faculty/Pages/item.aspx?num=48352 (Accessed: 2 January 2020).
7 Vitality Program Features | Wellness For Your Health (no date). Available at: www.weatrust.com/buy-from-the-trust/vitality-wellness-program/program-features (Accessed: 2 January 2020).
8 Vitality (2015). *What's Your Vitality Age?* Available at: www.vitalitygroup.com/insights/what%C2%92s-your-vitality-age/ (Accessed: 2 January 2020).
9 WSJ (2006). "In South Africa, Insurer Gives Points For Healthy Living", *WSJ*. 21 February 2006. Available at: www.wsj.com/articles/SB114048591562678630 (Accessed: 3 January 2020).
10 Govender, D. (2019). Personal interview.
11 Discovery (2018). "Discovery's Vitality Open gets more South Africans active and driving better", *Discovery*. 11 December 2018. Available at: www.mynewsdesk.com/za/discovery-holdings-ltd/pressreleases/discoverys-vitality-open-gets-more-south-africans-active-and-driving-better-2812813 (Accessed: 2 January 12).
12 Ibid.
13 Britain's Healthiest Workplace | Vitality (no date). *Vitality Health and Life Insurance*. Available at: www.vitality.co.uk/business/healthiest-workplace/ (Accessed: 2 January 2020).
14 Shaun, S. (2019). Personal interview.
15 *Britain's Healthiest Workplace | Vitality* (no date). *Vitality Health and Life Insurance*. Available at: www.vitality.co.uk/business/healthiest-workplace/ (Accessed: 2 January 2020).
16 Shaun, S. (2019). Personal interview.
17 The Vitality Institute. Available at: http://thevitalityinstitute.org/ (Accessed: 4 January 2020).
18 Millard, F. (2019). Personal Interview.
19 Shine (no date). *Culture of Health*. Available at: https://shine.sph.harvard.edu/culture-health (Accessed: 5 January 2020).
20 Vitality (2017). "The Vitality ObeCity Index", *Vitality*. Available at: www.vitalitygroup.com/wp-content/uploads/2017/10/2017-Vitality-ObeCity-Index_final.pdf (Accessed: 4 January 2020).
21 Vitality (2018). "Vitality Apple Study – World's biggest study on physical activity", *Vitality*. Available at: www.vitalitygroup.com/vitalityapplestudy/ (Accessed: 4 January 2020).

22 Vitality (2018). "Vitality-linked insurers to get 100 million people 20% more active by 2025", *Vitality*. Available at: www.vitalitygroup.com/press-release/vitality-linked-insurers-get-100-million-people-20-active-2025/ (Accessed: 5 January 2020).

23 Millard, F. (2019). Personal Interview.

24 Nepgen, A. (2019). Personal Interview.

25 Porter, M. E., Kramer, M. R. and Sesia, A. (2014). "Discovery Limited". Available at: www.hbs.edu/faculty/Pages/item.aspx?num=48352 (Accessed: 2 January 2020).

26 Millard, F. (2019). Personal Interview.

27 Patel, D. *et al.* (2011). "Participation in Fitness-Related Activities of an Incentive-Based Health Promotion Program and Hospital Costs: A Retrospective Longitudinal Study". Available at: https://journals.sagepub.com/doi/10.4278/ajhp. 100603-QUAN-172 (Accessed: 5 January 2020).

28 Mer, M. (2017). "Man versus Machine – the rise of the robo actuary" *Deloitte Australia | Human capital, Actuaries Summit, Deloitte Australia*. Available at: www2.deloitte.com/au/en/pages/human-capital/articles/man-machine-rise-of-robo-actuary.html (Accessed: 5 January 2020).

29 Hughson, G. (2017). "CD4 cell counts", *aidsmap.com*. Available at: www.aidsmap.com/about-hiv/cd4-cell-counts (Accessed: 5 January 2020).

30 Accion (2017). "Insurtech Leader AllLife Raises Funds to Expand Coverage to People Living with Diabetes and HIV". Available at: www.prnewswire.com/news-releases/insurtech-leader-alllife-raises-funds-to-expand-coverage-to-people-living-with-diabetes-and-hiv-300450114.html (Accessed: 5 January 2020).

31 Porter, M. E., Kramer, M. R. and Sesia, A. (2014). "Discovery Limited". Available at: www.hbs.edu/faculty/Pages/item.aspx?num=48352 (Accessed: 2 January 2020).

9   Carling Black Label #NoExcuse

An alcohol brand counters violence against women

With some brands, the connection to public health is easy to make. Lifebuoy soap and LIXIL toilet cleaners improve hygiene, Durex condoms prevent infections and Discovery insurance promotes healthy diet and exercise. But what if people criticise your brand for contributing to social problems? How can you take on a social purpose while protecting your business? Isn't that extremely hypocritical?

That was the challenge taken up by Carling Black Label, the largest-selling beer brand in South Africa. Since 2017, its marketers have worked to reduce the disturbingly high rates of violence against women in that country – without demonising its mostly male customers. Rather than merely write cheques to non-profit organisations, they put the resources, expertise and R&D of the company directly to work on the problem. It is too soon to pronounce their efforts a success, but the work shows how a controversial brand can tackle a social problem without damaging its commercial prospects.

How Carling embraced the fight against domestic violence

The Carling brewery began in Canada in 1818 and developed the Black Label brand of lager in the 1920s. Through a series of mergers, it gained the scale to expand to Britain and throughout the Commonwealth. While the Molson Coors company controls the brand in Canada, Britain and the United States, South African Breweries (later SABMiller) took it on in its market in 1966.

The brand has long targeted male customers, and its messaging has worked to define masculinity in changing contexts.[1] In the 1980s, it ran television ads associating the beer with the popular Western shows and movies. The cowboy represented a hero who deserved a cold Carling Black Label as a reward for a long day's work.[2] The messaging changed in the 1990s, to reflect a nation of builders as South Africans abolished apartheid. Ordinary men were now the heroes, strong, honest and hardworking. Then in the 2000s the brand connected the beer with entrepreneurs and the rising generation of "self-made men". In the 2010s, the brand thus took on a multi-dimensional identity of a "New Man" and, shortly after, the "Champion Man", ready to be a role model for others.[3] With each image of masculinity, the message was that every man deserved a Carling Black Label at the end of the day.

The best-selling beer became a household name in South Africa, and people affectionately call it Zamalek. The nickname arose from the 1990s when a soccer team from the Zamalek district of Cairo, with the same uniform colours as the beer, defeated the Kaizer Chiefs, a local team. This connection to a sports team's name is just one indication that masculinity, sports and alcohol are inseparable in the minds of South Africans.[4]

That's where things stood when AB InBev, the largest beer corporation in the world, bought SABMiller in 2016. Andrea Quaye, the Marketing Director at SABMiller, knew the value of Carling. She called it "a unique brand with a clear purpose. It really is all about instilling pride in masculinity."[5]

It was also a key brand for AB InBev, which eyed Africa as vital to future growth. Having covered much of the world with hundreds of brands, the world's largest brewer (US\$54.6 billion in 2018 revenues) wanted a strong position in the continent's largest market for beer.[6, 7] Lager sales dominate the alcohol industry in South Africa, accounting for 80 per cent of the volume and 56 per cent of the revenue.[8] Carling accounted for a fifth of total beer sales in Africa, which in turn covered 7 per cent of total sales worldwide.

But with her promotion to AB InBev's Vice President of Marketing for Africa, Quaye knew she could not continue business as usual. As the acquisition was going through, local researchers were calling out the downside of the country's fondness for beer. South Africans had the highest alcohol consumption in the continent. At the equivalent of 9.3 litres of pure alcohol (equal to 400 12-oz bottles of beer), it was double the overall average. Also it was highly gendered: men consumed 16.2 litres while women had only 2.7 litres.[9, 10] The World Health Organization reported that 58 per cent of all deaths from South African traffic accidents were alcohol-related, the highest in the world and far more than in Canada (34 per cent), the United States (31 per cent) and Australia (30 per cent).[11]

Even worse, the estimated rates of murders (femicide) and overall violence against women, while declining since 2000, were five times the global average, with alcohol commonly present.[12] More than half of the women murdered in 2009 (56 per cent) were killed by an intimate partner.[13] Overall, one in five women has suffered violence from a partner, and in some groups perhaps as high as one in two.[14, 15]

The consumption of alcohol also promotes risky sexual behaviour, including the transmission of HIV. In bars and pubs, alcohol combines with the venue's atmosphere to increase men's sense of power, which fuels aggressiveness towards women.[16] Some men drink to gain courage to beat their partner when they feel it is socially expected.[17] Heavy drinking affects cognitive and physical functions and diminishes the ability to negotiate non-violent resolutions when faced with conflict. Excessive drinking also makes it harder for men to manage finances, care for children and relationships generally.[18]

Alcohol thus increases the rate of intimate partner violence and sexual assault.[19, 20] Two-thirds of South African women suffering from spousal abuse indicated that their partner always or sometimes used alcohol before the assaults, higher than the United States (half) and Britain (a third).[21] Another study suggested that a third of South African men had committed violence against their intimate partner, with alcohol abuse as a main factor.[22] Between 6 and 10 per cent of men report having perpetrated violence overall in the last year, and an estimated 40 per cent of men in their lifetime.[23]

This violence risks the public health of women. Young men who engage in violence against women are more likely to be living with HIV than those who do not.[24] South African women who suffer physical or sexual violence were much more likely to develop depression, suicidal thoughts or to abuse alcohol themselves, even two years after an incident.[25] Studies stretching back to 2004 have found that "hegemonic masculinity", a cultural norm connecting men to power and economic achievements, promotes alcohol abuse and gender-based violence, globally and in South Africa.[26, 27]

In response to these statistics, Carling Black Label's team worked on a message. Grant Pereira, Brand Director, Carling Black Label, said that:

> We are aware that, while the vast majority of our consumers drink responsibly, there are some men who commit acts of gender-based violence after having abused alcohol. As a brand that promotes responsible drinking at all times, we acknowledge that abuse of any kind, including gender-based violence, is unacceptable.[28]

Yet Quaye and her colleagues decided it was now time to do more. Newspaper headlines were raising awareness of the extent of the problem. The marketers needed to take some responsibility, and risks, to ensure both the safety of South African women and the future brand's growth – yet stay true to the brand's heritage. As Quaye put it,

> We've known that masculinity in South Africa, and I think across the world, is under huge pressure, so we felt that it was our role to instil pride in masculinity. But how could you be proud of being a man with the levels of gender-based violence, or when the association people have with masculinity is one of violence?[29]

Quaye explained AB InBev's thinking:

> As a company we talked about the idea of a social cause. Our dream was to be a reference company – a company against which all of the companies were measured. Part of that growth is bottom line expansion and engagement in terms of staff. But it was also about the company's reputation and being a company that does well in society.[30]

As for Carling Black Label, Quaye pointed out that:

> It is our biggest brand with the most scale and therefore the most influence. So if you want to have an impact on society, you need to pick your biggest weapon. We've targeted the men who are used to hearing from us. We want to bring them on board because gender-based violence is a man's issue.[31]

She notes that:

> It was a very risky area because alcohol is seen as a cause of gender-based violence. The moment we acknowledge that [as part of the alcohol industry], we have a role to play. We wanted to be part of the solution and not just the excuse for gender-based violence.[32]

But it was going to be a special challenge. Catalina Garcia, formerly with SABMiller and now Global Director of Corporate Affairs at AB InBev, pointed out that the biggest critics of the brand are those who are against alcohol, and "they're everywhere. They do not accept that we can be part of the solution."[33]

Behaviour change

Beer was so ubiquitously enjoyed in South Africa that whatever solutions Carling developed, it needed to protect the bottom line and the overall industry. One idea was to produce beer with reduced alcohol content and alcohol-free beer, part of the overall AB InBev's commitment of US\$1 billion in social marketing and social norms programmes by 2025.

The company supports the World Health Organization's goal to reduce the harmful use of alcohol by at least 10 per cent in every country. It aims to have no- or low-alcohol beer become 20 per cent of their global beer volumes, and to place a guidance label on all beer products by the end of 2020 to increase alcohol health literacy.[34, 35, 36]

Its leaders tackled the social problem head-on, by following the brand's own tradition of adapting masculinity to new situations. Masculinity is a complex and context-specific concept, but in South Africa it badly needed to be reimagined. Carling's own research found that half of South Africans said beating a woman is sometimes acceptable.

Quaye laid out the brand's goals:

> Our dream is to significantly reduce gender-based violence in South Africa. There are a few men who are abusive towards women in many different ways, and there are lots of good men who say nothing and accept it. We want the next generation of all South African men to believe that it is unacceptable.[37]

The first behaviour-change programme involved the Smart Drinking Squads, groups of AB InBev employees responsible for working with taverns to promote responsible drinking. This ongoing programme began in 2018 as a pilot in two communities. Focusing on poorer communities, the squads identify and train men to become models for the good use of alcohol, in the taverns and the wider community. By early 2019, the squads had engaged with 4000 men.

The squads helped to spread awareness of the problem, but to bring about transformational change, Carling went deeper with the Champions for Change programme, also starting in 2018. This programme emerged from a partnership with Craig Wilkinson, a local social entrepreneur aiming to restore men to true masculinity and authentic fatherhood through experiential education.

The programme worked not just with taverns but also soccer associations and technical colleges, to identify 100 willing men. It took them on a two-day intensive camp with a mix of adventure-based challenges and life skills training. The activities forced the men out of their comfort zone and prompted them to take responsibility for others. From this group, Wilkinson and Carling's representatives choose ten men with the greatest potential to be influencers and gave them three days of special training. Those ten men returned to their communities to speak with men over the next several months.

The goal was to reach 1500 men over five months. Wilkinson and the marketers sought to learn about men's engagement within the household and beyond, and see how behaviour can shift.[38] Wilkinson explained, "We work with local structures in each community. The whole idea is to ignite a fire, to create a movement that does not need a big infrastructure or constant involvement from us."

He added,

> One of the challenges with men is that we don't talk. The suicide rates are internationally between four or five times higher than women. And one of the reasons is we feel we have to be strong, that we can't be vulnerable, and we bottle it all up. We're creating conversations so men share in ways they've never done before. The philosophy is to transform and heal, and to provide them with tools and materials so they can go network.

The programme focuses on men's woundedness. Wilkinson explains,

> A lot of men carry deep wounds, especially around fathers, but they've never actually dealt with them. So, we have another man stand in proxy for the man's father, who was either absent or abusive, and ask for the man's forgiveness. There's a whole restoration healing process – there's a bit of psychology involved in that. We also appeal to the nobility in men.

You can either be a gift or a curse. Men are not born rapists or abusers; they become that way through brokenness, fatherlessness, bad role modelling, and distorted messaging about masculinity.

The work started with taverns, which have a mix of "drunk, rowdy, and disorderly" men, but Wilkinson is empathetic: "You see tremendous pain there. These are the guys that are damaged by society, often despairing and they're finding comfort in a bottle. You're dealing with the most deeply wounded people in the community."
Wilkinson adds,

> Sometimes it feels like it's just a drop in the ocean, but we're starting to see some wonderful stories come out of it, of men changing. What we teach and preach is that first there is never an excuse, no matter what a woman does or does not do. The second thing is that the real mark of a man is not how much muscle you've got or how much money you've got. It is how you use your strengths, and primarily masculine strength is given as a responsibility to love, serve, and protect the safety of those around you.[39]

Advocacy

Carling Black Label also worked aggressively on larger communications, mostly on social attitudes rather than lobbying governments. In November 2017, soon after the AB InBev acquisition, the brand ran the #NoExcuse campaign with television and social media advertising. It sponsored a men's march that drew 8000 people, and released five million #NoExcuse cans of beer. The campaign called on South African men to take a five-year pledge to work against gender-based violence.[40]

Quaye was nervous about such a public campaign. "I thought I'd be fired, but it actually was the leadership that people were waiting for. People are waiting for brands, big companies, to make change."[41] Surveys were finding that of the four main sectors of society – government, business, media and non-profit organisations, half of South Africans trusted businesses the most.[42] They also reported that 82 per cent of South Africans believed "a company can take specific actions that both increase profits and improve the economic and social conditions in communities where it operates", higher than the global average of 73 per cent.[43]

Still, some people were sceptical that an alcohol brand could truly work against alcohol abuse. During interviews on radio programmes, Quaye says she was "lambasted by listeners who said this is just a marketing ploy and you're not serious".[44]

Undaunted, Quaye and her colleagues took the campaign to another level. For several years, the brand had offered the Carling Black Label Cup at the Soweto Derby, a biannual soccer match that transfixed much of the country.

The same two teams played every year as part of the biggest soccer rivalry in the country, and the event often turned violent – with some people trampled to death.[45] The brand encouraged fans to purchase specific versions of the beer to send a message on which players to play – which resulted in millions of votes.[46]

Leading up to the 2018 match, the brand worked with Ogilvy, the global media communications firm, and indaHash, an influencer marketing firm.

Figure 9.1 Carling Black Label #NoExcuse campaign at the Soweto Derby, 2018.

Just before the match began, a group of women formed a circle in the centre of the field and began singing Asambe Nono, the soccer anthem for South Africa. But they changed the lyrics: the song now described a man coming home after his team had lost a match and reacting violently against his partner in frustration. The song's chorus kept repeating: "No excuse for woman abuse".

The two soccer teams, the Orlando Pirates and the Kaizer Chiefs joined in as well. The players wore #NoExcuse-branded armbands during the series of games and posed with a banner at the end (see Figure 9.1).[47]

The event reached a greater audience of South Africans than the opening of the 2010 soccer World Cup in Johannesburg. indaHash placed influencers at the stadium capturing the event, posting reactions, photos, videos and stories across Instagram and Twitter.[48] Analysts reported that the Soccer Song for Change campaign reached 45 million people, increased Carling Black Label's brand mentions by 820 per cent, and generated over US$2 million in earned media.[49]

Partnerships

To sustain this momentum, Carling set up a variety of partnerships. It developed a five-year #NoExcuse initiative with Takuwani Riimel, a community-based organisation that mobilises men's associations.

Carling's challenges with partnerships were similar to those that other brands on a mission have faced. Quaye noted that:

> We are a big corporation and when you work with NGOs it can take a bit of time because we're such different beasts. We've got the timeline, the budget, the execution, while NGOs have a different model that engages with different parties. It took a bit longer than we expected.

She believed that especially as an alcohol brand, Carling Black Label first needed to show commitment and gain trust from other parties. Eventually other local companies joined in, such as First for Women, an insurer with products to uplift and empower women.[50]

The partnership with Craig Wilkinson happened at this time in 2018. He independently planned a meeting with AB InBev to pitch his idea, with the head of corporate social investment for Africa. Quaye happened to be at the meeting, and immediately decided to work with him for Carling Black Label.[51]

Wilkinson brought strong ideas on impact. He believes that #NoExcuse and other social media initiatives, with the backing of celebrities to create awareness, are:

> a very good thing, but mostly offer little in the way of solutions. Gender-based violence is not something that will self-correct. It will take

empathetic, strategic, and sustained action based on an understanding of its true causes, to break the cycle.[52]

He also pushed the brand on its messaging: "What is a Champion Man? There's a lot of confusion [in society] around what it means to be a man and what it does not mean, a lot of false messages out there."

At the corporate level, AB InBev has partnered with Lifeline, a 24-hour counselling line. This anonymous and confidential service offers emotional support and advice in identifying options and choices for a variety of issues, including alcohol abuse and violence.[53, 54] The company has also worked with academic institutions on product labels to promote alcohol health literacy.[55] It aims for "a world where communities thrive because harmful use of alcohol no longer presents a social challenge and every experience with beer is a positive one".[56]

Measurement

Carling's leaders understand the importance of measurement, on long as well as short-term impact. They look for changes in knowledge, social norms and behaviour.[57] They have contracted with Nudge, a South African market research firm, to carry out this work, but it's too soon to judge the effectiveness of the programmes.

The news so far has been mixed. Most important, these risky initiatives have not backfired on the brand. Positive sentiments on social media almost doubled, with few calls for boycott. On the other hand, Nudge found no major changes in attitudes or behaviour after two months of the #NoExcuse campaign.[58]

The campaign has certainly succeeded in engaging employees, a key secondary goal for brands on a mission. Thousands of AB InBev employees in South Africa have led community meetings tied to #NoExcuse when they talk about masculinity. That's important, points out Quaye, because "We're a beer company, we have access to rural areas. Our employees in those spaces are uptaking the campaign, working with local police, working with the government. So it's owned by everybody – it's not just a marketing campaign."[59]

Quaye attributes that success partly to the brand's efforts not to stigmatise men:

> It's important to not shame and blame because what we desire is a positive outcome. We desire people to take action. We've kind of inspired them to do something about it, and I think that's where the magic comes in.

Carling Black Label has deemed these efforts enough of a success to roll them out elsewhere in Africa, with adaptations to the local context.[60] As in South

Africa, partnerships will be essential. What seems to be lacking is a strong academic partner to help evaluate the impact on society, beyond what a market research company can find. Whether more brands with controversial industries can be brands on a mission remains debatable, but one thing is certain verifying impact is absolutely crucial.

Notes

1 Milani, T. and Shaikjee, M. (2013). "A new South African man? Beer, masculinity and social change", *Gender and Language in Sub-Saharan Africa: Tradition, struggle and change*, (33), pp. 131–148. Available at: https://doi.org/10.1075/impact.33.10mil
2 Ibid.
3 Ibid.
4 Taylor, D. (2010). "Watching Football, Drinking Beer – A South African Tradition", *Voice of America*. Available at: www.voanews.com/africa/watching-football-drinking-beer-south-african-tradition (Accessed: 31 December 2019).
5 Quaye, A and Garcia, C. (2019). Personal interview.
6 Taylor, D. (2010). "Watching Football, Drinking Beer – A South African Tradition", *Voice of America*. Available at: www.voanews.com/africa/watching-football-drinking-beer-south-african-tradition (Accessed: 31 December 2019).
7 AB InBev (2018). *2018 Annual Report – Shaping the future.* Available at: www.annualreports.com/HostedData/AnnualReports/PDF/NYSE_BUD_2018.pdf.
8 Report Buyer (2017). "The Liquor Industry in South Africa 2017". *PR Newswire.* Available at: www.prnewswire.com/news-releases/the-liquor-industry-in-south-africa-2017-300541554.html (Accessed: 31 December 2019).
9 World Health Organization (2018). *Global Health Observatory data repository – Total consumption with 95% CI by country.* Available at: http://apps.who.int/gho/data/node.main.A1036 (Accessed: 31 December 2019).
10 Fihlani, P. (2017). "South Africa's battle with the bottle", *BBC News*, 13 January. Available at: www.bbc.com/news/world-africa-38587655 (Accessed: 31 December 2019).
11 Ibid.
12 Head, T. (2019). "Femicide rates: South Africa vs the rest of the world", *The South African*. Available at: www.thesouthafrican.com/news/how-many-women-killed-south-africa-femicide/ (Accessed: 6 January 2020).
13 Abrahams, N. *et al.* (2013). "Intimate Partner Femicide in South Africa in 1999 and 2009", *PLOS Medicine*, 10(4), p. e1001412. doi: 10.1371/journal.pmed.1001412.
14 The preliminary results of the South African Demographic and Health Survey (2016) show that one in five partnered women have ever experienced physical violence by a partner. Prevalence varies widely by geographic location, marital status and education, and climbs up to 39 per cent in certain groups of women; the MRC's Three Province Study (1998) and the Gender Links & MRC study of Gauteng (2010) show prevalence between 19 per cent and 33 per cent.
15 Dunkle, K. L. *et al.* (2004). "Gender-based violence, relationship power, and risk of HIV infection in women attending antenatal clinics in South Africa", *The Lancet*, 363(9419), pp. 1415–1421. doi: 10.1016/S0140-6736(04)16098-4.
16 Watt, M. H. *et al.* (2012). "'Because he has bought for her, he wants to sleep with her': Alcohol as a currency for sexual exchange in South African drinking venues", *Social Science & Medicine*, 74(7), pp. 1005–1012. doi: 10.1016/j.socscimed.2011.12.022.
17 Jewkes, R. (2002). "Intimate partner violence: causes and prevention", *The Lancet*, 359(9315), pp. 1423–1429. doi: 10.1016/S0140-6736(02)08357-5.

18 World Health Organization (2006). *Intimate partner violence and alcohol.* Available at: www.who.int/violence_injury_prevention/violence/world_report/factsheets/fs_intimate.pdf.

19 Townsend, L. *et al.* (2011). "HIV Risk Behaviours and their Relationship to Intimate Partner Violence (IPV) Among Men Who Have Multiple Female Sexual Partners in Cape Town, South Africa", *AIDS and Behavior,* 15(1), pp. 132–141. doi: 10.1007/s10461-010-9680-5.

20 Simbayi, L. C. *et al.* (2004). "Alcohol use and sexual risks for HIV infection among men and women receiving sexually transmitted infection clinic services in Cape Town, South Africa", *Journal of Studies on Alcohol,* 65(4), pp. 434–442. doi: 10.15288/jsa.2004.65.434.

21 World Health Organization (2006). *Intimate partner violence and alcohol.* Available at: www.who.int/violence_injury_prevention/violence/world_report/factsheets/fs_intimate.pdf.

22 Hatcher, A. M. *et al.* (2014). "Intimate partner violence among rural South African men: alcohol use, sexual decision-making, and partner communication", *Culture, Health & Sexuality,* 16(9), pp. 1023–1039. doi: 10.1080/13691058.2014.924558.

23 Machisa, M. *et al.* (2011). "The War at Home: The Gauteng GBV Indicators Research Study". *Gender Links and the South African Medical Research Council.* 10.13140/RG.2.1.4295.0007.

24 Ibid.

25 Jewkes, R. *et al.* (2013). "Prevalence of and factors associated with non-partner rape perpetration: findings from the UN Multi-country Cross-sectional Study on Men and Violence in Asia and the Pacific", *The Lancet Global Health,* 1(4), pp. e208–e218. doi: 10.1016/S2214-109X(13)70069-X.

26 European Institute for Gender Equality. Accessed 25 June 2019. https://eige.europa.eu/thesaurus/terms/1236.

27 Hatcher, A. M. *et al.* (2014). "Intimate partner violence among rural South African men: alcohol use, sexual decision-making, and partner communication", *Culture, Health & Sexuality,* 16(9), pp. 1023–1039. doi: 10.1080/13691058.2014.924558.

28 Pereira, G. (2019)

29 Quaye, A and Garcia, C. (2019). Personal interview.

30 Ibid.

31 Ibid.

32 Ibid.

33 Ibid.

34 AB InBev (2018). *How we're changing the way people think about Smart Drinking.* Available at: www.ab-inbev.com/content/abinbev/en/news-media/news-stories/How-we-are-changing-the-way-people-think-about-Smart-Drinking.html (Accessed: 31 December 2019).

35 AB InBev (2018). *Making Progress in Our City Pilots Program.* Available at: www.ab-inbev.com/content/abinbev/en/news-media/smart-drinking/making-progress-in-our-pilot-program.html (Accessed: 31 December 2019).

36 AB InBev (2018). *Reducing the harmful use of alcohol and improving road safety: AB InBev's Progress Report on its global Smart Drinking Goals and contribution to UN SDGs 3 and 17.* Available at: www.ab-inbev.com/content/dam/abinbev/what-we-do/smart-drinking/landing-page/GSDG%20Double%20Website%2012.09.18.pdf.

37 Quaye, A and Garcia, C. (2019). Personal interview.

38 Wilkinson, C. (2018). Personal interview with Celine Mazars.

39 Ibid.

40 AB InBev (2018). *#NoExcuse Campaign Tackles Violence Against Women.* Available at: www.ab-inbev.com/content/abinbev/en/news-media/smart-drinking/noexcuse-campaign-tackles-violence-against-women.html (Accessed: 31 December 2019).

41 Quaye, A and Garcia, C. (2019). Personal interview.

42 Kamva Somdyala, K. (2018). "Trust in SA government dips, businesses most trusted – survey", *News 24*. Available at: www.news24.com/SouthAfrica/News/ trust-in-sa-government-dips-businesses-most-trusted-survey-20180619 (Accessed: 31 December 2019).

43 Edelman Trust Management (2018). *2019 Edelman Trust Barometer – Global Report.* Available at: www.edelman.com/sites/g/files/aatuss191/files/2019-03/2019_ Edelman_Trust_Barometer_Global_Report.pdf.

44 Quaye, A and Garcia, C. (2019). Personal interview.

45 Said, N. (2017). "The Soweto Derby: A rich history and a tragic past", *ESPN.com.* Available at: www.espn.com/soccer/south-african-premiership/story/3236258/ the-soweto-derby-a-rich-history-and-a-tragic-past (Accessed: 31 December 2019).

46 Shazi, N. (2017). "Here's Maybe Why The Soweto Derby Continued Even After The Death Of Fans", *Huffington Post*. Available at: www.huffingtonpost.co.uk/ entry/heres-some-reasons-the-soweto-derby-continued-even-after-the-de_uk_5c 7e8905e4b048b41e38fd29?guccounter=1 (Accessed: 31 December 2019).

47 De Villiers, J. (2018). "How Carling Black Label reached more than 45 million people worldwide to fight violence against women", *BusinessInsider*. Available at: www.businessinsider.co.za/carling-black-label-noexcuse-anti-gender-based-violence-campaign-reach-45-million-people-loerie-award-2018-8 (Accessed: 31 December 2019).

48 Straton, A. (2018). "indaHash proud partner of Cannes Lion Award winning #NoExcuse campaign", *MyPR*. Available at: https://mypr.co.za/indahash-proud-partner-of-cannes-lion-award-winning-noexcuse-campaign/ (Accessed: 31 December 2019).

49 Ogilvy Cape Town (2018). *Soccer Song for Change*. Available at: http://sites.wpp. com/wppedcream/2018/public-relations-public-affairs/business-to-business/soccer-song-for-change (Accessed: 31 December 2019).

50 *1st for Women*. www.firstforwomen.co.za/ (Accessed: 31 December 2019).

51 Wilkinson, C. (2018). Personal interview with Celine Mazars.

52 Wilkinson, C. (2018). "Gender Based Violence – why it happens and what we need to do to stop it", *Daily Maverick*. Available at: www.dailymaverick.co.za/ opinionista/2018-04-20-gender-based-violence-why-it-happens-and-what-we-need-to-do-to-stop-it/ (Accessed: 31 December 2019).

53 LineLine. Home Page. https://lifeline.co.za/ (Accessed 20 June 2019).

54 Wilkinson, C. (2018). Personal interview with Celine Mazars.

55 AB InBev (2018). *Reducing the harmful use of alcohol and improving road safety: AB InBev's Progress Report on its global Smart Drinking Goals and contribution to UN SDGs 3 and 17*. Available at: www.ab-inbev.com/content/dam/abinbev/what-we-do/ smart-drinking/landing-page/GSDG%20Double%20Website%2012.09.18.pdf.

56 AB InBev (2018). *How we're changing the way people think about Smart Drinking*. Available at: www.ab-inbev.com/content/abinbev/en/news-media/news-stories/How-we-are-changing-the-way-people-think-about-Smart-Drinking.html (Accessed: 31 December 2019).

57 Quaye, A and Garcia, C. (2019). Personal interview.

58 Stadium Management South Africa (2018). "#NoExcuse – Bold new movement against gender based violence", *Stadium Management SA*. Available at: www. stadiummanagement.co.za/2018/07/noexcuse-bold-new-movement-against-gender-based-violence/ (Accessed: 31 December 2019).

59 Quaye, A and Garcia, C. (2019). Personal interview.

60 Ibid.

10 What do numbers really mean?

The challenge of measurement and accountability for brands on a mission

Measurement is key for brands on a mission. They need to be confident that the social purpose is helping the brand grow while doing genuine good in the world. By tracking the resources devoted to different projects, and then how much each resource moves the needle on key goals, brands can build models with the likely return on investment, and then budget with confidence. Beyond budgeting, the measurements give project teams essential feedback for improving their social mission work over time. If an initiative is not effective, brands often know it quickly and can adapt and improve their approach.

When it comes to boosting public health and other social purposes, however, brands struggle to integrate measurements of both business and social impact into their plans. Whilst the SDGs are now clear on goals and sub-goals, what to measure is not always clear. Academics and non-profits disagree on what numbers to watch. It is also partly because measurement on the social side is harder, more expensive and less reliable than commercial measures of sales, penetration and consumer loyalty. The tools are still being developed and the science is constantly evolving.

Yet some degree of measurement is essential. One reason is simple: accountability. Investors, governments and non-profits – not to mention the general public – tend to be sceptical of commercial brands claiming to actually care about working towards sustainable development. Reliable measurements reassure stakeholders and customers that corporate efforts are actually doing some good and are not just purpose-washing.[1]

Another reason is that we want to make sure that what we are investing our time and money into is actually working. Most commercial projects operate in a familiar environment with common tools and techniques refined by decades of operation. Successful brands are, by definition, very good at working out what makes for sales success. But there is no guarantee that this operational skill translates over into effective social purpose and impact without building the capability to do so.

Along with tools to assess social impact, brands are still working on how to connect these effects to business results. The connection is essential to building the business case to stakeholders. How do you quantify the benefits of purpose among customers, employees and stakeholders?

This book is calling for a new vision where business models can boost public health, but we cannot realise that vision without heightened accountability. The United Nations will not, and should not, be content with a brand's loose claims to be furthering one of the Sustainable Development Goals (SDGs). Clarity of which goals and sub goals to align themselves to here gives brands some credibility with the public sector for them to jointly define programmes that are better targeted. Even when reliable measures of specific outcomes exist, it's often difficult to tie the work of brands directly to those metrics. Sceptical outsiders can attribute the gains to other causes, and usually it is a combination of efforts that amount to these reductions.

In all these areas, we are still figuring out good practices on measurement. What follows, more than in other chapters, is a summation of current thinking from brand leaders and partners. It has two overall messages. First, do not let perfection be the enemy of the good, as brands are on a journey to learning and trialling. Second, measuring inputs offers more benefits than you might imagine.

What to measure

To sustain its efforts, a brand on a mission needs to go beyond the direct social impact and measure its effects on multiple levels – that of the brand (within the company), the organisation overall and the ripple effect the work is having in the public sector at large. Besides the effects on consumer behaviour around the social purpose, there are three important levels:

1. Brand level: the brand's commercial bottom line. Are your efforts boosting unit sales, margins, and market penetration? Are you increasing purchase intent through communicating to your consumers about your social mission to your consumers? Ideally your social mission should boost sales of your product or at least build your brand equity.[2, 3] At Lifebuoy the goal was that the least vulnerable populations use the brand. But also important is whether the social mission is differentiating the brand from its competitors and boosting consumers' preference. Conventional brand tracking metrics can work here. Consumers should be able to articulate the brand's purpose and associate it with the brand's distinctive assets. And as we educate consumers and translate what ethical consumerism means to developing countries, they should be able to distinguish between brands that are genuinely investing to make a difference versus those just riding the purpose wave.

If we can demonstrate that a social purpose is of importance to consumers, then, if only for selfish financial reasons, that purpose is immediately important for retailers. This opens up new channels for purpose to reach consumers (such as product coupons) and a better way to collect data (through retailers via coupon redemption). In a collaboration with Spar, the largest retailer in South Africa with 850 stores, Lifebuoy linked the schools programme with a money-off coupon by asking communities to choose which schools would benefit from refurbishment of infrastructure. There was a subsequent sales uplift in targeted versus nontargeted communities. Getting the communities involved in the social mission was a big plus.

As argued in Chapter 1, a social purpose should help with the salience of your brand generally, in an increasingly commoditised world. When many brands offer the same functional benefits, a purpose will help differentiate them. This is one area where you keep an edge on your brands. Educating your target consumers is hard, especially if they are in rural areas or have just given birth (in the case of new mothers). But purpose well-deployed and then well-articulated to consumers boosts the equity of the brands. If you have a proposition that is differentiated in the minds of consumers, and it is also something that resonates positively with them, that is half the job in driving a brand's long-term growth through equity. This will in time be translated to sales growth.

It is important to track consumer attitudes, to better anchor yourself in what consumers actually think.[4] At Unilever, when we started tracking sustainability in metrics on brand equity, we were surprised to see that we lagged some competitors. As Stephen Lovelady, who leads Unilever's Global Centre of Excellence for Marketing Analytics, recounted; "We had to get Unilever employees out of their own heads and instead make them think about 'what purpose means for my consumers.' "[5]

Lovelady continues:

> Indeed, employees tend to believe that big brands do the most good for society, because most marketers work for the big brands, and if they weren't doing the most good, why would all these talented people be working for them? By contrast, consumers tend to think that big brands do the most damage to society, in terms of environmental impact, consumption of raw materials, effects on health and well-being, and running the little guy out of business. By tracking these metrics, we can observe how consumer attitudes to our brands shift as we make purpose central to our brand strategies.[6]

2. Organisational level[7]: here we are tracking the team's engagement with the mission. If brand managers and leaders remain with the same brand for a while, it's often because they really want to see a programme through, to find out the impact of their efforts and they're motivated by the purpose. Another measure here is how well employees can articulate their brand's purpose and get their friends and family engaged in the various purpose programmes. Many Unilever employees, for example, have gone to teach handwashing in their own children's schools and read a story on the importance of toothbrushing. It is always an added plus when you link your work with something meaningful to contribute to the lives of your children.

This kind of engagement has an indirect payoff for the larger company. It boosts productivity, reduces attrition and improves camaraderie in the workplace. People feel satisfied with their work, and more readily share what they do all day with their family and friends. Human Resources departments should be able to correlate that brand engagement with existing measures on productivity, absenteeism and retention – which in turn helps feed the business case for social purpose.

3. Wider appeal to the public sector: here the focus is on the brand's effect on public discourse and resources. Is the brand attracting resources from partners and from direct support to blended financing? Is the brand getting favourable recognition for its efforts, such as awards or statements of praise, all tied to its social purpose? Is the brand social mission opening up networks that would not exist if the purpose programmes were not being deployed? For example, with the right behaviour change programmes, access might be granted to clinics to talk to new mothers about handwashing. In the case of LIXIL, the Gates Foundation has supported them to expand the Sato brand.[8] With Lifebuoy, millions of euros of external resources have been mobilised, in addition to the brand's marketing resources, to pilot, test and expand programmes.

Social media has opened up the conversations that consumers are having with each other, giving companies a less filtered view into their attitudes. The channels also enable marketers to ask consumers directly about a brand, and then interject to clear up mistaken notions. Many companies now have sophisticated tracking methods to make sure that you can listen to the public conversations about brands and to enable them to quickly respond. Nothing fuels conversation like a purpose advertisement.

Measure inputs, not just outputs and outcomes

Brands on a mission are trying to improve the lives of people. Ideally, they connect their work with accepted improvements in human well-being, such as lower incidence of disease or better mental and physical health generally. However, it is very hard to do that, and often very expensive in a hard equation of tight profit-and-loss statements.

The SDGs are a convenient set of goals for brands on a mission to refer to, but each goal in its entirety is too broad for any brand or organisation of any kind to tackle. We therefore need to look at the target level. Global Compact have released all the Goals and Targets of the SDGs which are business relevant.[9] At Unilever, whenever a brand picked an SDG to tackle, the team were challenged to focus on specific sub-goals (targets and indicators). With Lifebuoy the focus was on SDG 3 – good health and well-being – developing partnership programmes that address the reduction of preventable deaths of infants and toddlers (sub-goal 3.2), and SDG 6, as mentioned earlier, which is focused on water, sanitation and handwashing infrastructures. By working on specific sub-goals, the brand can narrow the range of possible programmes. For instance, a new mothers programme targets an important teachable moment that could lead to a large reduction in infant mortality and can contribute to sub-goal 3.2. If companies review the most appropriate SDG for their sector and then review all the targets and SDGs for those material goals, then they can plan initiatives to help meet those targets per territory. It will also help the sustainability teams report into the Board to feed into the group's KPIs.

In Public Health, there is a well-defined set of experimental methodologies to show both cause and effect, not just effect. If you claim to be contributing to the cause – at least publicly – you need to do so to the same standard. Internally, it is a different story, as you need sufficient evidence of cause for a good decision to be taken, not strict proof (i.e. Do we do this again? Do we do more? What do we do differently?). If strict measurements fail to demonstrate substantial gains early in the purpose journey, marketers can lose confidence. If, for example, our handwashing programmes can save one life, and prevent thousands from getting colds and diarrhoea, then our efforts would have been all worth it.

As a result of these difficulties, most brands will want to focus on their inputs, rather than outcome measurement. When my Lifebuoy colleagues and I wanted to reduce childhood illness we set a goal, not around health, but around the number of people we would like to reach with our handwashing programmes and how we changed handwashing behaviour. The goal was set to reach a billion children and adults with the brand's handwashing behaviour change messages, and some of the programmes would reach SDG3.2 directly or SDG6 with infrastructure development. In measuring effectiveness, the focus was on the number of people exposed and on the intensity of the messages that were being delivered. Lifebuoy is a good example because it had the clarity required from a data and measurement point of view, following from clear, measurable articulation of its social purpose. If it is not specific enough, you cannot measure the input, and hence you cannot show cause and effect. Measuring inputs is also important in proportion to how much people will value the Brand Do, not just the Brand Say. If the brand is growing, and has purpose at the heart, then the Brand Do should proportionally grow.

With Lifebuoy, other measures of well-being outcomes were considered. The first thought, of course, was to track soap sales. If Lifebuoy (and other soap makers) were selling more units in the targeted countries, then it could be reasonably assumed that people were changing their behaviour and protecting themselves against infection. But the public sector tends to dismiss business data. At the time, I remember joking that there's only so much that one can do with a bar of soap – yet the critics had a point in this case. People already used soap in the bath but did not see a need for it before meals or after the toilet. Since bathing consumes far more soap than handwashing, total soap sales do not provide clear evidence of advances in public health. Maybe higher sales meant that Lifebuoy was just getting more people to use soap for bathing.

The easiest and cheapest handwashing measure is self-reported behaviour, yet this is subject to large reporting biases.[10, 11] When you ask people if they washed their hands with soap after coming out of the toilets, almost everyone says yes, regardless of whether they actually did it. This is true for basic hygiene questions in all markets and across all strata of the population.

A common alternative is structured observation (directly observing people's behaviours).[12, 13] In the introduction I described spending two years in Senegal, observing thousands of pupils coming out of toilets to see how many washed their hands with soap. While I learned something about behaviour, my approach was not sustainable and my presence surely affected how the kids behaved.

Lifebuoy tried using electronic loggers embedded in soap bars. These used real time clocks and accelerometers to record the time and nature of soap movements in field trials. The data pattern of soap provided an indication of soap use and even allowed the brand team to discriminate between likely body washing and handwashing. While this method was less intrusive than structured observations, it was still too expensive for broad use.[14] Inserting loggers in soap also means a lot of education for consumers who can become suspicious, wondering if there is spying going on.

Eventually Lifebuoy settled on the sticker diaries described in Chapter 6. Each child recorded their use of soap with the stickers provided. The approach relied on children recalling their actions and probably did not eliminate reporting bias. However, the approach was tested in partnership with academics at the London School of Hygiene and Tropical Medicine. The results were good enough to give the brand actionable information.[15] Data collection methods are evolving and can be much more creative than in the past, and better than standard questionnaires. What is challenging is the cost of designing expensive trials that brands at their individual levels can find hard to fund or can do only once in a decade depending on the size of the brand of course. Even many public health researchers would say that these should be reserved for limited cases. Of course, there are some new metrics that could be of interest, such as the happiness measures for brands such as foods and even oral health.

To sum up:

- You may be tempted to just use the easiest measures that can be deployed across markets.
- If you want to be confident and show to the world your impact, you need to understand the best measures to use for different stages of building evidence.
- While such a process is not easy, it is necessary to know what kind of impact you're having.

Partnering for measurement

Academics can help brands improve their measurement, both in coming up with new ways to track results and in validating the metrics that are chosen.

They are also good at helping marketers learn from experiments. But those same partnerships can slow your progress. It is important now, with only ten years to go to deliver the SDGs, that we find a way to report against globally recognised metrics. Academics require rigorously designed studies with randomised comparisons. They work to very high standards that can withstand scrutiny and require generalisable results. Marketers typically need only enough confidence to generate good investment decisions. But if you are going to operate in public health marketing you are going to have to step up the game. Little of Unilever's work, for example, has made it into academic journals, although the company has lately been trying to improve the publication journey on its purpose brands and keep transparency high. Obviously it depends on industries – if you are developing a vaccine, a high level of accuracy is absolutely required.

As Jeff Bezos wrote in his 2016 shareholder letter: "Most decisions should probably be made with somewhere around 70% of the information you wish you had. If you wait for 90 percent, in most cases, you are probably being slow."[16] Those decisions include the work on social purpose, and cost and time are major constraints. Academic standards can sometimes be too high or take too long to comply with. That does not mean you should work with academics only in an advisory role. It's just important to understand the different motivations for academics when you partner with them on measurement. As a marketer, I have to prove the value of purpose work in comparison to all the other things we could be spending our time and money on. The research does not need to be perfect; it just needs to be convincing enough to make the leaders decide whether to allocate money there or elsewhere.

That's especially true at a company like Unilever, which has pushed for social purpose work at the highest level. "Having gained overall permission to invest in purpose, we've needed only to make a case for certain kinds of programmes", says Stephen Lovelady.[17]

During my time on Lifebuoy, we benefitted from academic evaluations on some large programmes. It was discouraging to receive the tough evaluation of our Bihar programme at Lifebuoy[18] (Chapter 6), which showed little real improvement in handwashing under that context and executed in those circumstances. But the brand team kept going and used the results as motivation to improve the brand's approach to changing behaviour.

Arathi Unni, Unilever's global manager for consumer marketing insights, goes further:

> Like most people in this company and industry, I hadn't dealt with academics [before the Lifebuoy work]. But now I would highly recommend that those working in purposeful brands consider engaging with academics and also look to publish. In addition to giving ideas, this approach strengthens your programmes and evaluations, building credibility and relevance in the external world due to the critical lens of scrutiny that academics pass things through.[19]

One caveat with academic partnerships in any capacity: for competitive reasons, brands may protect specific knowledge related to their purpose work.

Proceeding with caution on external validation

Some of the larger purpose-driven corporations have begun to audit their efforts to gain credibility. Unilever engaged Price Waterhouse Coopers (PwC), the accounting giant, in 2010 to audit the work on its Sustainable Living Plan. The audit process itself was intensive; it felt like a non-stop counting exercise that risked losing the human touch and reasoning behind the programmes. Every brand and country manager had to meet certain requirements (the non-negotiables on the purpose programmes) to be included in the externally agreed and validated results. As Atul Patel, a director of stakeholder assurance at PwC, explained, "We needed to make sure that we understood what it means to improve health and well-being, and what it means to reach people."[20]

I remember how difficult it was for us at Lifebuoy to comply with the PwC metrics. This risked demotivating the team, which would see this as a mere counting exercise removed from actually making a difference in the world. There was also a risk of upsetting external partners and participants. But it also meant that reaching one billion people was verified and could be announced to the world to show the brand's commitment to reaching the goal.

At Unilever there has long been tension over the proper measurement of programmes. Corporate leaders want a very prescriptive, detailed and performance-orientated approach to measurement and capturing information. They know that the world is tough on companies trying to do good, especially with the science evolving all the time. The marketers and programme managers, by contrast, favour a softer approach that captured several kinds of evidence, qualitative and quantitative.

Strict measurement can also discourage participation on the ground, especially with children. They (or their parents) may not want their photos taken or their names registered, but then it is hard to rigorously count them towards targets for people exposed to an education programme.

For all PwC's efforts at clarity and rigour, Patel realised that social impact indicators are still primitive and that brands get better at measurement over time. The firm came up with a "maturity model" for measuring brand impact. This is where brands that are in the embryonic stage in social purpose are assessed using lower measurement standards than brands with greater maturity.[21, 22] This model can help companies decide how to communicate progress to the public despite questions over the reliability of the measurement.

So yes, it is good to get outside auditing, but be careful to find the process that works for your team.

I expect digital technology will play an important role in doing the heavy lifting of monitoring, reporting and verification (MRV) of companies, and providing this data to decision makers. Advances such as Blockchain, IoT and AI will support data creation, collection and verification and track progress at a much lower cost than current approaches.

Innovative measurement: World Wide Generation's G17Eco platform

In 2018 Unilever launched an intriguing partnership with a "fintech" company, World Wide Generation (WWG). WWG's technology platform, called G17Eco, is underpinned by Distributed Ledger Technology. G17Eco is an interoperable data platform connecting companies, assurers, rating agencies and investors together. Within the G17Eco platform is an MRV Tool that helps companies collect data with ease and provenance direct from source. It then processes this data against standardised frameworks including the SDGs for comparability and disseminates this data in the most efficient and trusted way. G17Eco tracks investments in contributions in real time. Unilever uses G17Eco to measure the impact of school-based interventions in South Africa on a variety of SDGs across three purpose brands (Lifebuoy, Domestos and Oral Care).[23]

The first phase in 2018 involved creating a full digital model of the programme, all the stages of the programme, delivery partners and beneficiaries. WWG then mapped Unilever's KPIs and wherever possible the outputs aimed by the specific SDG. This created a digital survey that could go to delivery partners, teachers, students and households to track progress. Phase 2 involved G17Eco sending out the surveys to 300 schools in Eastern Cape to create a baseline of data, i.e. "what did the world look like" for these beneficiaries before the intervention. Phase 3 was the same digital survey sent after the intervention to measure the impact and change in behaviour from before and after. The programme was also operationally tracked on G17Eco to see if capital and resources were being deployed in the most efficient way.[24]

The use of blockchain technology ensures that data claims are immutable and fully traceable and thus reducing corruption and increasing transparency and accountability. Unilever is also able to draw correlations between other data sets, such as access to Wi-Fi, facilities and SPAR stores, to drive behaviour change and performance of the programme. G17Eco could also correlate the beneficiary data to who redeemed tokens in store as a result of the programme.

As the technology develops, this software platform could assess the impact of brands (products/services, operations and CSR Initiatives) at an enterprise level and down to specific brand-based interventions per country. G17Eco also tracks every SDG deficit in every country. As brands start reporting their enterprise and project data, G17Eco will be able to help them understand how they are contributing to the SDG deficits per country. It will track and measure year-on-year progress in a standardised way.

At the end of 2019, WWG completed an industry wide pilot with 30+ leading brands mapping, monitoring, measuring, managing and marketing their data and efforts on G17Eco. WWG received significant excitement and buy-in from all stakeholders regarding G17Eco's capability, and now they are getting ready for scale in 2020, with several governments supporting the rollout.

The future of measurement for social purpose

Three challenges exist for measurement around social purpose. The first will come as brands integrate their purpose-based work with the overall business strategy and marketing effort. Bringing the two together could make measurement easier, but only if the messages are consistent. At Lifebuoy, it is important that the soap is marketed as a premium brand. Yet to help people increase handwashing, we have found it helpful to draw on the emotions of disgust around using toilets. How can Lifebuoy introduce elements of disgust and germs while presenting a premium image? Or to take another example, can we talk about reduction of iron deficiency anaemia when talking about flavour for a bouillon cube? How do you reconcile the two? When consumers think of flavour, they do not generally want to hear about nutrition. I have found that the Brand Do is the answer very often as it targets the consumer differently.

The second challenge will be the use of consumer data. As consumers become sensitive to corporate use of personal data, brands may find themselves limited in using this data even for a social purpose. This challenge has already arisen for Google's Project Nightingale, a partnership with the second largest health insurance company in America, in which Google was using data analytics on individual health records to develop better correlations on disease and treatment. The problem is Google is necessarily using data without explicit consent of patients and at such fine granularity that it can compromise individual anonymity.[25]

The third big challenge will be about acquiring new data sources that show a bigger, clearer perspective. This could be linking purpose-led programmes with national scale measurement programmes, such as demographic and health surveys which are internationally standardised surveys used by governments to measure progress related to the SDGs and other targets. These calculations could also connect purpose-led programmes with overall brand equity to see whether investments in purpose led programmes are having an impact in countries' national programmes.

Disentangling the business growth attributable to an aspect of a marketing campaign from other factors is very difficult to do, but determined brands are making good strides. They realise the importance of trust in how consumers and other stakeholders perceive the brand's social purpose and how data and measurement can assist with that. They are also understanding that this is a long-term gain and that building a brand's equity can take decades.

Exercise

How measurement can help you see the big picture

It's important to measure an intervention along four dimensions: impact on the stated social purpose, brand-level effects, internal organisational impact and effects in the public arena. Data on these dimensions can give you a holistic perspective on the intervention.

For example, if the intervention is promotion of handwashing in order to improve public health, you would look at the following areas:

- Impact on the social purpose: To what extent is your intervention changing handwashing behaviour at key public-health moments (before eating, after toilet)? Who is the intervention reaching? Is it likely to drive any public-health impact?
- Brand level: Is your social mission responding to a business need of the brand? (For example, are you trying to drive volume by getting more people to wash their hands with soap?) Or will your social mission drive a clear differentiation from competitors? And if so, what will this be? Will your social mission help drive sales?
- Organisation level: Is your social mission engaging the teams? Do you think you could get your brand managers to want to stay longer on the brand? Is the social-mission challenge big enough to motivate brand managers to want to think more creatively about solving it?
- Public level: Is there genuine interest in the public sector for your contribution? Which doors would the intervention open? What is the intervention's ability to attract attention, win recognition, earn outside support and gain external resources?

For each of the four dimensions, review the literature and carry out four interviews to be sure you understand the potential impact of the intervention on the chosen social purpose. Then look at three timeframes: short, medium and long term. Identify clearly how you will measure progress of your programmes in each of these time frames. Are you able to articulate how the intervention moves the needle?

Notes

1 Lars Holm (2018). "Brand Purpose Is Increasingly Essential: It's Time We Measured Its Impact Properly", www.campaignlive.com/article/brand-purpose-increasingly-essential-its-time-measured-its-impact-properly/1455250?utm_source=website&utm_medium=social (Accessed 29 December 2019).
2 David A. Aaker (1996). "Measuring Brand Equity across Products and Markets". *California Management Review*, 38, 102–120. http://dx.doi.org/10.2307/41165845

3 David A. Aaker (2009). *Managing Brand Equity*. New York: Simon and Schuster.

4 David A. Aaker (1996). "Measuring Brand Equity across Products and Markets". *California Management Review*, 38, 102–120. http://dx.doi.org/10.2307/41165845

5 Lovelady, S. (2019). Personal interview.

6 Ibid.

7 Nina Montgomery (2019). *Perspectives on Purpose – Leading Voices on Building Brands and Businesses for the Twenty-First Century*. Abingdon, Oxon: Routledge.

8 Montesano, J. (2019). Personal interview.

9 *UN Global Compact* (no date). Available at: www.unglobalcompact.org/ (Accessed: 4 January 2020).

10 Robert Rosenman, Vidhura Tennekoon, Laura G. Hill, Robert Rosenman, Vidhura Tennekoon and Laura G. Hill (2011). "Measuring Bias in Self-Reported Data", *Int. J. of Behavioural and Healthcare Research*, vol. 2 (Measuring bias in self-reported data, Inderscience Publishers), https://doi.org/10.1504/IJBHR.2011.043414.

11 Ibid.

12 W. P. Schmidt *et al.* (2019). "Comparison of Structured Observation and Pictorial 24 h Recall of Household Activities to Measure the Prevalence of Handwashing with Soap in the Community", *International Journal of Environmental Health Research* 29, no. 1 (2019): 71–81, https://doi.org/10.1080/09603123.2018.1511772.

13 Divya Rajaraman *et al.* (2014). "Implementing Effective Hygiene Promotion: Lessons from the Process Evaluation of an Intervention to Promote Handwashing with Soap in Rural India", *BMC Public Health* 14, no. 1 (December): 1–10, https://doi.org/10.1186/1471-2458-14-1179.

14 Richard L. Wright *et al.* (2015). "Use of Electronic Loggers to Measure Changes in the Rates of Hand Washing with Soap in Low-Income Urban Households in India (Loggers to Measure Hand Washing with Soap in Urban Households in India)" *PLOS One* 10, no.6: e0131187, https://doi.org/10.1371/journal.pone.0131187.

15 Schmidt, W. P. *et al.* (2019). "Comparison of structured observation and pictorial 24 h recall of household activities to measure the prevalence of handwashing with soap in the community", *International Journal of Environmental Health Research*, 29(1), pp. 71–81. doi: 10.1080/09603123.2018.1511772.

16 Charan, R. (2019). *How Amazon Does It: Decision Making Inside The World's Most Daring Digital Company*, *ChiefExecutive.net*. Available at: https://chiefexecutive.net/how-amazon-does-it-decision-making-inside-the-worlds-most-daring-digital-company/ (Accessed: 4 January 2020).

17 Lovelady, S. (2019). Personal interview.

18 Henrietta E. Lewis *et al.* (2018). "Effect of a School-Based Hygiene Behavior Change Campaign on Handwashing with Soap in Bihar, India: Cluster-Randomized Trial", *The American Journal of Tropical Medicine and Hygiene* 99, no. 4: 924–933, https://doi.org/10.4269/ajtmh.18-0187.

19 Unni, A. (2019). Personal interview.

20 Patel, A. (2019). Personal interview.

21 Mary Beth Griggs (2019), "Google Reveals 'Project Nightingale' after Being Accused of Secretly Gathering Personal Health Records", *The Verge*, 11 November, www.theverge.com/2019/11/11/20959771/google-health-records-project-nightingale-privacy-ascension (Accessed: 3 January 2020).

22 "PwC Insight Report", Available at: www.thecrownestate.co.uk/insight-report/index.html. (Accessed 4 January 2020).

23 World Wide Generation (2018). "Global SDG targets get a boost with launch of World Wide Generation's, G17Eco platform", *World Wide Generation*. Available at: www.worldwidegeneration.co/ (Accessed: 3 January 2020).

24 Manjula Lee. Personal Interview with Manjula Lee, CEO, World Wide Generation November 2018.
25 Mary Beth Griggs (2019), "Google Reveals 'Project Nightingale' after Being Accused of Secretly Gathering Personal Health Records", The Verge, 11 November, www.theverge.com/2019/11/11/20959771/google-health-records-project-nightingale-privacy-ascension. (Accessed: 3 January 2020).

11 How LIXIL is changing the narrative on sanitation

Sanitation is an issue close to my heart. My career in public health started there, and it made me especially sensitive to human dignity. Maybe it all started when I was ten years old in Mali, when I accidently fell into a septic tank near school that was not properly closed. Some passers-by had to help get me out. That was terrifying in itself, but worse was the public humiliation of being water hosed in front of the school community, and then carrying that smell for weeks. My grandfather later joked that this was why I had gone to such great lengths and faraway schools, to learn about how people relieve themselves.

For much of the world, sanitation is still a grim business. Some 2 billion people, close to a third of the global population, lack basic sanitation facilities.[1] Of these, 673 million still practice open defecation, meaning that they do not use any toilet at all, and hundreds of millions use facilities shared by multiple families – which are hard to keep sanitary.

During the day, 620 million children lack access to a proper toilet in their school. Rural areas lack the scale to justify proper sewage or septic systems, and urban schools cannot handle the scale of demand. Toilets may exist, but because of inadequate cleaning and maintenance, they often do not work properly.[2]

Poor sanitation is a major public health challenge, causing more than 280,000 deaths annually,[3] while contributing to nearly half of undernutrition worldwide.[4] Poor sanitation makes it hard to keep any valuable foods down. It is also the cause of enormous economic losses, estimated at US$200 billion annually from stunted cognitive development of children, as well as direct health care costs.[5]

Open defecation is particularly dangerous. Women often go into fields at dark, for privacy, but this is when they are most vulnerable. Many girls avoid school in the weeks when they menstruate, because they lack toilets with the privacy to take care of themselves.

A full solution, through conventional means, is a long way away. To reach the UN's Sustainable Development Goal for sanitation by 2030, we would need to spend US$1 trillion. That's triple the current rate of investment by donors, governments and multi-lateral organisations.[6] Investment is likely to pick up as public health organisations emphasise the payoffs from sanitation; recent figures suggest that a country gains US$5.50 in benefits from every dollar invested.[7] But we need the private sector involved as well, and it is encouraging that recent research has shown that by leveraging consumer demand, the private sector can help close the gap for many who lack adequate sanitation.[8, 9]

LIXIL's innovation

The LIXIL Group might seem an unlikely pioneer in sanitation, as toilets are only a part of its overall operations. This Japanese group was formed in 2011, from the combination of Tostem, a maker of window sashes, doors and other building materials; Shin Nikkei, a manufacturer of supplies for skyscrapers and large buildings; Sunwave, a maker of kitchen products; Toyo Exterior, a supplier of residential exterior materials; and INAX, a toilet and bath systems manufacturer. LIXIL has become perhaps the world's largest player in what's called water technology, including owning major plumbing suppliers such as American Standard and Grohe. It is now a US$16 billion company operating in over 150 markets around the world.

Back in 2011, the company used social purpose as one of the ways to engage employees from legacy businesses to feel part of a unified company. Jin Montesano, the chief public affairs officer, said "We found, early on, that to be 'one LIXIL' we needed a true north to engage employees and align them in the same direction."[10] The guiding mission was to help every person on the planet to have a better home.

That includes some of the most vulnerable people in the world. As Montesano explains,

> If that better home is a new kitchen for a young couple in Tokyo, that's fantastic and we can help them. But it should also be for the family in Tanzania that gets their first basic toilet when they hadn't had one before.[11]

LIXIL's marketers saw many organisations raising awareness, but consumers that sought better sanitation lacked an appropriate product.

Accordingly, in 2013 LIXIL developed SATO, short for "Safe Toilet", designed from the ground up to be desirable and affordable for many who lack a basic toilet, costing between US$3–5 retail (see Figure 11.1). This is a crouching, "pour-flush" toilet, where faeces and urine that collect on the self-sealing trap door are flushed through with a small volume of water, some of which remains on the trap, forming an air-tight water seal. LIXIL tested the product for quality and durability up to the standards of American Standard's labs in New Jersey. As of 2018, 1.8 million SATO pans have been installed and used by 9 million people in 25 countries across Africa and Asia. Some additional products provide sitting toilets or connections to multiple toilet pits or piped sewer systems.

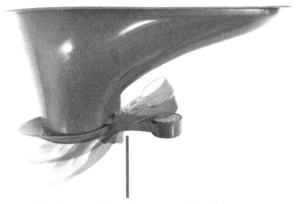

Self-sealing trap door - keeps away flies, insects,
odours, and saves water

Figure 11.1 The SATO toilet, developed by LIXIL, 2013.

LIXIL launched SATO as a sheltered, five-year investment. The Gates
Foundation provided supplemental funding, as SATO met two key objectives: it required no central plumbing infrastructure, and it was affordable to
the poorest communities. After all, one of the problems with providing free
toilets to schools and other institutions is that the recipients would sell the
toilets for cash. LIXIL put the product under a separate social sanitation initiatives department, with the goal of becoming a break-even brand after five
years.

The goal was to use company expertise to develop what the world needs
for the poorest of the poor. But LIXIL also saw basic sanitation as a long-
term business growth opportunity – where a single company would make a
US$5000 toilet and a US$5 toilet.

Behaviour change

LIXIL's marketers designed the SATO pans according to the behavioural
context of its users. After all, a key advantage of the brand-led approach is
that the company sees the intended audience as consumers making their own
choices, not as beneficiaries. Therefore they spent time understanding the
situation on the ground, as you do not want product innovation that radically
changes the customs and traditions of a community.

The marketers therefore rejected the usual messages of improved health as
a reason to use a toilet. Researchers had already found these ineffective in
many settings.[12, 13] Instead they focused on the improved experience of using
the toilet. With SATO, it was smell- and fly-free, as well as easier to clean
than traditional cement slabs. It could therefore be used within or close to the

Figure 11.2 The key marketing messages for the SATO toilet.

home. To overcome the scepticism against putting a toilet there, they put out materials that showcased the product in homes. These messages helped users overcome their reservations and experience the great difference in the user experience (see Figure 11.2).[14]

Through this combination of an innovative product and strong messaging, SATO pans encouraged mass behavioural change on sanitation. People could now use an affordable, high-quality, easy-to-clean toilet instead of cement slabs, shared latrines or open defecation. This home-based approach complements the work of Domestos, described in Chapter 1, in boosting sanitation by enabling better cleaning of school facilities.

SC Johnson's Mr Muscle is another brand of bathroom cleaner that similarly addressed sanitation. In 2007, it worked with partner NGOs in Kenya to improve urban sanitation through the Community Cleaning Services (CCS) model in Nairobi slums. The model co-created toilet-cleaning "microfranchises" with underemployed youths, who received training, supplies and marketing support.[15] The goal was to expand services based on SC Johnson products to create entrepreneurial opportunities and provide cleaner, safer homes.

Cleaning toilets shared by multiple households creates challenges, as most often there is some kind of cleaning rotation amongst users, and these are hard to enforce and frequently lead to conflict. Instead, hiring an outside service that everyone pays for equally may solve this challenge. To get costs down, packaging had to be re-usable and shipped in bulk. SC Johnson packaged the optimal existing formulas of Mr Muscle cleaners and sent them to Kenya in barrels, not in cases of consumer packaging. Because the toilets were shared by multiple families, so was the cost of the service. The average residential client paid US$0.18 per week, less than a bottle of soda.[16] Over time the programme worked well enough for local governments and NGOs to ask for an expansion to public (pay per use) toilets.

In 2010, however, SC Johnson decided to stop investing in the programme. While the programme had delivered local impact, it was not meeting financial objectives as a business and could no longer continue as a solely mission-based project. CCS continues to operate in Nairobi, without direct SC Johnson support, and is looking to partner with other toilet-based brands. By 2012, the programme had trained more than 200 young people in sanitation service provision and business management, with the CCS mobile cleaning team cleaning nearly 800 toilets.

As the leader of the initiative, Justin DeKoszmovszky says:

> What strikes me the most in retrospect about the CCS experience is that we iterated and co-created with the community, which was challenging and the resulting model was complex. But that complexity gives CCS the resilience and agility necessary to drive impact in dynamic communities and on multiple key issues, including: youth employment, health & hygiene, circular economy, packaging waste in consumer goods.[17]

More recently, Firmenich, the second largest flavour and fragrance company in the world, co-sponsored a study with the Bill and Melinda Gates Foundation on malodour and sanitation decision-making in low-income communities.[18] The study itself was interesting for dispensing with conventional research approaches. Conducted by Archipel&Co, a consulting firm, it used young, under-employed adults from underprivileged communities to interview their peers. This peer-to-peer approach can offer more reliable qualitative and quantitative data by embedding epistemic privilege in the survey design, implementation and analysis.

The study concluded that bad odour and dirtiness were major reasons for people choosing open defecation over using existing toilets. Aid organisations had a misconception that poor people were not bothered about smell. David Menasce, Managing Partner at Archipel&Co, explained,

> What we are now able to show is that even if we have daily exposure to it, we are repulsed by the smell of human waste and will choose more dangerous sanitation solutions, like open defecation, to avoid it. It is completely logical but somehow had been forgotten by many working in sanitation – infrastructure and hardware won't solve the problem without maintenance and software.[19]

Firmenich has responded to the sanitation challenge by developing new fragrance technologies to combat malodour, some of which are now available to low-income consumers in Bangladesh, India and South Africa.[20]

Advocacy

LIXIL has been a major supporter of the UN's World Toilet Day, held annually on 19 November. Many people in affluent countries do not understand the effects of poor sanitation, so the company explains that it affects education, gender equality and safety. There is a multiplier effect when families can access a basic working toilet – it can change entire communities. The company has also co-hosted the annual World Toilet Summit, and it works especially on generating awareness in Japan – a large market for fundraising partners such as UNICEF.

LIXIL's other main path for advocacy is the Toilet Board Coalition. Established in 2015, the coalition is a business-led platform focused on bringing business solutions to Sustainable Development Goal 6: universal access to sanitation. The coalition began with its flagship programme, the Toilet Accelerator. CEO Cheryl Hicks explains,

> For future growth, many businesses need every person on the planet to have access to a toilet and a bathroom. Large businesses know how to achieve scale, and small businesses understand the innovations needed on the ground in their local markets. Partnerships between large and small businesses to scale new innovative approaches to access to sanitation is a win–win.[21]

LIXIL was a founding member representing toilet hardware, with Domestos/Unilever for cleaning products, Kimberley Clark for sanitary paper and Firmenich for odour control.

The coalition members see the sanitation economy as a new marketplace for innovation. To make toilets economically viable, businesses need to identify new value streams from sanitation – such as the capture of waste for reuse and conversion into water, energy or nutrients. Digitising sanitation and capturing data is another way to derive value and to ensure that sanitation systems work more efficiently. The coalition also argues that inadequate sanitation limits the growth of business in the area, so the surrounding companies should have a strong interest in sanitation just as in other aspects of environmental sustainability.

To verify these ideas, LIXIL carried out a three-year research programme on the true cost of poor sanitation[22] in partnership with WaterAid and Oxford Analytics. The study estimated that inadequate sanitation cost the global economy US$222 billion in 2015. The Toilet Board Coalition estimates that the Sanitation Economy – the business value from toilet infrastructure, products, toilet resource reuse and data capture, could be worth US$62 billion a year in India alone by 2021.

From this initial work, the coalition has been engaging multi-lateral organisations and governments, from the World Bank to UNICEF. It has also worked with additional companies, emphasising the need to go beyond writing cheques. As Hicks argues,

> At the Toilet Board Coalition our members focus on the value proposition – solutions that business can bring to sanitation. And increasingly we look at solutions that new sanitation economy approaches can bring to the broader business – via circular sanitation and smart sanitation. Sanitation is every business's business, beyond CSR to material core business issues. We say, "Sanitation needs to be a part of every company's sustainability strategy. Businesses employ millions of people who all need sanitation, and whose toilet resources could provide water, energy and nutrients back to the business."[23]

After all, she added, "the sanitation economy has the potential to transform sanitation from unaffordable public costs to sustainable business opportunities".[24]

This sanitation economy is starting to take off, with a variety of growth opportunities. These range from individual end-user products, to processing by-products in a "circular sanitation economy", to using data for better service delivery in a "smart sanitation economy".

Sanergy, a Kenyan start-up, introduced high-quality public toilets in Nairobi, and they were so popular that landlords leased the toilets to provide an efficient service to their tenants.[25] Pit Vidura, a Rwandan start-up, developed tools to automate the high-risk manual emptying of faecal pits, and to capture the value of the removed material.[26] And entire cities might embrace smart sanitation with sensors in sewer lines to detect disease outbreaks, as well as to optimise service delivery and maintenance across a widely distributed network of public toilets. More possibilities will emerge as poor sanitation is framed as an opportunity, rather than a problem.

Partnerships

LIXIL has other partners besides the Gates Foundation. UNICEF had been promoting its own model of providing subsidised toilets, but with LIXIL it shifted towards a co-creation approach with the private sector. The goal now is to create a competitive sanitation market, where the best products flourish and consumers choose the best solution for them.[27]

To help get there, as toilets become more affordable, governments are exploring ways to subsidise the products for different income levels. Several national-level partnerships have recently started, from Swachh Bharat in India[28] to the National Sanitation programme in Tanzania.[29]

LIXIL benefits from its size in negotiating partnerships. As Montesano points out,

When organisations enter into a conversation with us, they're really interested in what is going on within SATO, but they're super attracted to partnering with us because it's owned by LIXIL. LIXIL is a bit of an insurance policy, with lots of financial security and also expertise. SATO isn't just a purpose-driven brand, LIXIL is a purpose driven corporation.[30]

LIXIL in turn benefits from the partnerships in testing new concepts for toilets and related hardware.

Measurement

SATO pans are still too new for LIXIL to have done much measurement. Another challenge is that the toilet itself is not enough to meet the SDG goal on sanitation. While SATO qualifies as a basic toilet, the goal also calls for safely managed sanitation, with the containment and disposal of human excrement through connection to a sewer, an on-site emptiable containment solution like a septic tank, or treatment and storage long-term on site. LIXIL is working with partners to connect the pan as a modular system with these disposal options. For example, several entrepreneurs in Ghana have already integrated SATO into their bio-digester designs and offerings.

Measurement would confirm two claims for the toilet. The first is that by having a more pleasant toilet, it should greatly reduce open defecation. The Firmenich study conducted by Archipel&Co on malodour and sanitation decision-making points to this being likely.[31] The second, for families now using cement slabs, is that SATO offers a more cleanable surface, and therefore reduces the spread of disease. Partnerships should help here, and UNICEF is already working with LIXIL on joint monitoring, and the Gates Foundation is supporting work to understand how SATO pans drive these two claims.

As for the business side, SATO marketers are using both financial and non-financial metrics such as sales targets, revenue generated and the number of lives improved through basic sanitation with SATO. And unlike with highly subsidised or free toilets, when families or communities buy the SATO toilets, they are much more likely to actually use them. Therefore, unit sales are a plausible indicator of improvements to public health. SATO's marketers are also assessing brand equity, given SATO's higher quality than previous toilets for low-income households, for which willingness to pay was found to be low.

LIXIL's primary objective for creating a social sanitation initiative is to support the goals of UN SDG 6, but other brands within LIXIL's portfolio are playing a role in supporting this objective. INAX, a US$6 billion brand in Japan and the maker of high-tech luxury toilets, launched a campaign in 2017 called "Toilets for All". For a six-month period, every LIXIL shower and toilet sold in Japan resulted in the donation of a SATO toilet in a developing country. Montesano says such promotions are especially effective with distributors.

> Our salesforce was motivated by the opportunity to have a very different conversation with their customers. Instead of talking about the difference in technical features between our products versus competitor products, we could talk about our commitment to tackling global sanitation challenges for the 1.3 billion people without access to a basic toilet. I think distributors supported our campaign because they were, in turn, contributing to the broader goals to tackle sanitation issues. They also viewed our commitment to sanitation as a unique or differentiating point compared with other manufacturers.

Looking ahead

LIXIL and other brands described here are improving sanitation in ways that governments and non-profits cannot. These products and programmes have yet to prove themselves as long-term solutions and scale up to match the severity of the problem. But more important than any single programme is the fact that brands are making progress in demonstrating the power of the private sector. Rather than wait for slow improvement from the other sectors, these brands have tackled the problem and developed promising commercial solutions. They have built momentum that should overcome the inevitable setbacks.

Besides the SATO pan, LIXIL is developing container-based treatment solutions for urban slum environments, improvements to sewer-style systems that more efficiently handle waste in urban environments, and new kinds of materials and products that can improve other aspects of sanitation at an affordable cost using only sustainable materials and resources. For example, they are making linings and superstructures from reclaimed ocean plastic that are durable and affordable. They have a team of material scientists, engineers and product developers working on reaching the world's poorest consumers with marketable products. That's the sign of a brand on a mission.

Notes

1 WHO (2019). *Sanitation – Key Facts*. Available at: www.who.int/news-room/fact-sheets/detail/sanitation (Accessed: 4 January 2020).
2 Tidwell, J. B. *et al.* (2019). "Theory-driven formative research on on-site, shared sanitation quality improvement among landlords and tenants in peri-urban Lusaka, Zambia", *International Journal of Environmental Health Research*, 29(3), pp. 312–325. doi: 10.1080/09603123.2018.1543798.
3 Prüss-Üstün, A. *et al.* (2014). "Burden of disease from inadequate water, sanitation and hygiene in low- and middle-income settings: a retrospective analysis of data from 145 countries", *Tropical Medicine & International Health: TM & IH*, 19(8), pp. 894–905. doi: 10.1111/tmi.12329.

4 Benetti, A. D. (2007). "Preventing disease through healthy environments: towards an estimate of the environmental burden of disease", *Engenharia Sanitaria e Ambiental*, 12(2), pp. 115–116. doi: 10.1590/s1413-41522007000200001.
5 LIXIL, WaterAid and Oxford Economics (2016). *The true cost of poor sanitation*. Available at: www.ircwash.org/resources/true-cost-poor-sanitation.
6 Hutton, G. and Varughese, M. C. (2016). "The costs of meeting the 2030 sustainable development goal targets on drinking water sanitation, and hygiene". 103171. *The World Bank*, pp. 1–64. Available at: http://documents.worldbank.org/curated/en/415441467988938343/The-costs-of-meeting-the-2030-sustainable-development-goal-targets-on-drinking-water-sanitation-and-hygiene (Accessed: 5 January 2020).
7 Hutton, G. (2013). "Global costs and benefits of reaching universal coverage of sanitation and drinking-water supply", *Journal of Water and Health*, 11, pp. 1–12. doi: 10.2166/wh.2012.105.
8 Tidwell, J. B. *et al.* (2019). "Understanding the Economic Case for Consumer-Driven Sanitation Quality Improvement Using Stated and Revealed Preference Methods in Peri-Urban Lusaka, Zambia", *Social Science & Medicine*, 232, pp. 139–147. https://doi.org/10.1016/j.socscimed.2019.04.046.
9 Tidwell, J. B. et al. (2019). "Understanding the Economic Case for Consumer-Driven Sanitation Quality Improvement Using Stated and Revealed Preference Methods in Peri-Urban Lusaka, Zambia", Social Science & Medicine, 232, pp. 139–147. https://doi.org/10.1016/j.socscimed.2019.04.046.
10 Montesano, J. (2019). Personal interview.
11 Ibid.
12 Jenkins, M. (2004). *Who Buys Latrines, Where and Why?* Water and Sanitation Program, pp. 1–12.
13 Jenkins, M. W. and Curtis, V. (2005). "Achieving the 'good life': why some people want latrines in rural Benin", *Soc Sci Med*, 61(11), pp. 2446–2459. doi: 10.1016/j.socscimed.2005.04.036.
14 Jin Montesano. Personal interview. January 2019
15 Council, W. B. (2012). "Tackling the challenges of urban sanitation: A social enterprise model", *Guardian*, 10 April. Available at: www.theguardian.com/sustainable-business/urban-sanitation-social-enterprise-model (Accessed: 4 January 2020).
16 Ibid.
17 DeKoszmovszky, J (2019). Personal interview.
18 Firmenich (2016). *Firmenich showcases its scientific excellence in mal-odor control on World Toilet Day*. Available at: www.firmenich.com/en_INT/company/news/World-Toilet-Day-2016.html (Accessed: 4 January 2020).
19 Menasce, D. (2019). Personal email.
20 Firmenich (2019). *Firmenich proves malodor control is a key lever in tackling today's sanitation crisis*. Available at: www.firmenich.com/en_INT/company/news/Firmenich-proves-malodor-control-is-a-key-lever-in-tackling-today-sanitation-crisis.html (Accessed: 4 January 2020).
21 Hicks, C. (2019). Personal interview.
22 LIXIL, WaterAid and Oxford Economics (2016). *The true cost of poor sanitation*. Available at: www.ircwash.org/resources/true-cost-poor-sanitation.
23 Hicks, C. (2019). Personal interview.
24 Ibid.
25 *Sanergy Nairobi*. www.sanergy.com/impact/ (Accessed: 4 January 2020).
26 Morales, D. (2018). "These women can really handle their shit…and yours too", *Medium*. Available at: https://medium.com/@PitVidura/these-women-can-really-handle-their-shit-and-yours-too-5e896154a5d3 (Accessed: 4 January 2020).
27 Montesano, J. (2019). Personal interview.

28 *Swachh Bharat* (no date). Available at: https://swachhbharat.mygov.in/ (Accessed: 5 January 2020).

29 *LIXIL Marks a Year of Partnership with UNICEF* (no date). Available at: www.3blmedia.com/News/LIXIL-Marks-Year-Partnership-UNICEF-Working-Together-Kenya-Ethiopia-Tanzania (Accessed: 5 January 2020).

30 Montesano, J. (2019). Personal interview.

31 Firmenich (2019). *Firmenich proves malodor control is a key lever in tackling today's sanitation crisis.* Available at: www.firmenich.com/en_INT/company/news/Firmenich-proves-malodor-control-is-a-key-lever-in-tackling-today-sanitation-crisis.html (Accessed: 4 January 2020).

12 Winning support within the corporation

Brands on a mission need to do more than win over partners and consumers. They must also convince their colleagues across the corporation to support their efforts. After all, brands rely on the larger organisation for budgets and special expertise. The imprimatur of the big corporation is often essential to gaining partnerships with nervous governments and non-profits.

In seeking corporate support, marketers need to keep in mind the structures and constraints that all large corporations work through. They need to become intrapreneurs roaming their large organisation in search of supportive leaders and colleagues. Big corporations can be difficult to navigate, but if you get its machinery going towards your social purpose, you can achieve everything that you need.

Supportive leadership

Ideally, your CEO or senior team has taken a strong stand in favour of social purpose. That is what we had at Lifebuoy, where Paul Polman in 2010 boldly committed Unilever as a whole to three main goals for sustainable living, including helping a billion people take action to improve their health and well-being. That goal gave the Lifebuoy brand strong headquarters support for our sub-goal of giving a billion people our messages on handwashing with soap. Polman agreed to travel across the globe, wearing a red Lifebuoy t-shirt and washing his hands with children in primary schools. His example won us enormous support from the rest of the organisation, although as you will see later in the chapter, we still had to struggle in some areas.

If you do not already have support from the leadership, you need to work on getting it. You can offer the arguments from Chapter 1 on why brands need social purpose now. You can say that executives in many of the most prominent companies are now rethinking what makes for sustainable success and are including new factors such as social purpose. They are also combining social and commercial impact with white-space strategies, such as building factories in emerging markets. In the short term, manufacturing costs will rise, but in the medium to long-term, those costs will come down, and the brand will gain more customers and have more success in changing behaviours among consumers.

Supportive, brave leaders see purpose as an investment, not a cost. They make sure the brand "do", not just the brand "say", are fully funded and feeding into each other, to guide the brand's overall journey for purpose. They help you think about holistic solutions, not just sales. They can listen and discuss how to push forward the solutions.

I asked Paul Polman about the characteristics of good leaders in a purpose-driven corporation. He said these are the same as the obligations we have with human rights. The first is to treat everyone with dignity. The second one is equity – that we help to give everyone the same basic opportunities. And the third is for compassion – putting yourself in the shoes of others who are less fortunate. He added that leadership is with the heart as well as the head.

Securing a proof point

One barrier to getting support might simply be your colleagues' inability to visualise a brand with purpose at all. If this is the case, it is helpful to land some kind of programme in a market early, no matter how small. People need to see how a social purpose can help a brand with sales, directly and indirectly. Otherwise they will assume it is no different from the usual CSR cheque-writing activity, and they will pigeonhole your work away. You may need to team up with other brands to better address a specific market.

As any purpose-driven marketer can tell you, making a real difference takes time, and lots of learning. It is vital to get a programme started early, to initiate the learning and to demonstrate a brand on a mission. That includes starting the measurement now – not because success depends on immediate results, but it helps with learning as well as early wins.

Justin Apsey embraced social purpose early, as General Manager for Unilever in East Africa. He oversees several brand teams, and he knows this is a long-term game – purpose requires longevity. He says, "I am not going to judge you on this after one quarter, or even one year. I am going to judge you over three years."[1]

From the start, however, he asks his teams some tough questions: What's the behaviour change you want to drive? What goals are you targeting that will drive affiliation and sales with your brand? How will you make money eventually – because if you do not, you will not be investing in any longer-term projects or finding resources for partnerships.

You may have to do some strategising about where to start. Suppose you are targeting an emerging market with enormous long-term potential. Do you start with urban areas, which are easier to reach and more likely to generate short-term gains? Or do you go for the rural consumers, to become the first mover and educate consumers on a behaviour that might not otherwise happen at all?

Different markets have different needs in terms of public health. We already discussed in Chapter 3 the Ethiopia challenge around lack of penetration of toothpaste and non-existent toothbrushing habits. By contrast, nearly all of the 29 million Ghanaians use toothbrushes and toothpaste. However, many of them brush only once a day, rather than the recommended two to three times.

If you are looking for a good demonstration project early on, do you go with urban Ghanaians, rural Ethiopians or somewhere in between? Each target involves a different mix of marketing messages and channels. This was a real decision for Unilever's Pepsodent brand (see Chapter 1). Also, do not forget logistics. Due to high import costs, for Ethiopia, Unilever had to build a local manufacturing facility for toothpaste locally.

Pepsodent started in Ghana where it combined the message about greater brushing frequency with a discount on a larger size toothpaste. Ghanaians got a 200-gram tube for the same price as the usual 175-grammes. The promotion boosted sales (and presumably brushing frequency) substantially, helping to defray the extra cost of the larger size. In addition, the behaviour change programme in schools and villages has been the largest in Ghana, sustaining the promotion with programmes and linking to schools and retailers.

To encourage this kind of innovation even if in another market, Apsey worked with executives to start Unilever's Brighter Future Fund. The fund is tied to a company-wide competition for the most innovative new projects that have potential for integration into the business. Projects must be linked to actual products, and therefore brands.

Another such project was "Jaza Duka" – Swahili for "fill up your store". Pepsodent and other Unilever brands teamed up with Mastercard to boost distribution through small retailers in Kenya. These micro-entrepreneurs lacked the cash to stock their shelves with products and expand their businesses, but banks required formal credit histories and collateral before granting loans. The project combined distribution data from Unilever with analysis from Mastercard to assess the inventory a store had bought from Unilever over time. The analysis showed that many of these retailers were good credit risks, so Mastercard recommended them for micro-loans at Kenya Commercial Bank. As a result, they no longer needed to borrow from informal lenders at high interest rates, which often trapped them in a cycle of debt; and Unilever's brands got better distribution.[2]

To secure enough resources, it is best to launch social mission projects in the first financial quarter, when leaders are in a more expansive mood. You need to convince the executives to take risks in supporting the programme and seeing it grow from one year to the next. Launching later in the year puts too much pressure on immediate results and can lead to purpose-washing – a showy demonstration of social purpose that actually makes little difference in society.

And whilst visionary leaders are not difficult to convince, not all leaders facing financial pressures believe in purpose or have the patience to go through the process that it takes to maintain that purpose.

One organisation is looking to make this process of "convincing" much more straightforward. Givewith describes itself as a social impact technology company, and its model leverages the power of everyday business transactions to generate new sources of funding for non-profit organisations. In November 2019 Givewith announced a partnership with SAP Ariba, the world's largest business-to-business network. The partnership will enable millions of buyers and sellers to easily embed social impact funding directly into their sourcing and procurement processes, as part of the nearly US$3 trillion in commerce and B2B transactions that flow through SAP Ariba procurement platform annually. Using Givewith's proprietary technology, their platform provides companies directly with the measured impact these social impact programmes have on each of the Sustainable Development Goals, in addition to Environmental, Social and Governance ratings (ESG), helping organisations to meet their sustainability goals, as well as creating business value.[3]

As Paul Polizzotto, CEO and Founder of Givewith explains:

> To illustrate how our platform works, I'll give you a real case study. CBS Corporation was looking to buy technology equipment, computers and printers from HP. As part of this new three-year deal, one of the incentives HP offered was to take 2% of the transaction and underwrite social impacts through Givewith. These social impacts aligned with CBS corporate values, helping them to contribute to the UN SDGs, to positively influence their ESG rating, in addition to positively influencing employee retention, investor relations and so on. The Givewith platform pulls together data from a large number of different sources, and provides appropriately matched programmes from our large network of non-profit partners.[4]

Holistic purpose – an all-in approach

While social purpose is likely the biggest opportunity for most consumer brands, marketers should not forget to take care of other important areas. If your brand is doing wonderful things for health and well-being, but filling the world with plastic, you will not be able to maintain your social purpose even within your organisation – not to mention hold an advantage over rivals.

As described in Chapter 2, Dove switched to cruelty-free product testing and lower-impact packaging at the same time it was developing the Real Beauty campaign. Sue Garrard, former Executive Vice President for Sustainability Development at Unilever, points out:

> Of course the marketing focus tends to be much more on the social piece, but consumers are looking at our credentials overall. We have to make sure we are doing the right thing for the planet as well as for mankind, and there isn't a trade-off between these two.[5]

These environmental adjustments are not just the right thing to do, but they also build trust. If consumers think you are doing something social at the expense of the environment, they will suspect you of purpose-washing. Thus Pepsodent, while fighting cavities, also worked with TetraPak for cardboard packaging that is fully recyclable. Other brands have joined partnerships to expand the recycling of waste. That is partly to protect themselves from potential legislation, and to test the use of post-consumer plastics. But it weakens the authenticity of any social mission if you do not address how your brand is polluting the environment.

Another Kenyan project involved supporting a supplier of recycled plastics. Unilever joined with some investor funds to fund the firm's expansion, so it could scale up with a strong and reliable network of waste suppliers. The project won solid support from corporate leaders even though brands outside of Unilever benefitted as well. And Danone also has a great circularity goal, where they aim to offer nutritious, high-quality food and drinks in packaging that is 100 per cent circular by 2025, keeping materials in use and out of nature. This means eliminating the packaging we do not need; innovating so all the packaging we do need is designed to be safely reused, recycled or composted; and ensuring the material we produce stays in the economy and never becomes waste or pollution.[6]

Managing risks to the corporate reputation

Many projects for social purpose involve risky activities that can backfire and damage the reputation of not just the brand, but the overall company. Either the programme itself might make something worse, or a partner might turn out to be disreputable. At Lifebuoy, one of the hardest parts of my job was working with Corporate Communications. Their job is to protect the corporate name, and their first answer to risk taking was most often no.

A particular friction point involved some of the local partnerships that the brand team set up for Lifebuoy. Corporate Communications are generally used to working with bigger budgets, with a CSR mentality and not necessarily linking the spend to business performance – and protecting the overall corporation reputation, trying to prevent any PR crisis and dealing with them if they do happen. Corporate Communication team members often tend not to have worked in a brand, in the field or in public health. Brave bosses were quite often needed to overcome their objections and try to manage the relationships with the external partners they were working for differently.

To overcome this impasse, it is better to have a corporate-level structure that nurtures purpose-driven brands and understands how the brands benefit from wider strategic interests. What happens when purpose goes wrong? What happens to the institutional knowledge? Given the huge amount of work involved in driving change that's needed to meet the SDGs, brands need expertise in communications, government relations, advocacy, policy change, employee engagement and stakeholder engagement, all stemming

from strong campaigning skills. To do this efficiently you need full confidence of the content, which in turn depends on working in an integrated
way with sustainability practitioners in the brand teams. In Unilever that team
doing this work was called the sustainable business team.

By merging or sending central experts into brands, corporations also create
a wider career path and build capability in-house, which is great because it is
very difficult to get this externally. These are people free from the responsibility of delivering for any brand, who can think across the whole company
and assess whether it is delivering. They in turn can hold the organisation's
leadership to account on social purpose, including communications. More
important than the size of this team is its freedom from short-term delivery
challenges. It likely also needs a capability to assess relationships with big partners at a global level, such as the UN.

Securing talent for the future: passion, training and rewarding purpose

Brands on a mission need support from corporate human resources as well.
Human resources (HR) are an important partner for brands on a mission.
The first requirement is people energised by commerce with a social purpose.
Passionate employees will knock down walls to solve issues; they will find
creative ways to succeed, because they are clear and motivated on the goal.
Passion will drive determination, inquisitiveness and curiosity, so long as
people have the licence to move ahead.

Social purpose requires blended disciplines, where business acumen goes
with a strong campaigning mindset and empathy for social justice. Marketers
need to be fully aware of the external world so they can move quickly to
address opportunities. Behavioural psychology is opening up a new world of
possibilities, and more cross-discipline learning is a good thing. Paul Polman,
the former Unilever CEO, has even recommended that marketers get two
masters degrees, an MBA and a master's in public administration, so they are
aware of public-policy dynamics.[7]

There is what I call competencies of the future when it comes to purpose
led brands, and human resources are crucial in fostering what that would look
like. Sangeetha Rajalakshmi, Global Learning Director – Sales and Marketing, says brand marketers need to make tough judgement calls in crafting a
purpose that is meaningful and authentic. And with that they still need to
blend in brand guardianship and brand equity.[8] Another key skill that HR
can help with is putting cross-sectoral collaboration as a key skill for marketers. Most marketers are used to working with agencies that they pay, which is
entirely different. Partners can be critics even as they carry out joint projects.
Purpose-driven brands also depend on influencers, so marketers need to work
with people with their own voice and point of view. Both kinds of relationships require extended commitments that run against the short-termism of
most marketers.

The second requirement from HR is to think of structures of the future which give these employees a wider career path, which will have more public-sector expertise embedded into divisions and brands, while developing in-house talent shared across the company. Purpose-driven marketers need to learn from public health research and stay connected to social impact on the ground. Corporations may also encourage time away in the non-profit and governmental sectors to build, share knowledge and understand the difference in pace of work and culture.

In turn, a strong social purpose will help companies attract talented employees. As Generation Z looks to enter the job market in the 2020s, they are likely to give social and environmental impact as much weight as financial rewards when choosing an employer. Wise businesses are recruiting based on alignment with values and passions over skillsets and experience. HR can help by tying financial rewards and recognition to delivering on the social purpose.

The more brands and companies commit to a social purpose, the easier it will be to develop people with these blended disciplines. Most corporations are set up for people with commercial skills. There's a clear career path based on the expectation that no one stays with a specific brand for long. However, people with the skills for social purpose do not have a clear path. The organisations who want to invest in purpose should think about career succession for these professionals.

The marketing mindset is very much about delivering in the short term and moving up the corporate ladder. That means it is hard to make marketers accountable on the purpose journey, to get them to innovate for the longer term. One reason we were able to achieve so much at Lifebuoy was that I stayed for ten years on the brand, serving as the "guardian of the good" as we kept innovating with the School of Five, digital messaging and television advertising. On Dove, Steve Miles also stayed ten years. It takes that long to really benefit from the maturity of the journey.

From my experience at Lifebuoy, I know that talented people in public health are attracted to working in industry. They realise the great things that big companies can accomplish. But once they arrive, they often burn out from the difficulty of working with the rest of the organisation. They spend a lot of time inspiring the business internally, but then they themselves need inspiration. Over time, they are likely to lose their passion and stop knocking over walls. They will lose their curiosity about the world around them – which is essential to work in brands. As Alan Jope, current CEO of Unilever, has said: "If you're not curious about the human condition and the hopes, fears, needs, dreams of people, you shouldn't be in marketing."[9]

The risk is also that these mission-driven people will stop inspiring creative people coming up in the traditional marketing path. Those people are just as important as the ones who start off with social purpose, because commercial skills will always be essential.

The final part of winning support from the corporation involves rewards for performance. Can you tie rewards and bonuses to building coalitions with the rest of the organisation, while keeping the brand's work on track? How do you get the rest of the organisation to respect your work on social purpose?

Internal company awards are one tool that can be used to recognise – and signpost to the rest of the organisation – good work and commitment to social purpose. But to ensure they are truly meaningful, these awards should be fully connected into the company strategy and connected to a career path.

Instead of relying on conventional rewards, marketers will need a good deal of self-awareness and exposure to different areas. Emmanuel Faber, the CEO of Danone, stresses this point about managers asking themselves the right questions:

> What are my areas of development? Self-awareness is necessary to take risks without fear. It's much easier to rely on a communications team, marketing guidelines, and a bright outside agency. But that's not how brands are going to act tomorrow. Marketers will need a backbone, not the traditional organisational support. They'll rely on their values and their collective awareness as a company, as a brand, as a tribe, and as a person.[10]

And far from dividing an organisation, he says, those identities should foster collaboration: "If I'm okay with who I am, then I'm okay with who you are, and we can discuss and create things together much more than today."[11]

Ideally, brands on mission would work in a corporate structure and strategy that helps them thrive over time. Having a clear corporate vision encourages brands to be creative with partners and donors, to try various models of blended financing, and to explore grassroots initiatives. The brands, and the larger corporation, in turn gain an edge over rivals that enables deeper engagement with consumers and partners. Publicly stated goals for social purpose – as for example Unilever announced in 2010 - provide a further boost because they make the company accountable for the success of these brands. Headquarters will help with sharing lessons across the organisation and in arranging partnerships.

That is especially important, of course, if you happen to work in a corporation which had a difficult past with the marketing infant formula but still has amazing brands in their portfolio. Knowing you can still make a difference is absolutely critical. Brands on a mission need to build that corporate awareness and enlist broad internal support.

Exercise

How to make a persuasive argument for your social purpose

If you are advocating in favour of a corporate commitment to a social purpose, it's important to be upfront about the challenges and risks, but also to emphasise the enormous potential benefits. Here is a blueprint for discussion, whether you are advocating to a department, a unit, the CEO or the board. Be clear about what you are asking them to do, write a convincing five-minute pitch on why they should do this and how the risk can be mitigated.

To be sure ...

Yes, there are challenges and risks:

> Achieving impact on a social goal takes time and a huge amount of work from functions as diverse as product development, marketing, sales, communications, legal, government relations, and human resources. Corporate-level commitment is a must.

> Projects might backfire; partners might turn out to be bad, you may want to drive a social purpose, but you first need to fix content of products.

> Stakeholders may accuse the company of inauthentic commitment. Brands need to do the real intellectual work of crafting a purpose that serves both vulnerable people and the business.

But think of the advantages ...

Across the spectrum of global corporations, brands are rethinking what makes for sustainable success, and more and more are focusing on social purpose.

Social purpose is an investment, not a cost. Focusing on social purpose may help the company:

- Differentiate itself in the marketplace – brands are usually rewarded by their customers.
- Gain customers.
- Stake positions in future markets and develop larger markets for the brand.
- Gain valuable knowledge and capabilities, such as how to aid start-ups and how to be more innovative about products and channels.
- Attract and retain talented employees – social purpose aids recruitment, makes employees feel better about working at the company and creates new career paths within the company.
- Demonstrate to the world many of its best qualities, including expertise, knowledge and commitment.

And the longer a company commits to a social purpose, the easier it gets and the bigger the rewards are, because you cannot even anticipate what the mission will do in terms of opening doors.

Notes

1 Apsey, J. (2019). Personal interview.
2 Mastercard (no date). "Jaza Duka", *Mastercard*. Available at: https://newsroom. mastercard.com/videos/jaza-duka/ (Accessed: 3 January 2020).
3 Polizzotto, P. (2019). "Walking the Talk: How Companies Are Delivering on the Promise of Social Impact", *Sustainable Brands*. Available at: https://sustainable brands.com/read/collaboration-cocreation/walking-the-talk-how-companies-are-delivering-on-the-promise-of-social-impact (Accessed: 6 January 2020).
4 Polizzotto, P. (2019). Personal interview.
5 Garrard, S. (2019). Personal interview.
6 Danone (2019). *Circular economy model*, Available at: www.danone.com/impact/ planet/packaging-positive-circular-economy.html (Accessed: 4 January 2020).
7 Polman, P. and Ruggie, J. (2019). "The Business Case of Sustainable Development: a roundtable discussion". *Harvard Kennedy School*, 11 April 2019.
8 Rajalakshmi, S. (2019). Personal interview.
9 Jope, A. (2019). Personal Interview.
10 Faber, E. (2019). Personal interview.
11 Ibid.

13 How processed food brands can gain a social purpose

The public health challenge of this century and the biggest opportunity for brands

So far we have looked at products with a direct link to social problems, such as soaps, toothpastes and condoms. It is easier to make a case for social purpose there. We have also looked at products that do not help directly with social problems, such as beer, but can raise awareness against challenges such as domestic violence. But what about products that have been part of the social problems in the past and want to contribute towards a better future?

Processed food has become a dirty word. It is tied to obesity, diabetes, cancer and heart disease – almost every major health issue plaguing wealthier countries. Poorer countries are coming under a double burden of malnutrition, with the lack of nutritious food and the abundance of junk food leading to stunted growth and obesity in the same populations. Something perceived as the opposite – whole foods have found their way into the names of everything from diets (for example, *Whole 30*) to even entire chains of retail stores (for example, *Whole Foods Market*).

Unfortunately, a diet free from processed food is unrealistic for much of the world. Whole foods can be more expensive and time consuming to prepare, and in some cases no healthier than the processed alternatives. Many people, especially in poorer countries, simply cannot afford to eat a varied and fresh diet. With fruits and vegetables unaffordable, and accounting for over 52 per cent of share of capita household income per day in countries like Bangladesh, India, Zimbabwe and Pakistan, processed foods are a part of daily life.[1] Beyond their direct cost savings, processed foods have given us discretionary time – the average time an American, for example, spends on food preparation has fallen from three hours a day in the 1920s to 37 minutes in 2014.[2] In addition, a huge benefit of processing is enrichment and fortification, making it easier and more accessible to get critical micronutrients.[3]

All whole foods are not created equal. Animal-based foods may have good nutritional properties (albeit in the west the portion sizes are often too high, and they are high in saturated fats and trans fats) but they have a relatively high environmental burden. Plant-based or lab-grown meat substitutes, for example, may have far less environmental impact than the equivalent meat. Moving away from processing can also lead to infectious disease outbreaks, commonly seen in raw milk. Another benefit of processing is the reduction in food spoilage, both directly by preserving fresh food and also through utilising less desirable parts by transforming them into palatable formats. Processing food is actually an old practice, involving drying, salting and often smoking. Modern methods for preservation are arguably healthier in many ways.

Indeed, "processed" is a blunt term. The NOVA classification[4] puts foods into four categories: unprocessed or minimally processed foods (seeds, fruits, eggs or milk); processed culinary ingredients (vegetable oils, butter and salt); processed foods made from combining these two groups (breads, cheeses or salted nuts); and ultra-processed foods (sugar-sweetened beverages, frozen dinners and deli meats). The proportion of ultra-processed foods has risen rapidly, mostly because of transnational food production and sales through retail and fast food service outlets.[5]

Common ingredients used in ultra-processed foods are indeed cause for serious concern. These foods often contain sugars, saturated fats and salts, all of which are associated with negative health impacts including obesity, hypertension, cardiovascular disease, diabetes and cancer.[6, 7, 8] These ingredients have been shown to increase consumption and some like sugar also have addictive properties. Salt intake is more associated with taste preference, decline in taste sensitivity, high blood pressure amongst other things. Processed foods, such as ready-to-eat meals, may reduce feelings of fullness, and come with higher glycaemic response leading to diabetes.[9] Products filled with salt, sugar and saturated fat lead consumers to desire products with these ingredients more, and drastically overconsume them. Our natural taste sensitivities, developed to ensure adequate nutrition in environments with limited foods, lead us astray in environments of abundance and ultra-processing. Processing of ingredients can enable less expensive replacements with similar taste and mouthfeel. Comprehensive reviews have found that the major food companies have aggressively marketed these products, influencing the beliefs, behaviours and health outcomes of children – while using little of their creativity, resources, and political and market heft to promote healthy diets.[10]

Yet debates over processing and health have often been waged not on the basis of evidence, but behind closed doors through lobbying and cover-ups. At a meeting in 1999, several major food companies and ingredient suppliers were shown mounting evidence of the harms caused by processed foods. Yet the food company executives present decided to do nothing, claiming that they simply offered a range of products to consumers, who could decide which best met their needs. Indeed, food companies waited a very long time to eliminate trans fats from their ingredients. Regulatory agencies are woefully under resourced and cannot meaningfully constrain companies. So, it is understandable that many consumers, not to mention NGOs and governments, look on food brands with suspicion.[11]

With this history of misinformation and broken trust, how can a food brand take on a mission of improving public health through better nutrition? Can a brand that sold unhealthy options in the past evolve to become a leader in securing our future?

For Lawrence Haddad, economist and executive director of the Global Alliance for Improved Nutrition, the answer is yes:

> I think you can, if you're honest and authentic about it. You can say look, the world was different back then. We now know a lot more about nutrition for mortality and morbidity. And even if consumer preferences don't change that much, we can be a driver of preferences as well as a responder to them. You can reinvent yourself. It's just whether it's done in a cynical or minimalist way, or in a wholehearted, "for the right reasons" way. The smart brands will want to position themselves as the number one healthy processed food company in the world.[12]

Brands can help to make whole foods tastier, encourage proper use of seasonings and portion sizes, and increase dietary diversity. They can forge partnerships to increase impact, though this may be challenging due to the scepticism of other actors and complicated by other brands in the same company having different positioning. They can advocate for a level playing field, so that promoting healthier foods does not lead to competitive disadvantage. Brands can even help in measuring nutritional impact beyond product ingredients, to understand how meals and whole diets are consumed. This chapter looks at initiatives from two processed food brands that I have had a chance to work on directly during my African stint. These are Blue Band and its owner Upfield and Unilever's Knorr brand.

Blue Band is a margarine spread first introduced in 1924, and part of the original group of brands that comprised the "Uni" of Unilever. In 2018 the company spun off all of its plant-based spreads as Upfield and sold it to the investment firm KKR in 2018. Upfield, which includes Country Crock, Flora and Rama, is the largest global producer of plant-based spreads, with sales in 95 countries. Over time, these brands have eliminated hydrogenated oils and trans fats, reduced salt and saturated fats, and added omega-3 fatty acids and plant sterols to reduce cholesterol.[13] Upfield have had a strong focus on incorporating only natural ingredients. Margarine is now seen as superior to butter for health and environmental impact. However, its consumption has been declining in developed markets and merely stable in emerging markets.[14]

Changing behaviour

As mentioned in Chapter 3, in the example of Knorr's bouillon mix, brands start with some credibility on taste and preference. Consumers are more likely to trust a brand's recommendation for healthy eating than a non-profit's, very simply because they offer a product. From that basis, brands can promote healthier eating in three ways. One is simply to make its existing product healthier. Second, it can boost consumption of that healthier food through marketing. And third, it can build on the understanding that people mostly eat several foods together, in a meal, and thus drive changes beyond the products it produces.

Walter Willet, professor at the Harvard School of Public Health, explains that "It helps to have a healthy product to start with but important to state that in the same company you can have healthy and unhealthy products in the portfolio of brands."[15] Take PepsiCo, for example, which has sugar-sweetened soft drinks and also Quaker Oats in its portfolio. The parent company can promote whole grains and other sound behaviours with Quaker Oats, but the economics can be challenging, due to the low cost to produce a can of soft drink. As Willett points out, he is all for marketing to promote foods that are both healthy and sustainable but "it's not an even match for the US$10 billion a year for soda promotion".[16]

Indeed, the main challenge comes down to economics. Kamel Chida, deputy director of Strategy, Private Sector Partnership Development for Nutrition at the Gates Foundation, laments that,

> A lot of the start-ups that have mushroomed over the last ten years are innovating for rich consumers. Diversifying diet comes at a cost, and lower income consumers don't have an incremental budget to pay for it. In pushing the public health message of "please diversify your diet" – all we're doing as marketers and brands is making the consumers feel even worse about themselves.[17]

While brands cannot change their ingredients overnight, they can begin a steady, intentional process towards health. Tim Verbeek, CEO Africa, Middle East, Asia at Upfield, says,

> We all know that too much salt is not particularly healthy for you, but it gives taste, and food is all about taste. So, we are gradually reducing salt, but if you do it too quickly, people will stop eating your product and switch to a saltier competition.[18]

This is especially a challenge in a competitive marketplace.

Consumers also have limited bandwidth to grasp the many competing claims, labels ranging from "natural" to "organic" to "sustainable", and different aspects of nutrition to consider and balance. As Verbeek describes:

> There's only a limited set of messages that you can get across even if you have a big budget. To actually get a message across to the masses at all takes a lot of time and effort. The most effective way to do so is to ensure that the message is simple, single-minded, and easy to understand rather than having five different messages.[19]

Brands have to think about how to unify their marketing approaches so that sustainability and health are not just confusing afterthoughts.

Beyond advertising, the design of packaging and the labels used are very important. Many countries provide feedback in the form of warning or colour-coded labels, which may help if designed well, but can also have limited impact. Chida describes one initiative in Chile, where black marks are put on products high in sugar, salt, calories or saturated fat:

> I think it's working a little bit for the products that have three black marks. For the products that only have one black mark, it was barely a blip on their sales. A stick approach does not move people. What moves people is their heart. And making nutrition and nutrition quality a matter of the heart is what we need to be working on.

On the positive side, taking initiative can pay off for a brand, according to Willet:

> Unilever got a head start in selling products that were trans-fat free, in the United States at least. Once it was on the label, being zero for trans-fat was a marketing advantage. I think Unilever's R&D efforts paid off there.[20]

Brands must also take a larger view of nutritional impact. For example, if they reduce salt in their product, and consumers respond with salting of their own in meals, then they have not really driven positive change. Knorr, for example, has one of the largest recipe databases in the world, and they offer

Figure 13.1 The Good Breakfast Challenge, Kenya.

selections to guide consumers to better choices. That is an easy way for people to take action on something they care about.

Blue Band's aim is: "to make a nutritious breakfast an everyday reality for half a billion schoolchildren in Africa, an essential step towards healthier lives and better school performance".[21] The brand team in Kenya initiated the multi award winning Good Breakfast Challenge, with school programmes, trade and social media to reach about one in three mothers there. Messages featured local sports hero David Rudisha, two-time Olympic and two-time world champion in the 800 metres track running event. The brand also helped form the Good Breakfast Alliance with global experts, local NGOs, government agencies, health professionals and the private sector.[22]

Marketing for the Good Breakfast Challenge promotes not only Blue Band's own healthy spreads, but also local whole grains and fruits (see Figure 13.1). They tell parents that sending children to school, without a good breakfast is not the optimum way to get kids' performance up in school and given that parents are sensitive to costs of education and performance then it hits a sensitive cord. Such an approach can result in overall improvements in health while helping the brand gain trust and credibility.

Partnerships

Given the scepticism that the food industry faces from governments and non-governmental organisations, is it possible to have a relationship that has benefits for both sides, and more important, for public health? Direct partnerships will certainly be challenging, and more so if the brand included trans fats in the past.

Necessarily the place to start is with a healthy product – trying to make claims about improving nutrition with a demonstrably unhealthy product will go nowhere. April Redmond, Global Knorr Vice President, reminds us:

> We are aiming to reframe "big food" to be a force for good as we have the scale to make a difference. We have to prove this through our products. No one's going to allow us to play that role in society unless our products are good, natural, nutritious, and better for the environment.[23]

Knorr is "big food" indeed, purchasing about 333,000 tonnes of vegetables and herbs, and Knorr products are chosen by consumers about 3.4 billion times annually.[24] Knorr launched the "Future 50 Foods" report in February 2019 in partnership with the World Wildlife Fund (see Figure 13.2).[25] This initiative was based on addressing several key unsustainable aspects of the global food system: First, that 12 crops and 5 animals make up about 75 per cent of food consumed globally, leading to a harmful lack of biodiversity. Second, humans consume too many animal food sources, as livestock account for about 60 per cent of greenhouse gas emissions related to agriculture, which in turn comprise about one-quarter of all emissions. Third, intensive

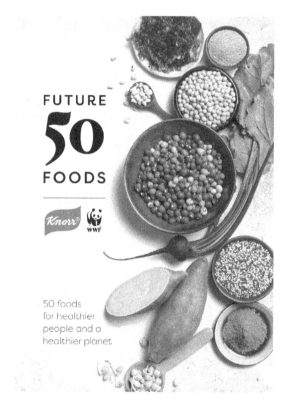

Figure 13.2 Knorr Future 50 Foods Report, February 2019.

monoculture farming practices can remove nutrients from the soil and leave crops vulnerable to pests and disease.[26]

The report identifies 50 foods we should grow and eat more of for the health of people and the planet. The Future 50 Foods have been selected based on their high nutritional value, relative environmental impact, flavour, accessibility, acceptability and affordability. The list includes algae, beans and pulses, cacti, cereals, and other plant-based foods. Knorr has committed to champion these foods to enable dietary diversity, more plant-based sources of protein and more vegetables. They will be promoted through products requiring new ingredient sourcing, improving access to these foods in local markets, and inspiring people to eat them through recipes created by chefs. Partnerships around making these foods available and acceptable will be key.

Partnerships are often essential for delivering messages, especially to children where laws properly limit the claims of brands. Non-profit organisations and governments may be better able to deliver benefits to vulnerable populations than brands, as well as having long running nutrition programmes in the curriculum, with nutritious cooking included in life skills.

In some cases, brands may want to lead the way in forming partnerships. This should not be done naively or without understanding what will truly lead to a benefit for the consumer and to others touched by the brand. However, it can build a foundation from which trust can be earned and future work will be more accepted by other actors. Verbeek explains that one powerful way that a brand can do this is through its supply chain:

> We went to see the Kenyan Ministers of Trade and of Agriculture in Nairobi to convince them to stimulate local farmers to switch to growing rapeseed (canola). We could then make oil containing Omega-3 and Omega-6, which are actually healthy for you. It also supports local farming communities whilst crop rotation increases yield of the land. If you want to make things happen, you have to start doing it yourself. It always starts with looking in the mirror. Only then can you get others involved to drive as much scale and reach as possible.[27]

The team went on to organise a couple of events that even included their direct competitors – including flour manufacturer, local porridge, cereals, fruits, bread – to just talk about the importance of a good breakfast and what role each brand could play with their product offering and portfolio, and how they could create a breakfast bundle to retailers.

Advocacy

Partnerships are hard enough, but can a processed food brand advocate for change? Have brands lost the right to talk about nutrition with the general public?

The easiest approach is to work on broad, inclusive campaigns. The SDG 2 Advocacy Hub is a consortium of non-profits, civil society, UN organisations and the private sector, organised to help reach the UN goal of reduced hunger. The hub facilitates the Chef's Manifesto, a community of 500+ chefs from over 70 countries championing and advocating for a better food future. The chefs argue that promoting the delicious use of healthy, sustainable foods is a better angle than trying to convince people directly to seek health or environmental benefits. By engaging with such a broad range of stakeholders, brands can help without standing out.[28]

Likewise, World Food Day on 16 October each year gives brands an opening to contribute their voice. In 2019, the theme was "Our Actions Are Our Future: Healthy Diets for a #ZeroHunger World."[29] Brands could get involved in explaining how they are responsible for delivering food affordably, while systemic factors are addressed by governments and others.

Brands can start advocacy campaigns themselves, but it helps to open the effort to others, even rivals. Knorr partnered with WWF to create Future 50 Foods. They are now partnering with WWF in South Africa to get local farmers to follow more sustainable growing practices.

In some cases, brands can even argue for regulation – often a scary word for the private sector. Many brands on a mission seek a level playing field – where brands that took healthy steps would find some protection through minimum standards on additives, preservatives, serving sizes and ultra-processed foods to young children. Even better than the stick would be carrots. Chida said, "I'd like to see food products that meet a certain health star getting rated as 'healthy' or 'part of a healthy diet.'" Other ideas, more speculative, include setting up incentives or zones similar to export processing zones for companies producing nutritious foods.

It is important to remember that it is not only SDG 2 that brands can impact. Food Brands can impact SDG 12.3 which has the ambition to halve global food waste. There is a great opportunity for brands to influence at all levels of the supply chain – from "farm to fork" – with consumer behaviour change campaigns like "Love Food, Hate Waste" in the UK,[30] and the Courtauld Commitments, a series of voluntary agreements that "bring together organisations across the food system to make food and drink production and consumption more sustainable".[31] Over the first four year period of the Courtauld commitment, 1.2 million tonnes of food and packaging was prevented, with a monetary value of £1.8 billion, and a saving of 3.3 million tonnes of carbon dioxide.[32] And at the global level, "Champions 12.3" is a coalition of executives from across every public and private sector, all dedicated to "inspiring ambition, mobilising action, and accelerating progress" towards achieving SDG target 12.3 by 2030.[33]

Measurement

Measurement is particularly hard for processed food brands. Health trade-offs between different ingredients and ways of processing are complex. Does adding fat to make up for reduced sugar make a product more or less healthy? It's also easy to game these metrics, by altering ingredients to just beyond an arbitrary cut off point, for example. But if systems are well designed, then brands substituting one unhealthy ingredient for another to maximise taste for a given level of healthiness is something that the R&D team can work on. It is a fine balancing act.

As evidence grows about the effectiveness of colour-coded food labels on consumers making healthier choices,[34, 35] brands should support and even lead in communicating to consumers where they are taking positive steps.

Here it's essential to consider the effects on consumers. If a brand uses less salt or sugar to the detriment of taste, then people might add so much of this ingredient that the food becomes less healthy. People do not eat ingredients, they eat meals.

Another interesting metric is the impact of food brands on the environment, and WWF and Tesco have formed a partnership with the shared ambition to make affordable, healthy, sustainable food available to everyone. The partnership goal is to halve the environmental impact of the average shopping basket – and they've defined a "sustainable basket metric" that can be tracked.[36]

Conclusion

Nutrition is a complicated area, but brands on a mission can make a difference. Upfront they can help people eat better, but in the long run they can also change the food system – from farm to fork and through retailers – by stimulating demand for healthier, more varied diets. They'll meet scepticism and distrust, as well as regulations and taxes, but brands are an essential part of the future public health involving nutrition. They can best show repentance for past misdeeds by joining with partners for a better future.

Notes

1 Miller, V. *et al.* (2016). "Availability, affordability, and consumption of fruits and vegetables in 18 countries across income levels: findings from the Prospective Urban Rural Epidemiology (PURE) study", *The Lancet Global Health*, 4(10), pp. e695–e703. doi: 10.1016/S2214-109X(16)30186-3.
2 Hamrick, K. (2016). "Americans Spend an Average of 37 Minutes a Day Preparing and Serving Food and Cleaning Up", *United States Department of Agriculture*. Available at: www.ers.usda.gov/amber-waves/2016/november/americans-spend-an-average-of-37-minutes-a-day-preparing-and-serving-food-and-cleaning-up/ (Accessed: 4 January 2020).
3 Allen, L. (2006). *Guidelines on food fortification with micronutrients*. Geneva: World Health Organization: Food and Agriculture Organization of the United Nations.
4 Monteiro, C. *et al.* (2019). "Ultra-processed foods, diet quality, and health using the NOVA classification system", *Food and Agriculture Organisation of the United Nations*. Available at: www.fao.org/fsnforum/resources/fsn-resources/ultra-processed-foods-diet-quality-and-health-using-nova-classification (Accessed: 4 January 2020).
5 Monteiro, C. A. *et al.* (2013). "Ultra-processed products are becoming dominant in the global food system", *Obesity Reviews*, 14(S2), pp. 21–28. doi: 10.1111/obr.12107.
6 Malik, V. S. *et al.* (2010). "Sugar-sweetened beverages and risk of metabolic syndrome and type 2 diabetes: a meta-analysis", *Diabetes Care*, 33(11), pp. 2477–2483. doi: 10.2337/dc10-1079.
7 Wanders, A. J., Zock, P. L. and Brouwer, I. A. (2017). "Trans Fat Intake and Its Dietary Sources in General Populations Worldwide: A Systematic Review", *Nutrients*, 9(8). doi: 10.3390/nu9080840.
8 Yang, Q. *et al.* (2014). "Added Sugar Intake and Cardiovascular Diseases Mortality Among US Adults", *JAMA Internal Medicine*, 174(4), pp. 516–524. doi: 10.1001/jamainternmed.2013.13563.
9 Fardet, A. (2016). "Minimally processed foods are more satiating and less hyperglycemic than ultra-processed foods: a preliminary study with 98 ready-to-eat foods", *Food & Function*, 7(5), pp. 2338–2346. doi: 10.1039/C6FO00107F.
10 McGinnis, J. M., Gootman, J. and Kraak, V. (2006). *Food Marketing to Children and Youth: Threat or Opportunity?* Washington DC: National Academies Press. doi: 10.17226/11514.
11 Freudenberg, N. (2014). *Lethal but Legal – Corporations, Consumption, and Protecting Public Health*. Oxford, New York: Oxford University Press.
12 Haddad, L. (2019). Personal interview.
13 Korver, O. and Katan, M. B. (2006). "The Elimination of Trans Fats from Spreads: How Science Helped to Turn an Industry around", *Nutrition Reviews*, 64(6), pp. 275–279. doi: 10.1111/j.1753-4887.2006.tb00210.x.

14 Nilsson, K. *et al.* (2010). "Comparative life cycle assessment of margarine and butter consumed in the UK, Germany and France", *The International Journal of Life Cycle Assessment*, 15(9), pp. 916–926. doi: 10.1007/s11367-010-0220-3.

15 Willet, W. (2019). Personal interview.

16 Ibid.

17 Chida, K. (2019). Personal interview.

18 Verbeek, T. (2019). Personal interview.

19 Ibid.

20 Willet, W. (2019). Personal interview.

21 Unilever (2016). "Blue Band unveils good breakfast initiative to boost school performance", *Unilever*. Available at: www.unilever.com/news/news-and-features/Feature-article/2016/Blue-Band-unveils-good-breakfast-initiative-to-boost-school-performance.html (Accessed: 4 January 2020).

22 Ibid.

23 Redmond, A. (2019). Personal interview.

24 Knorr and WWF (2019). "Future 50 Foods Report", *Knorr*. Available at: www.knorr.com/uk/future50report.html (Accessed: 4 January 2020).

25 Ibid.

26 Unilever (2019). "Knorr and WWF-UK introduce 50 future foods", *Unilever*. Available at: www.unilever.com/news/news-and-features/Feature-article/2019/knorr-and-wwf-uk-introduce-50-future-foods.html (Accessed: 4 January 2020).

27 Verbeek, T. (2019). Personal interview.

28 SDG2 Advocacy Hub (2017). "Chefs' Manifesto", *SDG2 Advocacy Hub*. Available at: www.sdg2advocacyhub.org/chefmanifesto (Accessed: 4 January 2020).

29 FAO (2019). "World Food Day 'Our actions are our future'", *Food & Business Knowledge Platform*. Available at: https://knowledge4food.net/event/world-food-day-our-actions-are-our-future/ (Accessed: 4 January 2020).

30 WRAP (2018). *Love Food Hate Waste*. Available at: https://lovefoodhatewaste.com (Accessed: 4 January 2020).

31 WRAP (2018). *Courtauld Commitment 2025*. Available at: www.wrap.org.uk/food-drink/business-food-waste/courtauld-2025 (Accessed: 4 January 2020).

32 WRAP UK (2018). *Courtauld Commitments – Tackling waste in the food supply chain since 2005*. Available at: www.wrap.org.uk/food-drink/business-food-waste/history-courtauld (Accessed: 4 January 2020).

33 *Champions 12.3* (2016). Available at: https://champions123.org/about/ (Accessed: 4 January 2020).

34 Ducrot, P. *et al.* (2016). "Impact of Different Front-of-Pack Nutrition Labels on Consumer Purchasing Intentions: A Randomized Controlled Trial", *American Journal of Preventive Medicine*, 50(5), pp. 627–636. doi: 10.1016/j.amepre.2015.10.020.

35 Trudel, R. *et al.* (2015). "The impact of traffic light color-coding on food health perceptions and choice", *Journal of Experimental Psychology: Applied*, 21(3), pp. 255–275. doi: 10.1037/xap0000049.

36 WWF (2019). *New measure to map environmental impact of food production*. Available at: www.wwf.org.uk/updates/Tesco-WWF-map-environmental-impact-food-production (Accessed: 4 January 2020).

Concluding thoughts

What a journey it has been to write this book!

I wrote this book partly to help those working in public health to harness the power of brands to do good. But also to reposition what it means to be a marketeer and to inspire the new generation of marketers, the future Steve Miles of this world, to come and work for a social purpose, for their own long-term satisfaction, as well as the strength of their brand. I believe many marketers are drawn to a social purpose, but they assume it is impossible in a corporate setting. In these pages I hope they have seen that it is already a practical career path – albeit challenging at times – and one that I think is likely to become a long-term corporate necessity.

Brands are critical contenders in the fight for social justice because they have the most powerful weapon of all – their consumers. It is important to also remember that corporations are made of people, who themselves are consumers, and they play an important role in this journey.

In reflecting on my work so far, on what I have learned and what I keep learning from Unilever and other companies, from governments and public sector, I have realised that I, too, am a brand on a mission. My mission, honed over many years of working, teaching and writing, is to continue pioneering models for social justice, to work with both the public and private sectors, and to never stop questioning the status quo.

In looking back, my work has been the combination of public health and marketing and this in-between space has not always been an easy one to occupy. I have also taken stock of how difficult it has been at times to live this in-between life, balancing the aims of the corporation with the necessities of people in need, as well as juggling a global career with the needs of my family. Wherever I go and whatever I do, I am always a bit different from everyone else. People like me, who stay in touch with their purpose, and who support the validity of applying private-sector resources and know-how to global problems, as I mentioned in Chapter 12, have often followed a lonely path. We have lacked a well-defined role. We are not public servants. We are not brand specialists. We are not communication specialists. But we are helping to change the world in a positive way and we are growing in numbers.

Mission-driven people desperately need to know they are not alone. That is one reason I wrote this book: to support intrapreneurs (a dreamer, who "does") who are looking for a boost. If there is one takeaway that I want intrapreneurs to gain from this book, it is that it is possible to live your purpose within corporations. I am the living proof of that. I do not think I would have lasted this long if it was not for Unilever's ethics and values.

It's not easy. But it *is* possible. Do not settle for "You can't do that" or "You can't be that". Challenging the status quo is exactly what the world needs. Keep demanding wider career paths that encompass diverse skill sets and that reward passion and commitment. Keep proving to your organisation that this merging of disciplines is crucial and absolutely key to the future success of the organisation.

Instead of relying on conventional rewards, intrapreneurs need to rely on themselves – on their own self-awareness and self-esteem, which are necessary for risk-taking.

This is a hard-earned lesson that has sustained me through the toughest times. By maintaining my self-awareness and ability to create trust across a variety of sectors, I have managed to continue moving forwards, keeping my passion, curiosity and integrity intact. In many ways I am still that same little girl from Mali, inspired by the example of her parents to fight for social justice and determined to make a difference in public health. I still want to be part of the development of Africa. I still have the same motivation to improve the health of mothers and children throughout the world.

Furthermore, I still feel the same excitement about the ability of consumers and brands to drive long-lasting change to contributing to some of these issues.

And what of the future? A call to action

The world needs more companies that commit to being a force for good, pulling out their swords to actively address social challenges rather than merely putting up their shields to defend themselves. Companies that simply avoid doing evil – creating less waste and less plastic, for example – will not retain consumers' loyalty in the long run. Consumers will become increasingly discerning and inclined towards brands that genuinely contribute to a better world for the children of tomorrow.

Being a force for good – waging effective altruism – will be essential as a way for corporations to pre-empt competition and build cross-company and public–private partnerships that will create lasting, collaborative, impactful solutions.

Brands cannot do everything – but they can kick-start a "purpose revolution" challenging governments, multilateral organisations and civil society to keep them at the table for good. Visualise the baobab tree that has been my guiding metaphor in this book – keep in mind the five roots that give social purpose its strength and nourishment: behaviour change, partnerships, advocacy, measurement and winning support within the corporation. This framework for conceptualising purpose-driven brands, which places the ultimate emphasis on "doing" rather than "saying", can serve as a research agenda that will last for decades and will continue evolving as we keep learning.

I predict an "all in" approach where brands address social and environmental impact holistically. Transparency and honesty will also become the norm as consumers expect more from the companies and brands they choose, and will love the ones that align with their personal values. Achieving a fusion of commercial and social ambitions is not some holy grail, I believe it is the *only* way businesses and brands will survive in the coming decades.

Figure C.1 A baobab tree, Senegal 2019 (copyright Alan Jope).

Afterword

The power of brands to act as catalysts and movements for social and environmental change is increasingly well understood. Indeed at Unilever, it goes to the very heart of our purpose-driven approach to doing business.

Few people have done more to pioneer such new ways of thinking – or develop the models to support them – than Myriam Sidibe. The drive and energy she brought in particular to the way Unilever works with non-profit organisations and governments to scale solutions has been instrumental in the way the company now works and collaborates with others. By living her purpose and by leading the way for brands to live their purpose, Myriam is now using her experience and insights to help others, as captured in this powerful book and collection of case studies.

As a business, we still have a lot to learn and contribute, and never has it been more vital that we collaborate with others – in the public and private sectors – to enable us all to do this in the most effective way for the millions in the world who need support. This book helps us all to challenge ourselves to do this – and take inspiration from the majestic baobab tree, a genuine "tree of life".

Alan Jope
Chief Executive Officer, Unilever

Index

Page numbers in **bold** denote tables, those in *italics* denote figures.